# THE ETHICS OF SPORT

## WHAT EVERYONE NEEDS TO KNOW®

# THE ETHICS OF SPORT

## WHAT EVERYONE NEEDS TO KNOW®

### ROBERT L. SIMON

OXFORD
UNIVERSITY PRESS

# OXFORD

UNIVERSITY PRESS

Oxford University Press is a department of the University of Oxford.
It furthers the University's objective of excellence in research, scholarship,
and education by publishing worldwide. Oxford is a registered
trade mark of Oxford University Press in
the UK and certain other countries.

"What Everyone Needs to Know" is a registered trademark of
Oxford University Press.

Published in the United States of America by Oxford University Press
198 Madison Avenue, New York, NY 10016, United States of America.

© Oxford University Press 2016

Library of Congress Cataloging-in-Publication Data
Names: Simon, Robert L., 1941– author.
Title: The ethics of sport : what everyone needs to know / Robert L. Simon.
Description: New York : Oxford University Press, 2016. |
Includes bibliographical references and index.
Identifiers: LCCN 2016004737 | ISBN 9780190270193 (pbk. : alk. paper) |
ISBN 9780190270209 (hardcover : alk. paper) |
ISBN 9780190270216 (ebook (updf)) | ISBN 9780190270223 (ebook (epub))
Subjects: LCSH: Sports—Moral and ethical aspects.
Classification: LCC GV706.3 .S59 2016 | DDC 796.01—dc23
LC record available at https://lccn.loc.gov/2016004737

*To Joy for her love, help, support, and encouragement*

# CONTENTS

ACKNOWLEDGMENTS                                               ix
PROLOGUE                                                     xiii

1 The Moral Significance of Sport                              1

2 Winning, Cheating, and the Ethics of Competition           28

3 Health, Safety, and Violence in Competitive Sport          68

4 Enhancement, Technology, and Fairness
  in Competitive Sport                                        90

5 Competitive Sport: Education or Mis-Education?             132

6 Sports, Equity, and Society                                180

7 Concluding Comment: The Two Sides of the
  Force, or Are Sports So Great After All?                   214

NOTES                                                        221
RECOMMENDED READINGS AND REFERENCES                          229
INDEX                                                        235

# ACKNOWLEDGMENTS

Just as it may take a village to raise a child, it also takes many people to produce a book. I am indebted to all those people whose assistance made this project so much better than it would have been without their help.

I especially want to acknowledge the students I have taught over the years in my course in "Philosophical Issues in Sport." Many of the questions raised in this book were initially proposed by students in my classes, particularly the class I taught in the fall of 2014, whom I told of this project and who suggested specific questions that I ought to pursue. However, all my students, many of whom have questioned my own views, have contributed both by their essays and through discussions, and by sending me new material on ethical issues in sport that they have encountered in their own reading.

I owe a special debt to Jackson Kushner, my student in the fall of 2014, whose criticism of Scott Kretchmar's defense of the duty to give bench warmers significant minutes in competition appears in a modified form in my discussion of the ethics of coaching. Another student, Zoe Mikhailovich, did an extraordinary job of not only proofreading sections of the manuscript but also of making many acute suggestions for improving the substance of my arguments as well. The students at my institution, Hamilton College, are superb, and it has been a pleasure to work with them for over 45 years. I'm sure I have learned as much from them as they have from me.

I want to thank the student-athletes at Hamilton College, who are true *student*-athletes, and who over the years have exemplified one of the major themes of this book: sport as a mutual quest for excellence. I am also grateful to Carolyn Mascaro, secretary *extraordinaire* for the Department of Philosophy at Hamilton College, who assisted me greatly in preparation of the final manuscript, always with encouragement and good cheer.

I have been blessed to have wonderful colleagues in the Philosophy Department at Hamilton, who have been tremendously supportive of my work on issues in ethics and sport. My colleagues in the International Association for the Philosophy of Sport, including some of those whose work is discussed in this book, have been equally supportive and encouraging. My colleagues in each area have the knack of being critical and helpful, and make philosophic inquiry into what I call a mutual quest for truth (in philosophy) and excellence (in sports); that is, a *cooperative* activity from which all of us gain.

I am deeply grateful to my editor at Oxford, Lucy Randall, for suggesting this project, for persuading me to take it on, and for all her invaluable help along the way. Her suggestions for revision improved the manuscript immeasurably. A prepublication review obtained by the publisher was full of acute suggestions to which I might not have done justice but which I tried my best to follow. I am grateful for the thoroughness of the review by Leslie Francis of the University of Utah and for the many insightful comments it contained. Of course, all the final decisions on substance were my own and the fault for any errors, or for at times not following the advice of others when I should have, is my own. I also want to thank the production team led by Nancy Rebecca and including copy editor Leslie Anglin and Caroline McDonnell who designed the cover.

I owe special thanks for the support and encouragement of my wife, Joy. She not only is a proofreader extraordinaire but also a coach, critic, and my best friend.

I have done my best to make this book accessible to readers who have not studied issues in sport in an academic setting, or who have limited familiarity with the world of sports, as well as for those already immersed in the realm. Readers interested in a more in-depth and scholarly approach to some of the themes discussed in this book, particularly the idea of broad internalism (interpretivism) and the idea of competitive sport as a mutual quest for excellence as discussed in Chapter 1, should consult *Fair Play* (2015), which I coauthored with Cesar Torres and Peter Hager. Sources listed in the Recommended Readings and References chapter also should prove helpful for those who wish to further pursue discussion of ethical issues in sport.

I especially hope that this book in particular shows that the analysis of issues in sport is not only of interest in its own right but also illustrates how critical examination can illuminate the questions at the heart of a major practice—competitive athletics—that affects and moves so many of us.

R.L.S.

December 2015

Clinton, New York

# PROLOGUE

*Why should we care about sports ethics? Aren't sports only games?*

I was on a flight from Orlando, Florida, to Albany, New York, just before the northeastern blizzard of January 2015. The chief flight attendant was going through the normal preflight safety instructions when, with tongue in cheek, he reported, "The runways in Albany are slick. No need to worry, however. Tom Brady is inflating the tires."

As many readers know, Tom Brady is the star quarterback of the New England Patriots, who were about to play in the 2015 Super Bowl, under the shadow of "Deflategate," the controversy generated by the discovery that the footballs used by the Patriots in their playoff win over the Indianapolis Colts were not inflated to the degree the rules require, making them easier to catch and throw. Was this an accident, caused by atmospheric conditions, as some claimed, or was it a deliberate attempt by the Patriots to gain a competitive advantage? If it was the latter, was it cheating or perhaps morally questionable gamesmanship?

As scandals like "Deflategate" remind us, questions about ethical issues in sports are pervasive. This is perhaps the best reason why we ought to give sports ethics serious thought. In fact, we find ethical problems in everything from doping scandals to debates over college athletics, to arguments over whether modern competitive athletics overemphasizes winning, to the requirements of gender equity in sports. As my flight attendant's remark illustrates, ethics of sport has become part of general public discourse. The attendant clearly expected virtually all the passengers on the aircraft, avid football fans or not, to recognize the reference to Deflategate.

We also need to pay attention to the ethics of sport due to their intellectual complexity. There is always more than one side to the story, and a surface understanding of the scandal or debate at hand is never adequate. For example, many of us have the intuition that the use of performance-enhancing drugs (PEDs) in athletics is a form of cheating. Perhaps it is if rules prohibit their use. But why shouldn't the rules permit use of PEDs such as anabolic steroids? Are the alleged benefits provided by such drugs any different in principle from advantages gained by techniques that are permitted, such as specialized weight training, the use of hyperbaric chambers to raise oxygen-carrying capacity, or the use of performance-enhancing equipment, such as improved golf clubs and balls, fiberglass poles for vaulting, or specialized running shoes? If everyone had access to performance-enhancing drugs, what would be wrong with using them? As we will see later in this book, the attempt to formulate a defensible position on the use of PEDs is a difficult endeavor, as we will find to be the case with many questions about ethics and sport raised in our discussions.

Third, sports have become a central element in our culture, for good or ill (a question we also will examine). Indeed, they captivate people worldwide, involving millions as participants, spectators, or simply observers. Youth sports alone are central to the lives not only of the children who play but also the adults and parents who organize leagues and transport players from contest to contest. Then at every level beyond that, the number of lives touched builds and builds when we take into account players, employees of the teams and athletic organizations, and the countless fans.

Finally, by examining such concepts as fairness, equity, justice, and virtue in the context of sports, we may generate insights into their nature that clarify issues in other areas such as social policy and education. Sports ethics, rather than being the mere application of very general ethical principles, may help us to formulate better principles of ethics in other contexts.

But, some of you may object, sports are only games. Isn't it ludicrous, such readers may claim, that so much attention is paid to such trivial pursuits?

Even if sports are trivial, which we will see is not the case, the ethical problems that emerge about and within them have undeniable significance. Sports are bound up with issues involving questions of what is fair or just, what is sportsmanship (or sportspersonship if you prefer), and why it is important. Is commercialization corrupting sport, as many would argue it has done to other aspects of our lives? Is it wrong to promote competition in children's sports, or is healthy competition a good thing for kids? What are colleges and universities doing in the athletic business anyway? Do sports build character, and if so, do they build the right kind of character or, as some scholars claim, do they make participants worse rather than better people? Even those who may not see the value of sports themselves will see the value of thinking through these conundrums.

Moreover, if sports raise these important questions, saying that "It's only a game" is unfairly dismissive to sports themselves. If sports are a form of striving for excellence, if they often instill in us important virtues like persistence dedication and courage, and reveal the beauty of what the human body can accomplish, to dismiss them as "only games" may be like dismissing a great painting or novel as "only art," because it does not immediately contribute to solving pressing social, political, or economic issues.

In what follows, we will explore different sides of major ethical issues that arise in sports, especially competitive athletics. Although we may not always come up with answers to which all reasonable people will assent, we will be able to clarify what values are at stake in the controversies and to explore in a critical but reasoned way the arguments presented by different sides or perspectives on sports. Critical inquiry, like sports, may affect the broader society for better or worse—say by clarifying the nature of social justice—but like sports it also is an activity that the participants engage in because of the value of the activity itself and the challenge it presents to our understanding of our culture and our world.

### What is your own background in sports and sports ethics? How did it prepare you to write this book?

I was born in Brooklyn, New York, in 1941 and grew up on the south shore of Long Island. My parents, who were more intellectual than athletic, became baseball fans in the late 1940s because of their admiration for Jackie Robinson, who broke the color line in Major League Baseball in 1947. Before Robinson's ascent to majors, they were strictly segregated; basically it was only white players allowed. Robinson showed tremendous courage and self-control in overcoming the often virulent racism that he faced.[1]

In any case, my parents became Brooklyn Dodger fans and I became an avid fan of the team as well. My favorite Brooklyn players besides Robinson were Duke Snider, Gil Hodges, Pee Wee Reese, Roy Campenalla, and substitute George Shuba, a strong hitter known also for an iconic photograph in which he, a white player, shakes Robinson's hand after Jackie's first home run for the minor league Dodger affiliate, the Montreal Royals.

Although I was no star, I played baseball, mostly just recreationally, and it was my first love. In fact, I met my wife on a blind date in 1965 when I took her to Shea Stadium to see the

Mets play the Cardinals. I was introduced to golf while I was in college, and golf soon replaced baseball as my favorite sport both to play and watch.

Much to my surprise, I became a philosophy major as an undergraduate at Lafayette College due to the influence of the wonderful teachers in the department there, and to my even greater surprise, I continued on to graduate school at the University of Pennsylvania. At that time, the mid to late 1960s, philosophy in most American and British schools was a very narrow subject, devoted to the analysis of language, logical problems in the sciences, and fascinating but technical issues in explaining the basis of our knowledge of the world. Sports were regarded by academics, as far as I could tell, as well outside the areas where serious research should be conducted.

I remember a time, early in my career in the 1960s, when an influential philosopher, Paul Weiss, wrote a book on philosophy of sport. A review of the book was posted on the graduate student bulletin board under a sign in large letters saying, "Write on this subject only if you already have tenure!" But it wasn't only sports that were thought to fall outside the proper sphere of philosophical or academic study. There were virtually no courses in medical or business ethics and indeed the study of ethics itself was quite narrowly construed.

Fortunately, philosophy soon became far less narrow and more relevant to public affairs, due in part to the desire of philosophers to contribute to issues raised by the civil rights movement and by the Vietnam War. It was during this period that through the influence of Paul Weiss and others, especially Warren Fraleigh, the International Association for the Philosophy of Sport (IAPS) was born at the State University of New York College at Brockport.

Despite these developments, I failed for a long time to connect my own philosophical interests in broad issues of public policy to my love of sports, and I also failed to realize that sport could be an object of intellectual study. Sports were just games and not to be taken seriously as an academic subject, right?

I'm not sure just what made me decide to bridge the gap between my athletic and academic interests, but challenges to my views on competition and the importance of winning by some colleagues at Hamilton College where I teach and attendance of some of the meetings of the IAPS encouraged me to get further involved in the developing area of sports ethics. Further encouragement from publishers led me to publish my first book in the area called *Sports and Social Values* (1985), later republished as *Fair Play*, now in its fourth edition (2014) coauthored by Cesar Torres and Peter Hager of SUNY Brockport, an institution that remains a center of academic sports philosophy.

At the same time, I was trying to become a competitive golfer and had some limited success and a far greater number of failures in local and regional tournaments. In 1987 the athletic director at Hamilton asked me to fill in for a semester as head men's golf coach, an appointment that turned out to last for 14 years. During that period our team, which competed in Division III of the NCAA, was frequently nationally or at least regionally ranked. My two sons played for me on one of our top teams.

Any delusions of grandeur as a coach were shattered, however, when during one summer, one of my sons won a qualifying tournament for the Syracuse Amateur Championship, no mean feat because many skilled college players and a number of former state champions were in the field. I served as his caddy, not his coach, because school was not in session. The Syracuse newspaper ran a story on us, the father–son team that won the event. I was brought down to earth, however, when my son was quoted in the article saying, "My dad thought he was doing great, but actually whatever he said I just did the opposite!" I must say, however, that as he became older, I have gotten a lot smarter, at least in his view.

My experience as coach and with athletics at Hamilton College has had a tremendous influence on me. Hamilton competes in Division III of the NCAA in which schools do not give athletic scholarships and athletes are truly students. Teaching many of these students who play sports has convinced me that in some contexts and *if conducted properly*, college athletics and academics can not only coexist but sometimes be mutually reinforcing. Whether that is still possible as well in the athletically elite and highly visible Division I athletic programs is questionable, a topic we will return to later in this book.

Although I have had experience as an academic who has written on sports, as a coach, as an aspiring but often unsuccessful golfer, and in various administrative capacities involving college sports, it is my background as a philosopher that I will bring to bear in this book, offering a critical examination of reasons or logical arguments that apply to various issues in sports. Although my own experience may provide a basis for the perspectives that are sometimes defended, it is important in critical inquiry as in sports themselves to be fair to all reasonable positions and to expose one's own views to criticisms when warranted. Keeping that in mind, here is a brief game plan or outline that I hope will be a useful guide to what follows.

### What issues does the book address and how is it organized?

We will start in Chapter 1 with some very general questions about sports and athletics. In particular, we will consider how to best characterize the nature of games, the relation between games and sports, the nature of sports, and the values they may embody or express. In Chapter 2 we will go on to examine questions about the value of competitive sport, the nature of cheating, the nature of sportsmanship, and ethical principles that ought to apply even in elite competition. Chapter 3 examines issues raised by technology and fairness in competitive sport, particularly moral issues involving the use of performance-enhancing drugs and genetic enhancement as well as the ethical evaluation of dangerous sports, especially boxing. Chapter 4 deals with the ethics of the connection between education and athletics, especially questions about whether higher education and intercollegiate athletics as presently conducted in the United States can be compatible. In the final chapter, we will consider a variety of social issues raised by athletics, ranging from questions about gender equity and Title IX in intercollegiate sport to concerns about the alleged corruption of athletics by commercial concerns.

Each chapter will examine a variety of arguments on different sides of the issues raised. In sports we are justified in regarding athletes as successful only if they compete well against worthy opponents and likewise in ethics, and more broadly in philosophy, we are justified in regarding our arguments as defensible only to the extent that our arguments can survive criticism in well-conducted discourse. Just as it is a mistake to underrate opponents in sport, it is a mistake to underrate objections to our own view simply because we want to protect our own beliefs from criticism. I hope the discussions that follow are fair to a variety of positions. Although I sometimes will suggest which positions I think are best supported by argument, I hope that this book will lead readers on to their own inquiry about issues in sport, and even more, to applying tools of critical analysis to important issues in whatever context they arise.

# THE ETHICS OF SPORT

## WHAT EVERYONE NEEDS TO KNOW®

# 1

# THE MORAL SIGNIFICANCE OF SPORT

*Why is it important to study and analyze sports rather than just enjoying them? What can an analysis of ethical issues in sports contribute to our understanding of sports, and perhaps of broader ethical concerns as well?*

In a fiercely fought qualifying match for the 2009 World Cup between France and Ireland, the French captain Thierry Henry admitted to a rival player that he had violated the rules and handled the ball in a play that led to France scoring the winning goal. Fans in Ireland were outraged that their team had been eliminated from the competition through an illegal play, and some fans in France argued that their own team should voluntarily forfeit the game.

This case raises a host of issues, many of which will be discussed more fully later in this book. For now, consider three different kinds of questions that could arise about the incident. First, there are factual questions concerning what actually happened. Did Henry use his hands to maneuver the ball? If so, did his illegal play lead to France scoring the winning goal? Second, there are explanatory questions. In particular, why all the fuss? Isn't it "only a game?" After all, will anyone even know or care about the game hundreds of years from now? Third, there are ethical questions. Did Henry cheat or was he just practicing permissible gamesmanship? Should France have forfeited the victory? Shouldn't players do everything they can to win and leave it up to officials to enforce the rules of the game?

It is important not to confuse these different kinds of questions with one another. In particular, ethical issues often concern questions about what is morally good or bad behavior, what is of moral value or disvalue, what is right or wrong, and what is fair or unfair or just or unjust. Although the relations between facts and values are often complex, when we ask what *explains* the intense interest so many people throughout the world have in sports, we are investigating a different set of concerns than when we ask whether their interest is a good or bad thing or whether an act was right or wrong. Why Henry violated the rules is one question, but whether he ought to have done so is quite another.

To navigate the complex and contentious moral questions that sports raise in cases like these, we can only get anywhere if we take a systematic approach. Participants, fans, and observers all have opinions that they express in various forums, ranging from local pubs to national media. Surely it is important that these views be open to examination, be based on evidence, and be able to survive critical scrutiny. Moreover, participants in sports may be called upon to face or publically address moral issues, whether they are professionals or amateurs. How is their response to be evaluated? Athletes, officials, fans, and critics of sport have to decide how to act in their various roles in the sporting world. If they are to avoid acting immorally, they need to have an idea of what morality requires of them, and they often need to be able to defend their behavior when it is exposed to criticism.

In what follows, we will identify and examine various moral issues that arise in sport. Many of these issues go well beyond the boundaries of sport and involve such broad issues as the nature of fairness and the manner in which we ought to treat others. Let us begin, however, by considering why sport is such a major cultural phenomenon. What, if anything, explains the fascination with sports across the globe? As we will see, even a preliminary examination of what makes sports so special to so many will shed some light on the ethical questions of whether such interest is justified and whether sports themselves are a valuable activity.

### What makes something a sport? Do all sports share common features that define them?

As readers will know by this point, in this book we will be concerned with ethical questions about sports and the ways that they are conducted. Before we look into the ethical questions that sports raise, however, we ought to examine the nature of sports themselves.

Is an inquiry into the nature of sport just a symptom of the unnecessary philosophical obsession with defining terms, which comes at the expense of delving into substantial questions? In other words, are we just going to be "nit picking"? Why should we be concerned with defining sports as such? Are there any characteristics that distinguish sports from other activities? Perhaps by investigating why certain activities are grouped together as sports, we can identify some features that are relevant to their moral evaluation.

Of course, various sports may have nothing in common when we look at them up close but only resemble one another in a variety of very general ways.[1] Perhaps influenced by the ancient Greek philosopher Plato (427–347 B.C.E.), who searched for the nature of truth, knowledge, and beauty, we might assume that all sports share common characteristics that make them sports, but perhaps that assumption is wrong. Plato influenced generations of thinkers who followed him in believing that there exist essential characteristics possessed by all and only members of certain classes of things or ideas. Sports might be an exception to this idea, as we will see.

Nevertheless, we distinguish sports from exercise; from games that have no necessary physical component, such as chess or Monopoly; and some forms of play, such as playing house, which may be a game but is not a sport. Surely, we might think, there is a basis for making such distinctions.

It might be useful, at least for our purposes here, to think of sports as games of physical skill. Games seem to be rule-governed activities in which a certain set of the rules define which moves are allowable within the game and which are not, what counts as winning and losing, and who counts as a player within the framework of the game. Such rules are called constitutive rules because they define what counts as or constitutes a play within the game. To give an example, advancing the ball through dribbling or passing is allowed by the constitutive rules of basketball, but running with the ball is not. As American readers will know right away, basketball is both a game and a sport.

On this view, sports are distinguished from games such as chess or tic-tac-toe because of the physical skill they involve. They differ from other rule-governed activities, such as taking an examination in college or filing a tax return, because the rules exist not for some practical end outside the game but simply in order to make it possible. As one writer has suggested, the rules make what otherwise would be an easy task challenging. It is easy to place a small ball in a hole in the ground, but golf is difficult because the constitutive rules require it be done through the use of golf clubs, which the former British Prime Minister Winston Churchill called "implements ill-designed for the purpose." Games, then, can be thought of as "voluntary attempts to overcome unnecessary obstacles," obstacles created by the constitutive rules, and sports are those games in which physical skill is needed to overcome the artificial obstacles that the rules create.[2]

We can distinguish between sports and mere exercise at least because of the obstacles created by the constitutive rules. Sports normally also differ from work because the justification for the rules is not practical (i.e., not designed to achieve some goal outside the framework of the game itself) but, again, simply serves to make the game itself possible. Of course, there are major challenges at work, but normally we take up these challenges for some other purpose, such as making a living, and not for the sake of meeting the challenge itself.

You may have doubts about this account of games and of sports as games of physical skill. For example, surely running marathons can be classified as a sport but is not normally *called* a game. Professional athletes play sports, but don't they accept the rules in order to make money, not just to make the activity of playing possible? Can't individuals at retirement age continue to work simply because they enjoy the challenges of their job?

Whether or not such objections are ultimately decisive is a matter of debate. So, even if marathons are not *called* games, they still have the structure of games, such as constitutive rules that create special obstacles to achieving a goal.[3] To give an obvious example, one can't complete a marathon by driving the route in a car. And though many professional athletes may play primarily for money, they earn their salaries through excellence of play in meeting the challenges created by the constitutive rules of their sport. The justification for having the rules is the creation of worthy challenges that professionals may excel in overcoming. Finally, individuals who continue to work only because they relish the challenges of their job may be treating their employment as something like a game and less like what is commonly regarded as work.

Even if our preliminary account of games, and of sports as games of physical skill, must be modified or corrected, major sports such as baseball, American football, golf, soccer, lacrosse, rugby, track and field, lacrosse, tennis, and volleyball all have constitutive rules designed to create a challenging activity. There may well be borderline cases. Does auto racing involve sufficient physical skill to be classified as a sport? What about online or virtual games that require dexterity and hand–eye coordination? Such cases, and others we might think of, may be difficult to resolve, but the account of sports as games of physical skill fits clear cases of what we regard as sports and, as we will see, will illuminate our attempts to explain the interest in sports and evaluate them.

Keeping these ideas in mind, without necessarily regarding them as the final say on the matter, we will now consider the question of why sports are so popular and arouse such interest in so many people around the world.

### Why do so many people care about sports?

If you didn't care about sports, even if only to learn about them or even criticize them, you probably wouldn't be reading this sentence. People express their interest in sports as spectators, as participants, and sometimes as critics. Even those uninterested in sports must wonder why others seem to care so much. But what explains this interest? Why sports rather than other activities?

Of course, there may not be one single factor that explains the interest in sports worldwide. Moreover, even if we can explain why sports are so influential and captivate so many, we also need to explore whether that interest is *ethical*. For example, do sports distract us from more important matters, creating indifference to broader social issues? Is the way sports sometimes are practiced, exhibiting a win-at-all-costs attitude, the problem? In particular, would a kinder and gentler version of competition in professional athletics be more morally acceptable than much of what we see in elite sports today? Do we put too much emphasis on children's sports, taking away time that they could dedicate to honing academic or artistic skills—or to simply being kids? Understanding what makes sports important, or at least seem important to so many, may help us address these ethical questions.

Many explanations of the widespread interest in sports have been proposed but often are less than satisfactory because they only scratch the explanatory surface. For example, people may participate in sports to make friends, for exercise and reasons of health, and to develop skills. People may watch sports in order to be entertained, to share the experience of going to a game with friends or family, or even to be part of a larger community. Individuals may even watch sports because a larger community to which they belong identifies with teams that, in their minds at least, embody a religious or ethnic identity.

Upon reflection, however, such explanations of why people are attracted to sports often prove unhelpful. Why get exercise through playing a sport rather than working out at the gym? Why try to make friends through a sport rather than through other activities such as a book club or hanging out with colleagues from work or friends from school? Clearly, sports are entertaining to spectators, but what makes them entertaining, even fascinating? What makes participants exert tremendous effort to compete, to improve, and to try to win? What keeps Charlie Brown, the character from the comic strip *Peanuts*, coming back for more after his baseball team loses again and again?

As all these questions indicate, many of the explanations of why people are drawn to sports, such as the desire to get exercise, are not fundamental. That does not mean there is some single factor that explains the interest in sports. Individuals may be drawn to sports for many of the reasons specified earlier. But there may be underlying characteristics of sports, especially competitive sports, that help explain why the less basic factors come into play.

Although many people who enjoy participating in sports may not stop to think about them, there are deeper features of sports we can consider in looking for the heart of sports' appeal. For one thing, sports contests and even seasons are what some writers have called "unscripted narratives." That is, they are stories where the ending—who wins games, who advances to the finals, and so forth—often is unclear until the very end.

As we have seen, sports normally involve people trying to meet special challenges constructed by the rules. For example, soccer balls must be advanced without use of the hands. In attempting to meet the challenge, athletes can succeed or fail under immense pressure, exhibit remarkable skills, and often demonstrate virtues such as coolness under stress or vices such as selfishness for all to see. A second possibility, then, is that it is the attempt to meet specially constricted challenges that explains at least a great deal of what makes sports so special to spectators and participants alike. Playing a sport or watching others play captures, on a small and specific scale, the human drama of striving to meet challenges and test one's abilities—something that, in all sorts of contexts, we confront every day and that indeed drives human civilization. When we look at it this way, it is no wonder that people around the world who may have almost nothing else in common can share a love of sports.

### Are sports a damaging distraction from the serious social problems of the world?

Many critics of what may be called our culture's infatuation with sport point out that it is essentially a frivolous activity that shifts our focus away from serious social issues or pursuits that may be better for our character. "It's only a game" is their slogan. After all, who will care who won the Super Bowl or the World Cup 100 years from now? Perhaps our interest in sports too often becomes way out of proportion when we think of the major social, economic, and political problems facing us.

If this critique is sound, however, it also applies to any form of entertainment, including much of the arts, that does not have an immediate practical or political goal. As noted in the Prologue, we might as well say "It's only art" as "It's only a game." Whether sports plays too big a role in our society is a genuine issue, but their significance or value cannot be simply dismissed because sports do not normally or directly address social or political issues and contribute to their solution. To be consistent, we also would need to question any other activity or practice that does not contribute directly to the solution of social issues. (I say "directly" because it will be argued later that sports, when conducted properly, embody and express values that are of broader social and political significance, however indirect.)

Indeed, it goes much too far to totally disconnect sports from broader social and political issues. Jackie Robinson breaking the color line in Major League Baseball, John Carlos and Tommie Smith giving the then controversial Black Power salute at the 1968 Olympics, and the philosophy of Olympism with its emphasis on world peace, all illustrate that sports do not take place in a moral, social, or political vacuum and can have a transcendent influence.

Sports also may help us to achieve important goals that play a significant role in moral education. That education instills in us the values we can then apply to pressing social and political concerns. For example, sports may function as a means for promoting social cohesion, as when fans of various religions, ethnicities, and political allegiances rally around their team, creating sporting communities. Sporting communities may even bring people of very different and opposing political and social views together and, as they get to know one another, help to diminish the hyperpartisan tone of contemporary political discourse.

On the other hand, sports also may serve negative social functions. For example, rather than promoting cohesiveness and social unity, they can divide us and promote fierce rivalries between different sporting factions. In some countries, even though sports themselves may not be the cause, sports fans all too often denigrate opponents with blatantly hostile and even racist chants and slogans. As philosopher John Russell points out, "fans of football around the world often regard their clubs as vehicles for expressing historical prejudices and animosities."[4]

### Do social function theories fully explain interest in sports?

In a classic game in the National Basketball Association Championship of the 1969–1970 season, the New York Knicks, under coach Red Holzman, who were known for their solid teamwork and consistent strategy of "hitting the open man," were facing off in Madison Square Garden against the Los Angeles Lakers. Leading up to the game, the Knicks' star center, Willis Reed, was injured; he had missed some earlier games of the playoffs, and it was uncertain whether he would be able to play.

But as the Knicks were warming up, Reed, in uniform, emerged from the locker room and took the floor. The spectators went absolutely wild, and their enthusiasm was contagious. Reed scored two early baskets and although he was unable to play many minutes in the contest, his dedication and commitment inspired the Knicks, who went on to beat the Lakers and win the championship by a score of 113-99.

The Knicks' excellence that season may have served the social function of uniting New Yorkers around their team and providing a community of fans to which they could belong. But surely that is only part of the story. What inspired the fans was the excellence of play their team demonstrated, the unselfishness they exhibited on the court, and of course the example set by Reed in that legendary championship game.

Social function theories characterize and analyze the importance of sports based on the social purposes that they serve. If we take this approach, we do not get the full picture. Although sports may serve social functions, including creating a community of fans supporting a team, the idea that interest in sports is largely due to their social function may put the cart before the horse, as the Willis Reed example suggests. Instead, sports arguably have the power to create community because of interest in the challenges they present and the human excellences displayed in meeting them. If so, sports have *value* independent of their social function; they can serve certain functions such as the creation of communities because of interest in their intrinsic character. (Similarly, we wouldn't attribute interest in art to its role in creating artistic communities, but instead we say communities of artists and audiences arise because of the interest in art itself.)

This suggests a possible overlap between an answer to the explanatory question of why people find sports interesting and the ethical question about what, if anything, makes them morally valuable or significant. Certainly people may have different motives for playing or watching sports. They may want to make friends, seal a business deal on the golf course, or just spend time outdoors. But what they are doing, even if only casually as in a softball game at the company picnic, is trying to meet the challenge of the sport. Likewise, as spectators of sports at any level, it's our interest in how the players meet the challenge that captivates us.

### What is the ethical significance of meeting challenges in sports?

What is so great about meeting challenges? Is there anything special about meeting them in sports? After all, we meet challenges in life all the time: at work, in civic and social life, and in personal relationships.

In sports, however, even if there are external rewards and results if players and teams win specific games or other sporting events, within the sport itself, they must meet the sport's challenges for their own sake. Even professionals who stand to become famous and get rich, and even other athletes who stand to make substantial gains of other types, for example scholarships and recognition, need to take the challenge set by the constitutive rules seriously in order to excel. Meeting challenges created by the constitutive rules is, in fact, central to the idea of sport.

What about competing in well-designed sports—ones that present us with worthy challenges? We should keep in mind here the useful distinction between tests and contests.[5] A test is an activity in which we try to score well at solving problems or completing some task, such as making 50 free throws in a row in basketball, trying to run a mile in under 5 minutes, or getting an "A" on a math exam. A contest is when we compete against others in solving problems or competing tasks, such as shooting baskets when guarded or trying to run a mile faster than other competitors. A contest involves the use of strategy in a more complex way than that involved in testing. Sports, when played competitively, are contests, not just tests. Hence, the challenge includes the obstacles created by the constitutive rules but also the strategies the rules allow, making the challenge strategic as well as physical.

The case that engaging in (and watching) sports is valuable, even morally valuable, rests in part on an analysis of what might be called human flourishing or the human good. It seems to be a fact that most people, given the choice, enjoy more complicated rather than less complicated tasks. Thus, children quickly outgrow the simple game of tic-tac-toe, which if played correctly always leads to a tie, and come to prefer more complex games. Similarly, in the workplace, workers tend to prefer jobs that call on their ingenuity and intelligence rather than simply requiring them to repeat the same task over and over again mindlessly.

Because sports are contests and not merely tests, the strategic complexity of well-designed sports provides a significant opportunity for humans to develop and flourish. On this view, meeting challenges for their own sake may well be part of the good life for humans. Surely, advocates of such a view would argue, using our intellectual and physical faculties to meet challenges that are fun and which stimulate us is a better life than engaging in repetitive tasks that can be repeated mindlessly without calling on our talents or skills.

To be sure, meeting challenges for their own sake also may have benefits, including educational ones. We can learn about ourselves and about others, as well as developing virtues such as dedication and a love of excellence, through participating in and perhaps even by watching sports. It is perhaps this insight that lies behind the controversial claim that participation in sports builds character. We will explore these points more fully in later sections, and we will consider criticisms of them. However, the idea that meeting challenges set by rules especially designed to create "unnecessary obstacles" surely is a major part of the explanation of why sports interest and even fascinate so many and may go a long way toward explaining their value as well.

### Does society place too much value on sports?

Even if sports help to instill and cultivate important values, they can still be overemphasized. The role of sports in educational institutions, such as colleges and universities, will be treated in depth in Chapter 3. However, we should note that the American model of tying competitive athletic teams to schools is very different from what generally is done in most other countries, where clubs playing at various levels of skill represent various geographical areas. Competitive amateur sport in those areas is not tied so directly to secondary schools or colleges and universities.

In the United States, one concern has focused on organized children sports, where critics argue there is too much pressure to win. Critics also worry that young people specialize in one sport too early and so not only fail to learn the lessons taught by playing many sports but also may focus on their athletic training at the expense of academics in hopes of winning an athletic scholarship. Some of this pressure comes from parents who critics maintain become too involved, and who too often become overly fixated on their children's play, perhaps turning games into work for some children and producing teenagers who "burn out" and leave sports as a result.

A more subtle issue concerns what ethics requires of competitors in the heat of battle. The ancient Greek philosopher Aristotle (384–322 B.C.E.) famously suggested that virtuous behavior consists of following a middle way, the Golden Mean, between two extremes. If we think in these terms, courage is a mean between being a coward and being reckless. Similarly, the fair person steers a middle way between considering only her own interests and giving into every claim made upon her, however outrageous.

But what is the "middle way"? What does it mean to act virtuously in the context of sports? It is not always easy to identify, especially in sports. What does sportsmanship require in various contexts? For example, suppose you are coaching a youth soccer team and the referees do not notice that your player tipped in the winning goal through illegal use of his hands. Your team and the fans all notice the infraction, but the official does not. Do you have a duty to tell the officials so that they can correct their call? Or, as many would say, should you just accept the win, perhaps figuring it is not your job to officiate the game? If you do remain silent and accept the victory, is the win something to be proud of? Have you really won in the sense of actually meeting the challenge defined by the constitutive rules of soccer, or have you only appeared to win in the eyes of others?

We will return to this issue later in this book. For now, note that while the idea of the Golden Mean might help us conduct ourselves virtuously as we confront many of the moral challenges that arise in our lives, at times the way it should be applied to sports is quite unclear. At times we may need to consider other ethical principles, as we will discuss later on.

In any case, the account of sports that emphasizes the challenge they present to us may be both an underlying or basic reason explaining much of the interest in them, and a clue to their value, at least when they are practiced in a balanced and fair way. In later sections we will explore what that balanced and fair approach might involve, and what might corrupt it, for example, as many critics claim, an overemphasis on winning at all costs.

*How do we go about examining ethical issues? Is reasoned ethical inquiry even possible given the diversity of ethical opinions? Isn't ethics simply a matter of personal opinion?*

As we noted earlier, to explain is one thing and to evaluate or to make morally defensible judgments about issues is quite another. A successful explanation tells us why things happen but not whether they ought to happen or whether what happens is morally valuable. The latter tasks, which are our focus, require reasonable argument about what we *ought* to do in various contexts and what sorts of activities are *valuable* and for what reason.

Some of you reading this book may be skeptical about whether we can actually come up with good reasons for our conclusions about ethics. After all, don't people disagree on many moral issues, even in sports? Should the soccer coach who sees her player tip the ball into the goal in the earlier example accept the win? Should parents let their children play football in view of the dangers of concussion or other serious injury? Is a losing season always a failure? Is competition in sports healthy, or does it breed a kind of selfishness and contempt or even hatred for the opponent?

Although it is true that people may disagree on these issues, it does not follow that reasonable positions cannot be distinguished from unreasonable ones. Still less does it follow that all moral issues are open to reasonable dispute, even in sports. For example, are there any grounds for regarding the alleged bounties offered by coaches on the National Football League's New Orleans Saints for injuring opposing players as ethical behavior? (In 2012, a National Football League investigation found that coaches on the Saints offered payments to their players for hard hits on opponents and for injuring them as a result.) Shouldn't athletes want to defeat the other team by meeting the challenges of the sport rather than by deliberately harming the best competitors so the challenge is reduced or even eliminated?

Our task then will be to consider and analyze the best arguments for different positions on major ethical issues in sport. Sometimes it may be difficult to determine which positions are strongest, but it does not follow that all positions are intellectually equal or that we cannot distinguish better from worse reasoning. Like any other positions, ethical positions on matters related to sports need defense, and we need to carefully examine such rationales to see if they survive the test of critical scrutiny.[6]

Although tools of ethical reasoning will emerge from our discussion, some points should be kept in mind right from the start. First of all, we need to base our ethical claims on facts. For example, we can't claim that a game was fair if replays of that game show that it was won by an illegal handball. We also may need to be impartial, at least in the minimal sense and try to understand and evaluate the arguments of others. We must resist the temptation to insult opponents, ignore their reasoning, or go into a discussion without willingness to consider criticisms of our own view. We need to demonstrate impartiality by fighting the urge to privilege our own perspective simply because it is ours. Moral views that can be accepted from an impartial point of view, and can be defended against the criticism of others, should win us over regardless of where our allegiance lies, just as a team that consistently defeats worthy opponents has a claim to excellence whether or not we are its fans.

Readers often will have to make the final ethical call for themselves, but I hope our inquiry will show that although reasoned disagreement on many issues is to be expected, we can at least narrow the range of reasonable opinions in a wide variety of cases, and in some make a strong argument for a particular resolution.

*But don't views on sports ethics and indeed on the nature of sports differ from culture to culture?*

Certainly views on a variety of ethical issues can differ from culture to culture. Moral stances toward bullfighting, for example, have been quite different in different places and at different times. The Academy Award–winning movie *Chariots of Fire*, which was based on the true story of two Olympic track hopefuls in nineteenth-century England, gives us a window into differences in moral beliefs about sports. One runner in the film, Harold Abrahams, is castigated by his teachers and fellow students at Oxford because he violated the gentleman athlete's ethic of the time by hiring a coach. Elite sports in England at that time were in many ways restricted by social class, and workers were sometimes prohibited from competing in many elite sports. Although no one would think twice about doing so today, hiring a coach was seen as a mark of professionalization and an unseemly interest in obtaining a reward rather than simply partaking in sport for the fun and the challenge of competing. Abrahams's act was considered too professional or even lower class by many of his contemporaries. "True athletes" were expected to rely on natural ability and inclination alone.[7] Most of us find this attitude toward having a coach as outlandish, but it was the norm in Abrahams's day among members of the British upper-class elite.

Although ethical opinions can differ from place to place and time to time, not all views are equally reasonable. What people *do* believe is one thing, but what is *reasonable* or *justifiable* for them to believe, what they *ought* to believe based on critical inquiry, is another. Cultural disagreements on ethical issues, including those that arise in sports, may not always admit of a reasonable resolution. If they do not, however, it is not merely because people disagree. Rather, it is because there is no decisive reasoning known to the disputants supporting one perspective over others. But whether there is reasoning supporting a resolution cannot be determined in advance of inquiry. Before embracing skepticism, we need to explore the issue to see if such reasoning can be discovered.

Some writers have suggested that standards of reasoning themselves differ from culture to culture so that there are no common standards for resolving cross-cultural ethical disputes. We will return to this issue at the conclusion of our inquiries when we discuss the power of reason to resolve ethical disputes. For now, we can conclude, even if tentatively, that the mere fact of ethical disagreement does not preclude a critical examination of the issues at stake.

### What sorts of considerations are relevant to critical examination of ethical issues?

Consider again the case of the youth soccer coach whose team benefits from an obviously missed call by an official. Suppose the coach decides to say nothing, even though all the players on the team know very well that their winning goal was achieved outside the rules and only by an egregiously bad call. (Of course, much depends on context. For example, did the referee make a simple mistake or deliberately favor the winning team? Is this a championship game or a recreational contest in an instructional league for beginners? Was the handball deliberate or accidental?)

One factor that surely needs to be considered is the *consequences* of the act. If the coach says nothing to the team, are the players being taught that it is perfectly all right to benefit from violations of the rules (or the law) if you are not caught? There are also general consequences of the practice of accepting bad calls in one's favor. If all coaches behave in a similar fashion, will the sport be better or worse? What will be the broader effects on players and spectators alike?

Utilitarianism, a philosophy often associated with its major proponents, Jeremy Bentham (1748–1832) and John Stuart Mill (1806–1873), and in our own day principally by Peter Singer, now of Princeton University, maintains that the morally right action, or in some versions the best set of rules to follow, are those with the best consequences for all affected, with everyone counting equally in the cost–benefit analysis. Of course, such an analysis is often hard to carry out, and there have been major debates about what makes consequences intrinsically beneficial or harmful. Is the criterion pleasure versus pain, as classical utilitarians have argued, or satisfaction of preferences, as some more contemporary utilitarians claim? Utilitarians view the question of whether participation in sports builds character, and if so what sort of character, as highly relevant to assessing competitive sports, for clearly a person's character has large effects on others both inside and outside the world of sports.

Are consequences all there is to ethics? Many would say no. Suppose the decision of the coach to accept the win and say nothing would not have an effect on the character of the players or have significant consequences outside the game itself. Some might argue nevertheless that the victory was not *fairly* gained—and that that is the more important ethical point here. On their view, fairness, justice, and equity are not values easily reconciled with utilitarianism. Some proponents of this view, influenced by the philosopher Immanuel Kant (1724–1804), would say that accepting an arguably unearned victory uses the opponents as mere means to external rewards, and it is wrong because it does not treat them as persons equal in moral status to members of our own team. It is unfair or unjust because the rules create a level or at least equitable playing field, and so it is imperative for all parties to protect that equitable framework if sport is to have any morality at all. Such a view stresses respect for people as a value over and above consequences and focuses on such notions as fairness, justice, and respect for the equal status or rights of others.

A third set of considerations focuses on whether actions exemplify such virtues as courage, honesty, compassion, and care for others. The idea that sports build character, if we take this approach, is more than a utilitarian calculation of consequences and instead focuses on the intrinsic value of the character that participation in sport allegedly produces.

Although each of these views has its champions, these views are not necessarily mutually exclusive. It is difficult to ignore consequences completely in any ethical assessment, but surely it is also important to not treat some people unfairly or ignore their rights simply to get better results. For example, it seems wrong, at least to me, for a coach to lie to a player about her chances of receiving meaningful playing time in games, simply because the coach wants to keep her on the team so there will be enough players to conduct practice.

Proponents of different approaches may try to absorb major points of other schools of thought into their own theory. For example, utilitarians may agree that justice and individual rights are important, but view individual rights and principles of justice as devices for securing the most utility. These utilitarians might argue that, generally, a just society will produce more human good and less harm than an unjust one. Moreover, all these approaches to ethics presuppose that we do not evaluate issues taking only our own interests into account but instead are impartial in at least a minimal sense: namely that we try to evaluate questions taking into account the perspectives and insights of others as well as our own.

Fortunately, we don't need to resolve long-standing debates in ethical theory here. Rather, we only need to keep in mind the kind of considerations that might prove relevant to our examination. Our task will be to examine ethical issues by providing considerations that make a claim to impartiality and do not merely reflect our own interests, to balance the kind of ethical considerations that might bear upon them, and to rigorously and fairly assess the criticisms that may be brought to bear upon our own proposals.

So should the soccer coach accept the win and ignore
the egregiously bad call that led to it?

We can distinguish at least three possible answers to this question. In considering them, remember, we are evaluating what
the coach should do in youth sports, and the issues might be
quite different in intercollegiate or professional sports.

One response is for the coach to reason that officiating
errors are just part of the game, and it is not the participant's
duty or obligation to challenge them. This coach might reason
that such calls balance out over the course of the game or the
season, and so in the long haul are fair to all. As one of my
students once said in class, "I would figure that officials have
made so many bad calls against me over my career, they owed
me this one!" However, bad calls do not necessarily even out
in the short term or in a short series of games, such as a playoff or in an overtime to decide a championship. A bad call in a
playoff game certainly can have more impact than one in a less
meaningful contest, so the latter cannot make up for or cancel
out the former.[8]

Moreover, if the coach simply accepts the win without
saying anything to the players, what lesson is being taught? Is
the lesson that it is perfectly all right to profit from injustice if
one can get away with it? The major purpose of youth sports,
we can plausibly argue, is not just to win games but to teach
important lessons about fairness, sportsmanship, and good
competition—about winning the right way. It is doubtful if si-
lence on the part of the coach contributes to such goals.

Alternatively, the coach could approach the referee immediately but politely and suggest the call was incorrect. The decision is then in the official's hands, and the coach will have
acted in an ethical manner. Although some players on the team
may resent the coach costing them a victory, this provides the
opportunity for an important teaching experience. The coach
can talk to the team about actually meeting the challenge of

the game rather than merely appearing to do so in the eyes of others, and about the value of a victory that is truly deserved.

The coach has yet another option. It may be defensible for the coach to accept the victory but then talk to the team about the reasons for doing so. Perhaps the coach does not want to "show up" the official or thinks the players need to learn to play their hardest whether the calls go for them or against them; in other words, their job is to play the game and not question referees. I myself favor the second view at the level of youth sports on the grounds that it is more important, at least at that stage of player development, to teach lessons about honesty and winning fairly by actually meeting the challenges of the game than it is to win.

Fortunately this kind of issue does not generally arise at elite levels of sport when referees can consult instant replay in the attempt to make calls as accurate as possible, but it can arise in high school, intercollegiate, and lower level professional sports when such technology is not available or its use is restricted by rules. Many would argue that winning should be regarded as more important at those levels than in youth sports. Although such a view has force, it also is arguable that winning ought to be the result of genuinely meeting the challenge of the sport and not because of egregious errors in officiating. In any case, we will discuss the degree of importance that ought to be assigned to winning more fully in Chapter 2.

### Is ethics in sports simply a matter of following the rules and applying them fairly?

Our discussion so far has emphasized the constitutive rules of sports and the challenges they create. But ethical issues in sports go well beyond conformity to rules. Should winning be the dominant value in competitive sports? How should coaches balance competitive success with giving all the players on the team a fair chance to play in contests? Is gamesmanship, activity that does not literally break the rules but aims at taking advantage of psychological weakness of the opponent, such as deliberately slowing the pace of play in a tennis match against an impatient player, acceptable?

Sometimes the rules themselves raise ethical questions. Should the rules themselves sometimes be changed on ethical grounds? For example, the legacies of such baseball sluggers as Barry Bonds and Alex Rodriquez have been called into question because of the allegations that they used performance-enhancing drugs to achieve their batting feats. Bonds and Rodriquez may have intentionally violated the rules or other norms prohibiting use of performance-enhancing drugs to gain a competitive advantage. (In Bonds case, explicit rules banning the use of certain performance enhancers had not yet been promulgated by Major League Baseball, although prohibition might reasonably have been inferred from other provisions already in effect.)[9] But are these rules themselves justifiable? Do prohibitions on the use of performance-enhancing drugs unjustly restrict the freedom of athletes to experiment? Are they necessary to preserve competitive fairness? We have to go beyond the rules to answer these questions and ask instead what rules we *ought* to have.

Following the rules doesn't only come into question when it comes to the bad things that athletes do; many acts of sportsmanship are not required by the rules but certainly seem to be admirable nonetheless. For example, Pablo Di Canio, in a Premier League Soccer game in 2000, refused to take a shot on an open goal so that the injured goalie, Paul Gerrard, might receive immediate attention. His act was widely applauded, and he received a FIFA award for fair play.

In assessing issues that may fall outside the rules, we can appeal to the kinds of ethical considerations already mentioned, such as the consequences of actions and policies, effects on character and virtue, and fairness and respect for individuals as autonomous persons. A number of writers, including me, have followed the lead of legal philosopher Ronald Dworkin

(1931–2013), who argued forcefully that the law is more than just a body of rules. In addition, in hard cases that do not easily fit under any rule, judges do and sometimes should appeal to principles that underlie the law.

Dworkin illustrates his position by citing an early New York State case, *Riggs v. Palmer*, in which the highest state court considered whether a young man who murdered his grandfather in order to gain an inheritance should be allowed to actually inherit. The majority of the court agreed the will was legally valid; it was signed by the legally required number of witnesses. Nevertheless, the court decided the murderer should not inherit appealing to the *principle* that no one should profit from his own wrongdoing. This principle was not a formal legal rule but a reason of significant weight that must be presupposed to make the best sense out of criminal law.

On this view, the law is not merely a body of rules. Rather, judges need to appeal not just to laws but to principles underlying the laws in deciding difficult cases. That is, they need a theory of the area of law that makes the law intelligible and coherent, and as morally sound as possible.[10] For example, the equal protection clause of the United States Constitution guarantees all citizens the "equal protection of the law," but what does "equal protection" mean? In deciding how to answer that question, the courts may need to formulate a theoretical account of the nature of equal protection that makes the most sense of precedent and that is morally defensible. The basic principles of that account then can be used as reasons by judges to help decide future cases. Such principles arguably are not merely the personal values of the judges but are logically drawn from the best theory of the area of law at issue. (Those who disagree with this approach claim that the personal values of the judges shape what is regarded as the best theory, thereby denying the objectivity of judicial decision making. This may be too glib, however. After all, people holding this view claim to be making an objective point, not just one that reflects their own personal preferences.)

An approach similar to Dworkin's arguably applies in sport. For example, referees in basketball have to decide how to apply the rule against physical contact or, in other words, decide how much contact constitutes a foul. A referee who is too strict and counts even minimal incidental contact as a foul risks slowing down the game to an unbearable extent, eliminating opportunities for creative play and turning it into a foul-shooting contest. A referee who allows too much contact risks turning the game into a wrestling match. What principle should the referees follow in interpreting the rules against fouling?

Another example from the history of baseball was cited by sports philosopher John Russell. In an 1887 American Association contest between Louisville and Brooklyn, Louisville player Reddy Mack crossed home plate to score and decided he was no longer a base runner, so the rule against runners interfering with fielders did not apply to him. He held down the opposing catcher, enabling a teammate to score. Russell points out that Mack's behavior was not explicitly prohibited by the formulation of the interference rule then in effect, but to allow Mack's behavior to stand would be, in effect, to turn baseball games into wrestling matches.

How are we to identify principles that should apply to such cases? Dworkin argues that the principles judges should appeal to in hard cases are not arbitrary and should not reflect their personal values but should underlie or be presupposed by key features of law. Similarly, John Russell proposed a general principle for use in sports: we ought to interpret the rules in such a way as to "preserve and foster" the excellences the sport is best construed as testing and in such a way as to preserve the challenge and, we might add, even the beauty of the sport.[11] For example, the introduction of the shot clock in basketball, which limits the time basketball teams can possess the ball without shooting, arguably is supported by Russell's principle, since without the clock, teams with a lead can stall or hold the ball without attempting to score, thereby preventing the other team from exercising important skills the game is arguably designed to test. Likewise, if Reddy Mack had been allowed to interfere with a rival fielder just because he had already scored, central skills of baseball such as throwing and catching might be replaced by the ability to assault opposing players—hardly a skill baseball was designed to test.

Principles differ from rules in that they are generally unwritten and sometimes must be weighed against one another. Rules such as "three strikes and you are out" apply in an all-or-nothing fashion. Consider, for example, whether we should allow more extensive body checking in men's ice hockey. This change might make the game more exciting to some spectators, even if it results in less emphasis on skating skills and the beauty they exemplify. The issue cannot be settled by appeal to the rules because it concerns what rules we ought to have. Instead, we must look for the best interpretation or theory of ice hockey and apply the principles it supports.

The appeal to underlying principles fundamental to sports sometimes has been called "broad internalism," because it takes a broad view of how the internal features of sport, such as the challenges created by the rules, are to be understood. It also has been called "interpretivism" because an interpretation of the fundamental excellences of the sport is needed to elicit the proper principles.

Is the choice of principles ultimately arbitrary or subjective? Does what counts as a good interpretation differ from person to person or culture to culture? Just as we may worry whether allowing judges to apply principles in hard legal cases gives them too much discretion, does the appeal to principle in sport do the same? Or is the choice of some principles over others defensible by appeal to reasons and, if so, to what extent?

These are questions the reader will need to ponder as we turn to the examination of concrete issues in sports. Be that as it may, we have developed a set of guidelines or tools that will help us in the examination of concrete issues arising in sports. These guidelines include the identification of the challenge created by the rules as a central aspect of sport, especially competitive sport, some approaches for picking out ethically relevant features of a case such as the consequences of acts or policies and fairness to all concerned, and the appeal to principles claimed to be presupposed by our best interpretation or understanding of sports themselves. The principle cited earlier, which enjoins us to protect the excellences and skills the different sports have been designed to test through challenge is an example. We now can make a turn from the more abstract to the more concrete by considering issues that arise from actual competition in sports and athletics.

# 2

# WINNING, CHEATING, AND THE ETHICS OF COMPETITION

## *What ethical issues are raised by competitive athletics?*

As we saw in the previous chapter, there are a host of moral benefits that we can reap by playing, supporting, or otherwise participating in sports, and there are also rich ethical questions that arise from sports. One of those questions—a central concern for our exploration of the ethics of sport—is whether competitive athletics, at the end of the day, have a positive or negative effect. Do we put too much value in winning? Is competition in general a bad thing? Is competition bad in sports in particular?

Critics charge that competition teaches us to view opponents as mere things or obstacles that get in our way and not as people in their own right. Although there are positive aspects of sports, for example, the values that it can instill in people, the beauty of skilled movement, and the friendships that often develop through participation, such critics think that the emphasis on competition makes us lose sight of all these things—and may even get in the way of their coming about in the first place.

This debate over competition in sports gets at a larger question: our fundamental conception of human nature. If one worries that humans always or at least generally act out of pure self-interest or selfishness, tendencies that need to be kept in check lest our relationships deteriorate and lest we find ourselves caught up in constant struggle, competition even in sports may be seen as reinforcing the worst tendencies of our innate character. On the other hand, if one views human nature as leaving room for the appreciation of a variety of values other than self-interest, one may be more inclined to view athletic competition as a cooperative mutual quest for excellence, as suggested later in this chapter. But let us cut to the chase and examine more closely a number of specific ethical issues concerning competitive sports by assessing the arguments that can be brought to bear upon them.

### *Some critics claim that competition in sports is morally indefensible. What are their arguments? Are such arguments sound?*

Although sports are sometimes played just for fun, as in pickup soccer and basketball games at local playgrounds, they are very often played competitively, with players trying their hardest to win games and defeat opponents. Some have suggested that we distinguish the largely recreational activity of sports from competitive athletics and even that different ethical principles apply to each case.[1] However, it is doubtful that a sharp bright line separates sports from athletics. More likely, there is a continuum with friendly pickup games at one end and professional, Olympic, and elite amateur competition at the other. (Because I believe in such a continuum, I will use the terms "sports" and "athletics" interchangeably. The level of competition at issue in different sections of our discussion should be made clear by context.)

Examples of sportsmanship and generosity can be found all along the spectrum, but any discussion of the ethics of sport certainly needs to be sensitive to relevant differences among levels of play. The degree of competitiveness appropriate in a professional championship is inappropriate for youth teams where children are just learning the fundamentals of a sport.

Critics of competitive sport maintain that the emphasis on competition and on winning at most levels of competitive athletics is ethically indefensible. In some cases, this stems from an objection to competition in general. However, many critics of competitive sport are most concerned with specific problems that arise from the emphasis on winning that is such a major part of contemporary athletic competition.

Part of their objection rests on assumptions that they make about human nature itself. We can learn about such assumptions by considering the political philosophy of a giant in the field of political theory, Thomas Hobbes (1588–1679). Hobbes's political philosophy can help us understand better some of the criticisms of athletic competition that will be examined later because of his view of what extreme unrestricted competition would entail.

Hobbes is known especially for his defense of law and order, which stemmed from his bleak view of what life would be like in their absence. In his major work, *Leviathan*, published in 1651, Hobbes described what he thought such a state of nature—a state with no law, no rules, and no one capable of enforcing them—might be like. Such a state, he theorized, would be one of relative scarcity of resources in which all human needs could not be fulfilled, and in which people would do virtually anything to secure their welfare. Hobbes, in other words, thought humans were by nature selfish, and that we would always put our own interests first. Even if that view is extreme, Hobbes might have assumed plausibly that each individual would reasonably fear that others might act on selfish motives with willingness to inflict harm on those in their way to obtain their goals. In the absence of law and order, he postulated, any alliances would be based on mutual advantage and would last only so long as it would be in the parties' interest to keep them. In other words, Hobbes's idea of a world without government was not far from what many read about and saw in *The Hunger Games*. We would be constantly at war with one another and, in Hobbes's famous words, our lives would be "nasty, brutish, cruel, and short."

Hobbes probably regarded the state of nature not as an actual period in human history but as hypothetical or imaginary. He used this model to illustrate why the legal system and the authority of the state were necessary. (He did suggest, however, that in the absence of an international government, the nations of the world actually might be in a sort of state of nature with one another, each pursuing its own national interest as its highest and perhaps only legitimate goal.) Hobbesian individuals in the state of nature tend to think of their own self-interest first, place a great weight on competitive victory over others, and focus less on the humanity of others and much more on their status as obstacles standing in the way of them securing their personal goals.

Although critics of competition in athletics surely recognize important differences between Hobbes's state of nature and competitive sport, their view of what competition entails may reflect some of the assumptions Hobbes makes about human psychology and about the state of nature. Thus, as already mentioned, one of their major points is that the intense pursuit of victory leads competitors, at best, to view opponents not as persons just like themselves but as obstacles. Many fear that competitive athletics breeds hostility, enmity, and even hatred of opponents. One writer, speaking primarily of spectators rather than participants, even suggests that the fans' regard for winners breeds a kind of contempt for the weakness of the losers that is "fascistoid" in character.[2]

A second major criticism of competitive athletics is that emphasis on competitive success, or winning, makes us too result oriented. We lose sight of the value of competition itself and the preparation for it, and we think only of outcomes. Just as in Hobbes's state of nature, winners are successful and losers are failures.

Finally, and perhaps most important, critics claim that athletic competition reflects, promotes, or reinforces a Hobbesian kind of selfishness where we put ourselves or our team first and place our own or our team's interests above all others. Competitive athletics, on the critics' view, teaches selfishness and egoism to a detrimental extent. If one believes with Hobbes that human nature itself is egoistic or selfish at its base, athletic competition might be seen as a mini version of the state of nature. Even if one does not go as far as Hobbes and leaves some room in one's views for humans to be good at their core, even when they aren't forced to be, athletic competition might be seen as reinforcing our worst impulses.

### Can athletic competition be defended against such criticism?

In evaluating such criticisms of athletic competition, we need to be careful not to blur very different points together so that important distinctions are not lost. In particular, we need to distinguish the way competitive athletics may actually be conducted from the way they *must* always be conducted and from the way they *ought* to be conducted. Thus, if sports are practiced a certain way, intense competition may indeed have the results critics fear. Players may come to dislike opponents simply because they are on the other team, and fans and players alike may express contempt for teams that rarely win. Success may be defined only as winning, and the value of other aspects of athletics, such as developing skills, improving, and persevering, despite being outmatched, are lost. I once asked the students in one of my classes what they thought the players on a local high school team that only won one or two games in their entire season got out of playing. One student, an outstanding athlete who played his sport professionally around the world after college, replied, "Absolutely nothing."

However, if sports are practiced with an emphasis on meeting challenges and what we can learn from trying to do so, winning can remain important as one criterion of success, but other important factors can also be recognized. For example, if a weaker team pushes an athletically more talented team to its limit in a game and loses due to bad luck—say, a sudden gust of wind blows an otherwise errant kick on a goal past the goalkeeper—doesn't the weaker team still have much to be proud of?

It is also doubtful that most players and most fans normally hate or despise their opponents, even in cases of intense rivalries: think of the way Yankee fans expressed support for Boston after the bombing of the Boston Marathon in 2013. Soccer in some European and South American venues may be an important exception, where rivalries are often expressions of deeper religious and ethnic differences, and fans too often target opposing players with racist chants. In many sporting contexts, however, spectators often respect worthy opponents or underachievers rather than feeling contempt for them. Chicago Cubs fans' love affair with their baseball team, despite the Cubs' longtime lack of competitive success, is just one example. Participants often respect each other, remembering that they have more in common than they have setting them apart from one another, as the traditional handshakes at the end of games in many sports symbolize. Hockey great Wayne Gretzky reportedly invited the top players from the leading Russian team of his day, which had an intense rivalry with his own Canadian team on the ice, to his home for a barbeque and even became friends with some of them. So we must keep in mind that athletic competition does not always and perhaps does not usually embody the disrespect and dehumanization of the opponent the critics fear.

The ethical question, of course, is what way of playing sport is morally most defensible? What kind of competition should we promote and what kind should we change or reform? If competition is regarded as a way of testing one's physical and mental skills, strategy, preparation, and one's heart, and of learning from both success and failure, athletic competition need not embody the Hobbesian worldview.

For example, we have to keep in mind that winning, while important, truly isn't everything. As I have argued elsewhere, we can view athletic competition as a mutual quest for excellence.[3] On this view, athletic competition is in many ways significantly cooperative and the athletes are not the analogs of the individuals in Hobbes's state of nature. Rather, we should regard opponents as having freely chosen to enter the contest so that both parties can test themselves through the challenge of competition as structured by the constitutive rules of the sport. Opponents facilitate each other's goal of being tested and are in an at least partially cooperative as well as competitive relationship.

But what if Hobbes is right? What if human nature either is basically selfish at root, or at the very least there are egoistic tendencies that sports bring out? What if, at the end of the day, sports are a loosely controlled series of fierce rivalries as much as they are a mutual quest for excellence?[4] If that is the case, sports are no worse than any other human practice, since, on the Hobbesian view, egoistic tendencies must be kept in constant check. Rivalries can be fierce in business, science, academia, and the arts as well as sport. More important, if the model of mutualism is emphasized in practice, a winning-at-all-costs attitude can be modified or controlled. We would be remiss to think that human nature is impervious to outside influence. Perhaps, if the idea of athletic competition as an activity from which all parties can and do benefit becomes a predominant norm, sports, properly conducted, can provide an important check on the excesses of an egoistic "me first" attitude in which winning, even crushing opponents, is everything. Perhaps they have the potential to benefit human nature rather than bringing out its ugly side.

**Are you suggesting that winning is unimportant? If winning is unimportant, why do they keep score?**

Even though we have to be careful not to overemphasize winning in competitive sports, it is important, and mutualism does not deny that. Winning requires the use of special skills over and above the normal play of the game. Winning normally requires the choice of appropriate strategies, including the ability to persist and keep one's cool when the opponent poses a challenge, and the fortitude to make a run from behind rather than give up when the game is not going as well as one had hoped.[5] The Seattle Seahawks of the NFL played very well in the 2015 Super Bowl, but a highly debatable strategic choice at the very end of the game may have cost them a victory. Accordingly their play in the game, despite the excellences they displayed, should not be regarded as an overall success. Strategic skills are often at least as important, or even more important, in competitive sport as purely physical ones. A good strategy or game plan is one that maximizes the chance of winning. Thus, winning is not something that can or should be taken lightly at most levels of play.

However, winning and losing must also be kept in proper perspective. Not all wins are unqualified successes, and not all losses are complete failures. When one of my sons was about 10 years old, his younger cousins Matthew and Rebecca came for a visit. During the visit, my son ran in from playing outside to announce proudly, "I struck out Rebecca five times in row!" "But Marc," I said, "she is only 6 years old!"

For a win to be truly significant, surely it has to be against a worthy opponent. A team that rolled up victory after victory simply by scheduling weak opposition would have less reason to take pride in its performance than another team that had a lower winning percentage but earned its wins against the best opposition it could find. Similarly, victories brought about by flukes, egregiously bad calls, or when playing poorly against inferior opponents, often called "ugly wins," surely should be accorded less significance and be a lesser source of pride than victories earned in well-played games against strong opposition.[6]

Does this sort of argument undermine the significance of winning? Shouldn't a truly excellent team or athlete be able to overcome bad luck or the occasional bad call? Isn't being able to win while having an off day against a weaker opponent a mark of excellence?

Consider the 1960 World Series in which the New York Yankees faced the Pittsburgh Pirates. In the seventh and deciding game, the Yankees apparently had victory well within their grasp when, in the final inning, a routine ground ball off the bat of Pittsburgh's Bill Virdon would, if fielded properly, end the game and give the Yankees a well-earned victory. Unfortunately for the Yankees, the ball struck a pebble and made an unexpected bounce. As a result, the ball hit the Yankee shortstop Tony Kubek in the throat, injuring him and giving the Pirates a second life. Pittsburgh took advantage of this fluke play to go on to score five runs, with the game-winning home run by future Hall of Famer Bill Mazerowski securing them the world championship.

Consider two reactions to this example. On the first, bad luck, the ball striking the pebble, played a crucial role in the game. Although Pittsburgh won and the Yankees lost, the Yankee loss was not a failure—they played as least as well as the Pirates and only lost because of a fluke—and the Pittsburgh victory was of less significance than otherwise would be the case because they benefitted from a lucky break.

On the second view, Pittsburgh still was behind after the bad bounce and still had to go on to score five runs to win. The Yankees were unable to stop them and so deserved to lose. Great teams overcome bad luck and, in any case, one fluke over a course of seven games did not decide the series.

My own view is that, in this case, bad luck did not radically diminish Pittsburgh's victory because of what happened afterward, especially the Pirates' dramatic come-from-behind rally. Suppose, however, that the winning run had scored on the very play involving the bad bounce into Kubek's throat. In that case, shouldn't we be reluctant to say that the hypothetical Pittsburgh win was fully deserved or at least be reluctant to claim that the Yankees failed? If so, it seems that we don't regard winning as the sole criterion of success but also consider how it was achieved and what contributory factors determined the outcome.

In any case, we shouldn't deny that winning is an important and often the most significant criterion of success in competitive athletics. But we also have to take into account the quality of the competition, the level of play exhibited, and the role of officiating and of luck. These factors can in some contexts either diminish the significance of wins or at least call the significance of winning into question. If we do so, we have to accept that the claim that "winning isn't everything, it's the only thing," often attributed (probably inaccurately) to famous American football coach Vince Lombardi, simply misses the point.

### Should winning be emphasized in youth sports?

Youth sports, which I will loosely define as organized competitions for children not yet at high school age (usually 14 years old in the United States), raise a host of issues. Sports at this level, such as Little League Baseball, are organized and coached by adults. Critics have maintained that parental pressure has led children to early specialization in one sport, perhaps because of parents' hopes that promising youngsters might be awarded an athletic scholarship to college. Indeed, the Little League World Series now is televised nationally and sometimes globally. In 2014, young Little League sensation Mo'ne Davis became the first girl to pitch a shutout in the Little League Series and was even featured on the cover of *Sports Illustrated*. Despite the inspiring example that she sets, the very existence of the Little League World Series illustrates the dangers of adult involvement in organized children's sports and the kind of pressure that can corrupt such activities when winning at the highest available levels of competition becomes a major focus.

In February 2015, the winners of the 2014 Little League World Series, the Jackie Robinson West team from Chicago, was stripped of its championship after an investigation alleged that team officials (adults) had falsified boundaries so they could place otherwise ineligible players on the team. This was heartbreaking because it was not claimed that any of the players on the team knew of the infraction. The team captured the imagination and affections of millions of fans, and it inspired the predominately African American neighborhoods where the players lived. Unfortunately, this was not the first such infraction involving national competition in Little League. For example, in 2000, a team from the Bronx, New York, was found to have used a player from the Dominican Republic who was too old for Little League Baseball and who violated other restrictions as well. The team had to forfeit its third-place finish, and the records set by its players, including the ineligible player, were erased.

Of course, most kids do not play on teams whose coaches take youth sports so seriously, and they often enjoy their participation in organized leagues in sports ranging from baseball and basketball to ice hockey, lacrosse, and, of course, soccer. Often authors who write for children and young adults, such as Matt Christopher, tell inspirational stories about how overcoming problems through participation in sports contributed to personal growth and maturity, and for many kids this is a reality. Although empirical research sometimes yields mixed results, which might be expected because sports for children are not conducted in identical ways depending on the sport and age group involved, there is evidence of significant positive benefit, especially for girls. (See, for example, the summary at http://www.aspenprojectplay.org/the-facts.)

The question remains, however. Should youth sports be treated primarily as recreational and instructional, with an emphasis on having fun and learning skills, or should competitive success and winning also be emphasized?

When dealing with children new to the sport, instruction and fun surely are crucial. Children cannot play competitively if they don't know how to play at all. But as they acquire skills, people differ as to the degree of competitiveness that is appropriate to their age and level of skill. Obviously we cannot deal with every set of circumstances that might arise. Nevertheless, it will be helpful to consider two opposing views and see if we might find an appropriate compromise or Golden Mean between them.[7]

On the first view, participation in sports, even for children, is preparation for life, and life itself can be harsh. A major role of sports, as advocates of this position maintain, is to prepare young athletes for life's pressures and not protect them in a cocoon that shields them from the pain of loss and the stress of trying to win. Youth sports, on this view, should be highly competitive and the young participants should be held to high standards of performance and commitment, at least once they have a grasp of the fundamental skills of the sport.

The second view, often championed by those who view themselves as reforming sports for children, argue that sports for this age group should be primarily about making friends, having fun, and learning skills appropriate to the sport. The reformers claim that most children are not prepared for the pressures of highly competitive sport and that it is wrong to make these youngsters feel that they have failed if they make mistakes that cost their team a game. Moreover, the reformers point out, excessive pressure at too early an age can cause burnout that leads children to drop out of sports entirely. Indeed, polls of participants in children's sports indicate that children themselves do not rate winning even near the top of their list of reasons for participating and consistently affirm that they would rather play on a losing team than sit on the bench on a winning team.

Although many observers and many parents criticize the overemphasis on winning and competitiveness in youth sports, there is something to be said for the first view. As proponents of this view maintain, why shouldn't the skills taught in children's sports include how to win and lose gracefully and how to exhibit skills in a competitive situation? Sports can be a medium for teaching youngsters how to deal with competitive pressures. The key is to do so in an appropriate manner for the age and skill level of the participants, however. Coaches can instruct and point out errors in play without screaming at their young charges. Rather than equating a mistake in play with the child being a failure, coaches and parents should use it as a basis for teaching how to do better the next time. As children grow in skill and experience, the competitiveness of the play can increase as well.

Of course, some youths are extremely talented, and pressure and sometimes criticism by parents and coaches may be needed to bring out their best. Golf star Tiger Woods was pushed to excel by his parents. However, they did not undermine his sense of self-worth and supported his efforts to do what he loved rather than push him against his will to excel in a sport he hated. This is no different from the way that classroom teachers also need to sometimes push their charges to excel and not allow them to think that they can get their best possible results without hard work and commitment.

Be that as it may, children can be driven out of sport entirely by excessive emphasis on winning. Bullying behavior by coaches is a form of abuse and should be prohibited. However, there likely is no strict formula or rule for determining how competitive coaches or parents of children should be. Our best recourse is good judgment.

The task in youth sports is to find an appropriate middle ground or Aristotelian Golden Mean, through which children can learn competitive skills without being discouraged or even crushed by competitive pressures imposed by overzealous adults. This mean, as Aristotle himself suggested, is not the same for everyone but may vary from situation to situation. Coaches and parents need to be sensible in balancing the stresses of competition against the values of fun and development of skills.

### What is cheating and why is it morally wrong in sports?

Calling someone a cheater normally is a way of morally condemning the person or the person's actions. (I say "normally" because, as we will see, it is possible to admire a clever act of cheating or use the term to refer to what some might call cheating but which the speaker regards as permissible. For example, a fan of the New England Patriots may say, "Deflating the football is cheating, but I see nothing wrong with it.") But what is cheating and what makes it wrong?

Like many moral terms, "cheating" is difficult to define, and some writers deny that it can be defined at all, regarding it instead as an all-purpose term of condemnation without determinative content.[8] On this account, to call an act cheating is just another way of calling it morally wrong. If we accept such a view, calling an act one of cheating would not constitute an independent reason for morally condemning it, as when one says the act is wrong *because* it is cheating. Rather, it would be just another way of calling it wrong or of merely repeating what was already said rather than justifying it.

Before we decide whether such a skeptical view is correct, let's examine whether we can characterize cheating at least relatively precisely. Clearly, cheating involves more than just violating a rule because many violations may be accidental or unintentional. A basketball player who fouled an opposing shooter in an attempt to block the shot has violated a rule but has not cheated. Moreover, even some intentional rule violations may not be cheating. Strategic fouling, or openly violating a rule with willingness to accept the penalty in order to gain a strategic advantage, arguably is not cheating.

Are deception and secrecy necessary elements of cheating? Many cheaters do not want to be caught and so cheat secretly or do so deceptively so as to avoid detection. But as Bernard Gert has pointed out in his book *Morality*, powerful cheaters can do so right out in the open as when a spouse who knows his partner is financially dependent on him cheats sexually quite openly, even flaunting his infidelity.[9]

An illuminating account of cheating draws on Gert's own analysis. On a rough sketch of this approach, one cheats when one violates a system of public rules central to a practice in order to gain a competitive advantage that would or could not reasonably be allowed as a general basis for making exceptions. That is, it would be unreasonable to allow everyone to exempt themselves from the rules in similar circumstances. For example, someone who cheats at golf by using a ball that is designed to fly further than the rules allow does so to gain an advantage over others, but this advantage would be lost if every competitor used the same illegal ball. Similarly, a soccer player who uses her hands to gain an advantage over opponents could not reasonably want everyone to use his or her hands to get such an advantage because not only would the benefit she gains be cancelled out by similar moves by opponents but, much more important, one of the primary skills of soccer, skillful use of the feet, would virtually be eliminated from the game.

What makes cheating wrong on this account is that cheaters make arbitrary exceptions for themselves; they place themselves above the law, so to speak, without any justification for doing so. Why should my opponent be allowed to use the illegal ball and not me? In a sense, cheaters do not win fairly by meeting the challenge set by the constitutive rules but instead avoid the challenge. In effect, they treat opponents not as persons in their own right but more as objects to be used for enhancing their own gains. On this view, cheaters violate Kant's injunction to never treat others only as mere means but always as ends, or equal persons, in their own right.

Useful as it is, this analysis may not cover all examples of cheating. Perhaps some acts of cheating are not violations of public systems of rules because no rule is at issue in the cases in question. In one example that has been cited by philosopher John Russell to illustrate this point, a baseball coach waters down the home field to soften it so an opposing team cannot take advantage of its superior speed.[10] Consider also a hypothetical example in which the coach of a volleyball team turns out the lights in the gym during the playing of the national anthem before home games after taking her team into a brightly lit locker room. The visiting players stand in the dark. The coach of the home team then turns up the lights in the gym as brightly as possible for the start of the game in the hope that her team would have an advantage while the opposing players would need time to adjust to the bright lights, thereby throwing off their perceptual judgment.

Do examples such as these show the need to revise our account of cheating? Do they show further that the concept of "cheating" has no determinative content but only is another way of saying the behavior in question is wrong? The jury remains out on both questions. However, my suggestion is that we can revise the account of cheating to cover the sorts of examples here. Whether this revision can withstand criticism remains to be seen, however. In particular, although neither watering the field nor darkening the gym violates specific constitutive rules of baseball or volleyball, each may well violate basic *principles* that apply to sports, which we discussed in the previous section.

The volleyball example might plausibly be viewed as cheating because the coach of the home team is trying to gain an advantage, but not through factors volleyball as a game is designed to test, such as strategy or physical skills like setting the ball up for the taller players to spike. Rather, the goal is to undermine the skills of the opponents by a tactic having nothing to do with the game. In other words, the home coach is trying to win not through her team displaying superior skills of volleyball but by preventing the opponents from utilizing their own skills by a trick irrelevant to the test presented by the sport.

The case of the watered baseball field is more complex. In fact, it is not at all clear that it is an actual case of cheating, since the watered-down field poses a problem for both teams. Moreover, the home coach can universalize by arguing that each team can set up its home field as it pleases to enhance its particular talents and skills. Darkening the gym, however, makes much less sense as a public practice because once teams are aware of it, they too would go into a lighted room before the game. More important, it violates the principle, formulated originally as we noted in Chapter 1 by Russell, that we ought to preserve and enhance the skills specific sports are designed to test. This principle arguably is not arbitrary but is presupposed by our best available interpretation of the very point of playing sports in the first place; namely, the testing of ourselves against the challenges of the sport. (Critics might respond that there is no single best interpretation of sports, a topic we will return to later.)

Surely this is just starting point for further analysis of the nature of cheating. What our discussion does suggest, however, is that there is a core conception of cheating that, even if it is controversial when applied to borderline cases, does seem to capture what is at issue in clear ones. Cheaters in sports, at least in clear cases, intentionally exempt themselves from the public standards (such as rules and principles) that reasonable and impartial persons would want applied in order to gain a competitive advantage without justification for such an exemption.

How does this analysis apply to cheating scandals that are related to sport but which take place off the field? To look at one such scandal, in the spring of 2015, key officials of the governing body of world soccer, FIFA, were charged with corruption of various kinds following an investigation by the FBI and Swiss authorities. Allegations arising from this complex scandal involve bribery, including in the award of sites for the World Cup and other major competitions, as well as other forms of misconduct, including serious charges against FIFA President Sepp Blatter.[11] The World Cup is perhaps the most widely watched and most lucrative event in competitive sport, and charges of corruptions in awarding sites for the event shook the sport to its foundations, as did claims of ethically dubious transfer of funds to FIFA officials.

Such corruption, as well as the bribery of game officials to fix the outcome of the contest, fit well under our account of cheating, broadly construed. Officials of FIFA, as well as referees in a contest, operate under a series of public rules designed to promote a fair outcome. Accepting bribes to award a site or fix a game clearly violates the public system of rules that apply in ways reasonable people could not agree to regard as legitimate exceptions. Why even have the contest or the process of bidding for sites of the World Cup if the result is in fact determined by factors deemed irrelevant by the rules of the procedure and the principles that support them? Cheating in sports can be as serious when it occurs off the field as when it occurs on it, and if the argument here is sound, it applies for much the same reasons in both sorts of cases.

### Can cheating sometimes make sports more interesting for participants and spectators alike?

Cheating on one's spouse or partner, one's business partner, on one's income taxes, and on tests in school clearly are serious matters and in some cases considered crimes. But sports take place in a special sphere where many actions not allowed in the outside world, such as tackling an opponent or throwing a baseball near someone's body, hard enough to injure the person, are not only permissible but encouraged in the framework of particular sports. These types of actions are in some cases part of the legitimate tactics that characterize skilled play. Should cheating be regarded similarly; that is, as something generally to be condemned outside of sport but sometimes a legitimate tactic to be employed inside of sport?

Perhaps, as one writer has argued, cheating is not always wrong because it sometimes can make athletic competition more interesting for spectators and possibly participants as well.[12] Will the baseball pitcher place an illegal substance, such as vaseline on the ball to make it behave erratically and therefore be harder to hit? Will the umpire detect the infraction? Will the offensive linesman in the NFL illegally hold the defender but do it subtly enough to avoid detection? Can the basketball coach get away with sending her best foul shooter to the line when a poor foul shooter was actually fouled? Will the squash player get away with calling an opponent's shot out when it was barely in? Can cheaters cheat with wit and verve that spectators and even fellow competitors can admire?

Perhaps we should conclude that some forms of cheating, such as the illegal pitch in baseball, sometimes make the game more entertaining. Indeed, some Major League pitchers, such as the great Gaylord Perry, became famous because of suspicion that they threw such pitches. The willingness and ability to occasionally throw an illegal pitch add to the repertoire of deliveries batters would have a split second to "pick up" or identify in order to hit, making the pitcher who does so an especially formidable opponent.

However, if we adopt the view that sports contests are not just entertainment but are designed to challenge the competitors to overcome the obstacles within a framework of constitutive rules, we should come to a very different conclusion. If we are engaged in a mutual quest for excellence through challenge, as outlined earlier, we should want to find out who are the best players, not who are the best cheaters. Thus, baseball players normally are evaluated on qualities the game is designed to test such as batting, throwing, and catching, whereas soccer players are ranked on their ball handling, defense, speed, and shooting abilities. Imagine a coach saying, "Although Cristina is my best basketball player in terms of the skills of the game, Elena, who is inferior in basketball skills, is actually my most valuable player because she is the best cheater."[13]

Of course, we could change sports to make cheating an accepted practice and perhaps never know the identity of the best cheaters because they would be so skilled their violations of the rules normally would not be detected. The price of such a change, however, would be that we would often not know if the winning teams or individuals were actually the most skilled in their sport—or even highly skilled at all—or whether they simply were the best cheaters. Isn't that price simply too high to pay?

## What is gamesmanship? Is it a form of cheating?

Although there probably is no uncontested definition of "gamesmanship," the term generally refers to attempts to distract or unsettle an opponent that are not prohibited by the rules. The term came to widespread attention after Stephen Potter published the satirical book *The Theory and Practice of Gamesmanship* in 1947. Potter refers to gamesmanship as "the art of winning games without actually cheating." Acts of gamesmanship include trash talking, deliberately slowing or speeding up play to disturb an opponent, providing false information, for example when a player pretends to be injured, and intimidation.[14]

Are acts of gamesmanship like this actually cheating? Some would argue that if it doesn't break the constitutive rules of a sport, it isn't cheating and may even be a legitimate tactic to be employed in a mutual quest for excellence. Cheating, remember, normally involves violating the public rules of a practice, without good reason for exempting oneself in order to gain an undeserved advantage. Gamesmanship, however, does not violate rules or principles of the game, but rather is normally an attempt to test the mental toughness of the opponent by use of more subtle psychological distractions.

Thus, if Tom Brady, the New England quarterback, insulted opposing defenders in an attempt to distract them, his behavior may have been unethical but, as we will see, he would not have been cheating. Deliberate violation of the rules, for example deliberately deflating the football, to gain an advantage over those who do follow the rules, if indeed that is what happened in "Deflategate," would be cheating.

On one view, gamesmanship, unlike cheating, is a legitimate part of the game. On this view, competitive sports test us psychologically as well as physically. Can we withstand the stress of close games and still perform to our potential? Can we maintain concentration when the opponent is trying to distract us? Gamesmanship tests competitors' discipline and focus and may even call out the best in them, for example when a verbal taunt inspires them to play harder and better.[15]

Are acts of gamesmanship ethically acceptable just because they don't violate the rules? For one thing, they still may violate a set of understandings among competitors, social conventions that are widely accepted by participants, sometimes called "the ethos of the game." Thus, in golf, trash talking (except perhaps among friends in a recreational match) would be at best morally questionable because it is not a practice consistent with the fundamental code of respect for the opponent, which lies at the heart of that game. On the other hand, calling a series of time-outs at the end of a basketball game to increase the nervousness of the opposing team's foul shooter seems widely accepted by all competitors and so does not violate the conventions of the sport.

More important than conventions, which after all might themselves sometimes be morally questionable, are principles that should apply to competitions. It is difficult to draw clear lines on this topic because much depends on context, on the sport in question, and on subtle nuances of play. Different principles might apply to different cases, or the same principle might apply differently to different sports. It may be helpful, then, to consider a specific form of gamesmanship, trash talking, in some depth.

### Is trash talking acceptable in competitive sport?

Proponents of trash talking argue that it provides a legitimate test of the target's mental toughness and ability to concentrate. Moreover, because all parties to a contest can trash talk, it doesn't disturb the equality among players.[16]

We certainly should acknowledge that psychological qualities as well as physical ones are tested by competitive sport. Indeed, the ability to focus, make good decisions, and maintain poise and confidence under pressure often may be more important to achieving excellence than physical skill. This doesn't show, however, that trash talking is a legitimate method of testing the psychology of the opponent. We surely can take it as a given that racial, ethnic, and religious slurs, as well as insults based on sexual orientation, appearance, family characteristics, and relevantly similar traits should be out of bounds. Athletes, like everyone else, should be treated with the respect due to them as persons. Moreover, we can view an athletic contest as the result of a tacit or even hypothetical agreement among athletes to test themselves through the crucible of competition. But although athletes may be presumed to have consented to participate in the contest, there are no grounds for assuming that they have consented to be the target of slurs and personal insults or any reason to believe that athletes *would* consent to such tactics under hypothetical but fair conditions of choice.

What about softer forms of trash talking that are directed at the opponent's abilities or that point out the pressure of the situation? For example, a defender in a football game might at a crucial moment say to a receiver something like, "This is a really big play so don't mess it up" or "Don't think about the pass you dropped in this situation last year." Shouldn't the receiver, especially at elite levels of the sport, be expected to concentrate? Don't attempts to disrupt concentration like these force opponents to focus? If players on the receiving end of such taunts can't focus, doesn't that demonstrate their weakness as athletes? They don't deserve to win if they are unable to block out distraction.

The case for soft versions of trash talking is not implausible, when such a practice does not violate either formal rules or widely accepted and ethically acceptable conventions of the sport at issue. However, there are that least three objections to such an account that may well be decisive.

First, the line between soft or acceptable forms of trash talking and unacceptable forms of trash talking is at best unclear. Because such a line is not in the rule book, and not widely agreed upon in informal dialogues, how are officials expected to enforce it? Players themselves may have different understandings of where the line is drawn, so what one side believes is acceptable might constitute "fighting words," words that reasonably can be expected to incite a violent response, for the other.

Second, the claim that trash talking is consistent with competitive equality because both sides can engage in it is a dubious one. Although it is true that both opponents can trash talk, some may be much more skilled and verbally adept than others, and hence have a competitive advantage over the less articulate or less clever. It is true, of course, that inequality is a legitimate part of sport; we play the contest in order to see which athlete or team is better. But shouldn't "better" be construed as superior in the skills the sport is designed to test? In softball, skills tested would be batting, throwing, and running, whereas in soccer they would include speed, footwork, and ability to understand what is going on throughout the field of play. Any interpretation of major sports that includes the ability to trash talk as a skill being tested seems strained at best and just absurd at worst. Imagine a softball coach saying of a player, "She can't hit, field, or throw very well but she is a great softball player because she is really good at trash talking." True, trash talking can help this player's team win, but is it really a skill of softball?

The third reason for denying that even soft versions of trash talking are acceptable, then, is that they do not test skills of a sport, only irrelevant qualities. But isn't that just what the proponents of trash talking deny? They consider the ability to focus and perhaps be stimulated to play even better in the face of trash talking a relevant psychological skill that make competitors better athletes. After all, sports test our mental as well as physical abilities!

Although the proponents certainly have a case, I myself doubt if sports are best construed as testing the ability to concentrate in the face of what amounts to taunting. Yes, mental toughness is an important psychological trait that good athletes should demonstrate under pressure. But the toughness should be a response to play clearly within the game, such as remaining cool when the opponent is on a hot streak or making smart choices when the opposition runs an unexpected play. There is nothing in the formal structure of major sports—in the constitutive rules, for example—that implies that skill in upsetting opponents through taunts and the ability to ignore them are among the traits being tested. Although the debate over trash talking will surely continue, because plausible arguments exist on different sides of the question, our own discussion suggests that the practice is problematic even in elite sports contests and does not belong in athletic competition.

### How does the idea of restoring justice play out in sports?

According to what we can call the skill thesis, the outcome of competitive athletic contests should be decided entirely (strong version) or largely (weak version) by the skills of the competitors that are relevant to the sport being played. Thus, a contest would be spoiled if a rules official or player were bribed to fix the outcome, if a player was deliberately injured to prevent him from exhibiting his skills, if the game was decided by an egregiously bad call, or if a game was decided by luck. (The weak version might modify such a view if a fluke of luck, the injury, or the bad call was not determinative and the outcome of the game still was largely the result of skill, as when the competitor's abilities allow them to take advantage of a lucky break.)

What should we say, however, if an individual or team tries to physically intimidate the opponent through violence, such as a dangerous illegal hit in football, a ball thrown right at the batter's head in baseball (a beanball), or a particularly dangerous high stick (a movement with the stick directed at hitting an opposing player rather than the puck) thrown by an "enforcer" (a player designated to intimidate opponents through physical contact) in ice hockey? Would retaliation be justified in such cases? For example, if your pitcher tries to hit our batters, should our pitcher do the same to the batters on your team?

What about from the point of view of the rules official, referee, or umpire? When officials realize they made a bad call, should they try to even things out by making a similar error in favor of the opponent? Some would argue that this type of measure would be a legitimate form of corrective or compensatory justice—in other words, a measure by which we try to make the victim whole by restoring the situation to what it would have been if the original miscue had not taken place. Let's explore this idea further.

### Is retaliation in sports morally acceptable?

In a major ice hockey game, a player on team A hits an opponent illegally from behind in an attempt to intimidate the target and affect subsequent play. A baseball pitcher continually throws inside of home plate to prevent opposing players from "digging in" or standing close to the plate. When the tactic doesn't work, he intentionally throws at the next batter in order to get a competitive advantage. A soccer player risks a penalty by illegally undercutting a leading scorer on the opposing team so the scorer will hesitate in future attempts to shoot on the goal.

In each case, physical force is being used in ways prohibited by the rules to affect the future play of opponents by inducing them to hesitate out of fear of injury in crucial game situations, thereby disrupting their ability to play their best. Often, the team or player targeted by such behavior will retaliate. The pitcher on the victim's team will throw at opposing batters, or the hockey team will turn loose its own "enforcer," a player who specializes in intimidating opponents often through illegal physical contact.

Retaliation for perceived violent play by the opposing team has become part of the code by which many elite athletes play. As former star Dodger pitcher Don Drysdale is reported to have said, "You hit one of mine, I'll hit two of yours. Let me know when you've had enough."[17]

But is this kind of retaliation morally acceptable? Clearly, there is a moral injunction against deliberately injuring opponents. Not only would deliberately injuring opponents treat them as mere means rather than as persons in their own right, violating the Kantian norm of respect for opponents as equal persons defended in Chapter 1, but it also would violate a major principle endorsed by a mutualist perspective on competitive sport. According to mutualism, athletes should want to play worthy opponents and demonstrate their superiority in the course of play rather than eliminating worthy opponents by removing them from the game by deliberately injuring them.

However, many acts of intimidation are not deliberate attempts to injure an opponent but rather are intended to help gain a competitive edge by making the opposition hesitate or give up an advantage in the course of play. For example, unlike a pitch thrown behind the batter (a beanball) that may cause the batter instinctively to duck backward right into its path, the brush-back is designed to move the batter away from home plate so it becomes more difficult to hit pitches thrown to the outside or away corner of home plate. Brush-back pitches arguably are a legitimate tactic within baseball because elite batters should have the reflexes to avoid them and be tough-minded enough to dig right back in and challenge the pitcher. Their moral status is different from that of the beanball, which is intended or at least likely to hit the batter and likely to cause serious injury.

What if a team is targeted by acts that reasonably can be viewed as violent attempts to inflict an injury or at least carry a significant risk of doing so? Is retaliation for acts like these justified? There seem to be at least three arguments for such a view.

To start with, and most obviously, if the original behavior does provide the agent with an advantage, retaliation provides a similar advantage in return, so the status quo is restored. Retaliation can be viewed as a form of corrective justice because it restores the competitive balance that existed before the original intimidation took place. This argument seems especially strong when we consider illegal hits in ice hockey and soccer, where the advantage gained by the perpetrator clearly was gained unjustly.

We must also keep in mind that retaliation may serve as a deterrent to dangerous behavior in the future. If athletes know their attempts to physically intimidate opponents will lead to similar behavior against their side, they will be less likely to engage in it, reducing the extent to which often illegal and often dangerous rule violations will occur.

The third argument is that players owe it to their teammates to retaliate. If my pitcher does not protect me by throwing at opposing batters, the pitcher on the other team will continue to throw at me and my teammates, putting us at risk. Our pitcher needs to protect us, his teammates, to whom he owes a special bond of loyalty. Similarly, if our enforcer in a hockey game does not retaliate for acts of intimidation by his counterpart on the opponent's team, our players will be vulnerable to injury. At the very least, retaliation might stop further acts of violence by the opposition and make the game safer for everyone, once the score has been settled, so to speak.

The first argument appeals to restoring the scales of justice to a proper balance, whereas the second focuses on reducing arguably dangerous behavior, or at least behavior that limits the exercise of skills of the sport, by intimidating the opposition. Similarly we can distinguish two separate grounds for the punishment of criminals: namely, restoring the scales of justice by depriving the criminal of any benefit gained from breaking the law and deterring future crime through instilling the fear of punishment.

But are these arguments sufficient to justify retaliation in sport?

In a perspicuous discussion of the issue, Nicholas Dixon points out that the arguments amount to an appeal to vigilante justice. Just as law and order would break down if we allowed citizens to take retaliation for crime into their own hands, so could sports deteriorate into a free-for-all if players took it upon themselves to mete out justice in order to deter future injustice. On Dixon's view, just as a strong government should enforce the criminal law, so should sports authorities protect players from violent plays and have procedures in place that result in appropriate punishment for transgressors.[18]

In addition, the three arguments for retaliation cited earlier all have weaknesses. Is it really likely that an act of retaliation actually restores a competitive balance to what it would have been had the original act of violence not taken place? The retaliator is perhaps as likely to over- or underreact as to respond in a balanced way. Moreover, similar acts of violence may be responded to differently by different retaliators. In effect, similar "crimes" will be punished differently. This supports Dixon's suggestion that it is better to rely on uniform, publically known, and consistently enforced procedures for dealing with violent acts in sport than on the judgment of individual retaliators exercised in the heat of the moment. Moreover, the public awareness of official penalties for violent acts is at least as likely to deter as hit-and-miss efforts by retaliators.

What about loyalty to teammates? Such behavior is expected, and failure to retaliate to protect teammates sometimes is punished within teams. In a 2006 Major League Baseball game, Chicago White Sox pitcher Sean Tract was pulled from the game after failure to hit Texas star Hank Blalock as retaliation for a White Sox batter being hit by a pitched ball. The White Sox manager, Ozzie Guillen, not only berated Tract but also demoted him to the minor leagues the very next day.

If we return to Dixon's suggestion that we can see the weakness of an argument for retaliation in sports by testing how it would work if applied to crimes, we can see the problem with this argument. This logic in the criminal context would justify family members taking the law into their own hands and attacking those who hurt their relatives as an expression of loyalty. So why would we tolerate this kind of behavior in sports? Indeed, at its worst, constant retaliation could turn sports into a series of ugly and sometimes dangerous brawls, an athletic analog of Hobbes's famous state of nature, a war of all against all in which life is nasty, cruel, brutish, and short.

This critique of retaliation in sports is powerful and, in my view as well as Dixon's, determinative. But what about cases in which sports organizations do not have a clear code with a set of penalties for violence in place, or where the code is at best loosely enforced by administrators and rules officials alike? Many would argue that this was the case in the National Hockey League for some time, and that the need for "enforcers" to protect teammates still exists today.[19]

In such instances, the case for retaliation is stronger than when organizational structures to limit and punish violence are in place and fairly enforced. Even then, although the point remains open to debate, the morally better course of action may be to lobby for organizational action to limit and punish player-on-player violence than to encourage each athlete or team to take the law into their own hands.

*Bad calls by officials may lead to one competitor receiving an unearned advantage over another. Should officials then make up for their bad call by making an equally bad call in favor of the other side? Are "make-up calls" acceptable or even required in such situations?*

Referees and umpires generally make correct decisions, even on hard calls, especially at elite levels of competitive sport. However, officials are only human, and sometimes they get it wrong. That presents them with an ethical issue. When they are aware of their error, should they make up for their bad call by making an equally bad call favoring the other side?

The principal argument for doing so rests on what we earlier called corrective or compensatory justice, the idea of rectification. For example, suppose a worker has been discriminated against because of her gender. She was denied a promotion that she had earned and which instead went to a less qualified male candidate. The aim of corrective justice is to right the previous wrong; in this case, to restore the woman to roughly the position she would have had if the discrimination had not taken place. For example, the wrongdoer, the discriminator, should provide her at least with the difference in salary between what she would have earned had she been given the promotion and what she actually was paid. Perhaps she also should be given the promotion or, if that is impossible, be paid further damages to make up for the loss.

Although this argument appears plausible at first, it is not decisive when applied to sports, in part for some of the same reasons that the argument for retaliation turns out to be weaker than at first glance. For one thing, there are some missed calls that just cannot be made up for. Consider again the 2009 World Cup between France and Ireland. Remember that French player Thierry Henry apparently used his hands while scoring the winning goal for France, but the official did not call the infraction. Ireland lost the game and it was widely felt throughout Ireland but even to some extent in France that they had been cheated out of the victory. What could count as a make-up call in such a case?

Similarly, in a Major League Baseball game played in June 2010, Detroit Tiger pitcher Armando Galarraga retired the first 26 Cleveland batters he faced and was one out away from completing a rare perfect game. Unfortunately, umpire Jim Joyce incorrectly called the next Cleveland batter safe at first base, a call that Joyce himself later admitted was a mistake. Joyce apologized for his mistake, and Galarraga also showed tremendous sportsmanship in his gracious response. Be that as it may, the loss of the perfect game would not have been rectified by an equally bad call made against the opposing Cleveland Indians because the perfect game was already ruined.

The compensatory argument at best applies only to a subset of missed calls. It is unclear, at best, whether rules officials can decide on the spot just which calls can be rectified and which cannot. Perhaps more important, however, are rules officials really in a good position to compensate for bad calls during the course of a game? More precisely, are they really able to tell if the make-up call actually restores the situation to what it would have been if the original bad call had not been made? Perhaps the make-up call doesn't quite provide an advantage equivalent to the disadvantage resulting from the original bad call, or perhaps it overcompensates. The game situation in which the make-up call takes place differs in significant ways from the context in which the first bad call occurred.[20] For example, a mistaken traveling call with 10 minutes to go in a basketball game normally has less effect than a make-up traveling call with 2 minutes to go when every possession is vital.

Perhaps an even stronger case against make-up calls can be made by focusing on the role of the official.[21] Officials who adopt the compensatory model of umpiring, in effect, transform themselves from experts trained in enforcing the rules and making correct calls to arbiters of the balance of justice, a role for which they might be ill suited and for which they are not trained. Indeed, I would add, if this was their proper role, they would be open to criticism not just for missing calls or interpreting the rules incorrectly, but for not balancing the scales of justice properly. Should referees be graded, for example, on whether their make-up calls actually do compensate for their earlier bad ones?

This does not mean rules officials should never appeal to considerations of ethics or justice in interpreting the rules. As noted in Chapter 1, sports arguably are governed by principles as well as rules. Principles are not in the rulebook but function as reasons inclining the umpire one way or another in difficult cases where rules either do not clearly apply or require interpretation. However, interpreting a rule is very different from deliberately making an incorrect decision to compensate for an earlier bad call that went the other way.

These considerations strongly suggest that rules officials should not try to rectify bad calls decisions with make-up calls. However, there is a kind of case that may be more ambiguous. What about a play where the official is in genuine doubt about what the correct call should be? The pitch in a softball game is on the edge of the strike zone, for example. Was that collision in the basketball game a charge or a block? Did the defender in a football game commit pass interference? Did the offensive player use his hand or was what happened too difficult to tell from the official's position on the pitch? Was the soccer player actually offside? In cases where the official is genuinely in doubt about what happened, what is the proper course of action?

The first step should be to consult with other referees on the officiating crew. Maybe one of the other officials had a better view of what actually happened. If instant replay is available, it can be consulted as well. But there still may be cases, such as calling balls and strikes in baseball, where no other official had a better perspective than the one making the call and where video replays either are unavailable or not decisive. In such rare cases of uncertainty, should a rules official attempt to balance out calls so one opponent does not get the preponderance of decisions in its favor?

One view that deserves further consideration might go something like this. Although the official should always try to make the correct call, in a contest (or perhaps a series of contests between the same opponents), where there are a number of plays in which the official is genuinely uncertain what the correct call should be, the official should ensure that no one opponent gets the benefit of the doubt to a disproportionate extent. Although such a view might not be correct—perhaps the officials should just do their best to be accurate and let the chips fall where they may—the case for striving for competitive balance under uncertainty seems less open to objection than the argument for deliberate make-up calls, although further discussion on both issues is clearly needed.

### What is sportsmanship? Should athletes be expected to be good sports? Isn't there a principal obligation, especially at elite levels of competition, to try to win?

At the 1936 Summer Olympics in Berlin, black track-and-field athlete Jesse Owens made history by undermining the racism of the Nazi Party, a particularly brave deed since Adolph Hitler personally attended the games. Perhaps less well known is the act of sportsmanship by German athlete Lutz Long that may have enabled Owens to advance to the finals of the long jump. In the preliminary round, Owens fouled on two jumps and would have been disqualified if he did not do well in his third and final attempt. Before his final attempt, Long advised Owens to adjust his take-off point to further behind the start line so as to ensure that he would qualify. Owens took the advice and qualified. He later praised Long for his sportsmanship and for showing the courage to befriend him right in front of Hitler and other leading Nazis.

Although we may admire gestures like Long's, which are undeniably admirable especially given the cutthroat nature of many sports contests (perhaps none more so than the Olympics!) we also can raise significant questions about sportsmanship. For one thing, is sportsmanship something that we ought to merely encourage or is it morally required? Perhaps it is what ethicists call superogatory, or over and above the call of duty. Perhaps sportsmanship is something that may have been valued in a kinder and gentler era but is rightly regarded as having no place in elite sports today. Imagine LeBron James telling a rival star about a flaw in his shooting technique just before the start of the NBA play-offs. Imagine the coach of Arsenal pointing out a flaw in the strategy used by an opposing soccer team and suggesting an easy way to fix it just before a crucial match. My guess is that such acts would be greeted with dismay and anger from fans today, as Long's act might have been criticized by the German fans of his own day, rather than garner praise like that which Long received from Owens.

Before turning to the ethics of sportsmanship, however, we need to try and get clear on just what we are talking about. We also need to establish that "sportsmanship" is being used here to apply to the behavior of both men and women. It can, of course, be replaced by "sportspersonship," but because "sportsmanship" is the traditional usage and is widely discussed under that heading, I will stick with it for purposes of this discussion.

The term "sportsmanship" should not be used so broadly as just another way of endorsing behavior as ethically permissible, morally correct, or ethically praiseworthy for going beyond the call of duty. If we conflate the concepts in such a way, we could not say an act was ethical or morally right because it was sportsmanlike, because to say the latter would merely be repeating the former. So if claims of sportsmanship are to have specificity, they must provide an independent reason for admiring, praising, and positively evaluating the behavior at issue other than citing its general goodness.[22]

The writer James Keating, in an insightful discussion of sportsmanship, maintained that we should distinguish two distinct activities often blurred together under the heading of sports. The first is "sports" in the sense of recreational play, where sportsmanship according to Keating involves generosity toward an opponent. Sports do not involve serious or intense competition but are games among friends. Thus, to use his example, in a friendly tennis match, one would give the opponent the benefit of the doubt on serves and call all serves "in" whenever there was any doubt about whether they actually landed within the lines. On the other hand, "athletics" refers to intense competition where generosity is neither expected nor given. Sportsmanship in the context of athletics is highly attenuated as, according to Keating, it amounts to little if anything more than abiding by the rules and playing fairly as the rules prescribe. A major mistake, Keating argued, is to expect athletes embedded in intense competition to act like friends in a sporting or recreational match.[23]

This may seem straightforward, but the idea that there is a sharp distinction between sports and athletics has been subject to significant criticism, as we noted earlier in this chapter. Many commentators, myself included, have suggested that there is no such sharp distinction but at most a continuum. Acts of sportsmanship can be found all along that continuum, as the example of Long in the 1936 Olympics illustrates.

What about the ethics of sportsmanship? Is sportsmanlike behavior something that is morally required of participants, is it simply permitted and to be encouraged, or is it just foolish at the highest levels of competition? Indeed, what is sportsmanship anyway?

Whether sportsmanship can be precisely defined is questionable. Perhaps, it is what has been called a family resemblance concept with different examples resembling each other in a variety of overlapping ways with no characteristics common to them all, just as member of a family may resemble each other in a variety of ways without sharing any one common characteristic.

Perhaps, however, some greater specificity is possible. On one view, acts of sportsmanship express an attitude toward athletic competition reflecting Aristotle's Golden Mean, the middle way between two extremes. On this view, the "good sport" is serious about the competition but also realizes "it's only a game"—that from the point of view of the cosmos, so to speak, the result has little significance. Thus, the good sport plays hard but does not view athletic contests as matters of life and death and so treats competitors with respect.[24]

This view is attractive but may need further refinement. For one thing, it may characterize the attitude of the good sport, but it does not necessarily distinguish sportstmanlike acts from the normal course of play. Conceivably, one could keep in mind the relative insignificance of the game in question and never even have occasion to depart from the normal course of play. If Lutz Long had not even noticed the flaw in Jesse Owens's technique, he never would have had occasion to help his competitor improve even if his attitude toward sports was appropriately moderate. Moreover, as Aristotle himself suggested, where the mean or middle ground is to be located may vary with context, so we may need further criteria in order to identify it in specific situations.

One suggestion worth pursuing is that a fundamental aspect of sportsmanship is respect for the ideal of competition as what we called a mutual quest for excellence in which each competitor challenges the other to excel within the framework of the game. On this view, opponents should want to play their competitors at their best so as be tested by worthy opponents. Lutz Long, for example, had a good moral reason to assist Owens, not simply out of generosity or because the Olympics were not matters of life and death (although in 1936 in Nazi Germany, they surely had enormous political significance), but out of respect for the value of good competition as a test for excellence. He may well have had political reasons for acting as well, but, on the view I am suggesting, what makes the act one of sportsmanship is that it was done out of respect for the values of good competition and challenge.

Sportsmanship, on this view, is something like respect for the basic principles that characterize the value of good competition.[25] It goes beyond simply following the rules and playing fair but in addition involves positive action to protect and enhance the worth of the competition itself. Normally, failure to exhibit sportsmanlike behavior is not punishable and is not morally required. Long was not duty bound to help Owens. Indeed, that is why his act is so special.

However, sportsmanship surely is to be encouraged because exhibiting respect for good competition and for good opponents helps distinguish athletic contests from ruthless competition. Acts of sportsmanship, on this view, illustrate that athletic competition can be a mutually acceptable practice in which competitors are treated as persons in their own right and the challenge presented by each sport is valued not just for the external rewards of victory but for the worth of the activity itself. Just where the line of what should be encouraged is unclear. Perhaps, to return to our earlier example, LeBron James should not be expected or encouraged to correct an opponent's shooting form just before an NBA playoff game, but what about during practice during the off-season? As Aristotle suggested long ago, much will depend on context. Clear cases of sportsmanlike behavior show respect for the values implicit in competitive sport, for worthy opponents, and for the principles of good competition. Although the boundaries of sportsmanship are fuzzy, our discussion indicates the concept is a morally weighty one. Normally acts of sportsmanship are not morally required and failure to act in a sportsmanlike way should not be penalized, but sportsmanlike behavior is to be encouraged in a way appropriate to the level of play and context at hand.

### What about bad sportsmanship? Should unsportsmanlike behavior ever be punished?

Our earlier discussion suggests that normally displays of good sportsmanship should be encouraged but not required. There may be exceptions, however. For example, in many sports, athletes are expected to shake hands with opponents after a contest as a gesture of respect. If a team refuses to shake hands with opponents after a game simply out of frustration at a loss, sanctions might well be warranted, although criticism and public censure often may be a much better remedy than formal punishments.

Formal sanctions, however, when appropriate, are more fitting for acts of bad sportsmanship than for failure to exhibit unusually good sportsmanship. Exhibitions of good sportsmanship normally are to be encouraged and not required, in part because it is difficult to see just what should be expected or required of athletes in competitive situations. But exhibitions of bad sportsmanship may sometimes need to be dealt with through formal sanctions. Perhaps "tanking" or deliberately trying to lose a game in order to secure a strategic benefit in the long run is such a case.

### Is tanking ever ethical?

At the end of the regular 2015 high school basketball season, two girls' high school teams from Tennessee, Riverdale and Smyrna, were disqualified from the postseason playoffs for each trying to lose a game against each other in order to draw a weaker opponent in postseason play. Similarly, badminton players from China, Indonesia, and South Korea were disqualified from the 2012 Olympics in London for trying to lose matches so as to obtain a better future seed. In 2015, I noticed on several Web sites that some fans of the Los Angeles Lakers of the NBA and the Buffalo Sabres of the NHL were urging their teams to lose on purpose, or "tank" as it is called, in order to gain an advantage in the draft of new players for the following season. (In an admirable effort to produce competitive equity among teams in the long run, teams with the worst records in the preceding season are given priority in drafting new players. The creation of an incentive to tank may be an unintended consequence of such a system.) Rumors of tanking also have been prevalent in other professional leagues in which losing teams can gain strategic advantages in the player draft by losing even more.

It is unclear whether tanking actually takes place at the professional level. After all, players and coaches have an incentive to protect their market value but not appearing inept, which losing on purpose may sometimes require. Nevertheless, it is worth considering whether such a practice is ethical. What, if anything, is wrong with tanking? Why isn't it just good strategy? At the professional level, sports teams are business, and if losing a few games now leads to much greater success in the future, why not do it? After all, isn't the goal of any business to make a profit? Doesn't doing so require looking at the long term, rather than focusing on meaningless victories in the present? In fact, not to do so may cheat fans in the long run by dooming their teams to competitive inferiority in the future!

But there is another side to this argument that I suggest carries the day. For one thing, losing on purpose cheats present fans who pay to watch games with the expectation they will see an actual game. Think of two losing teams playing each other, each trying to lose on purpose, presumably without being detected. Would anyone pay to see such an anti-contest? Furthermore, in addition to disappointing the fans, tanking undermines the ethic of meeting challenges so central to the idea of a sporting contest. In fact, one could argue that "games" between teams trying to lose are not really contests at all: the goal is to fail rather than meet the difficulties created by the constitutive rules. Tanking, then, is at best, ethically questionable and, at worst, is a form both of cheating the fans and of disrespecting the game.

### What are the principal conclusions we can draw?

In this chapter, we have suggested that mutualism is an ethically defensible model of the manner in which competitive sport might be conducted. We also have examined what can go wrong if athletic competition is conducted in a questionable way, with cheating being a primary example. Positive acts of sportsmanship can help balance the scales. Such acts illustrate that competition in sports, at its best, can reveal behavior that goes beyond duty to protect and enhance the fundamental principles that support the value of sport itself.

# 3

# HEALTH, SAFETY, AND VIOLENCE IN COMPETITIVE SPORT

*What concerns about health and safety might be raised about the social effects of recreational and elite sport?*

There are many concerns that might be addressed in response to this question. In this section, we will focus on three. First, what issues arise in assessing the contribution of sports to public and individual health? Second, what moral value, if any, should be assigned to high-risk sports: sports such as mountain climbing that carry an especially high risk of injury to participants and sometimes to spectators as well? Third, can we identify and assess the principal moral issues raised by sports that involve violence directed against opponents, ranging from boxing and extreme combat to sports such as football that many observers also regard as violent by nature? Other areas of risk in sport include danger to spectators, for example at auto races; danger to animals, for example in dog racing or cock fighting; and dangers to the environment, for example from water use on golf courses in the American Southwest. However, in this chapter, we will focus on the three main areas specified.

*Are sports and physical activity major contributors to the overall health of the participants?*

Recent data show that Americans in particular are increasingly at risk of developing early diabetes, obesity, and heart disease, and at a younger and younger age. For example, the Centers for Disease Control (CDC) reports that childhood obesity has more than doubled in children and quadrupled in adolescents in the past 30 years, that in 2012, more than one third of American children were overweight or obese, and that obesity is a major risk factor for cardiovascular disease and diabetes among other conditions harmful to their health. Indeed, the rate of childhood diabetes, a disease almost unheard of when I was growing up, has skyrocketed over the last 20 years. Lack of exercise and a diet high in sugar and carbohydrates are among the factors that are thought to be significant contributors to this development.

Considerable data show that exercise, including participation in sports, has significant benefits for children, including the promotion of stronger bones and muscles, lowering the risk of developing type II diabetes, reducing blood pressure and cholesterol, and even improving sleep. Benefits of participation in sports for girls may be especially significant, including decreased drug use and higher scholastic achievement. One study recommends that children engage in physical activity for 60 minutes a day, most days per week, to maximize health benefits, a goal that parents know is challenging when so many kids remain glued to their electronic devices for what may be unhealthy periods of time each day.[1]

Of course, we need to distinguish between sports and exercise. Running on a treadmill, doing crunches, or doing resistance training all are forms of exercise and can contribute to a healthier lifestyle, but they are not sports. Sports, as we have seen, normally involve unnecessary obstacles created by constitutive rules, and the challenge the obstacles (including the opponent) create. Because sports generally are games of physical skill, they do involve exercise but are not mere exercise because they also involve overcoming challenges created by the constitutive rules.

Sports also can be dangerous, with a range of risks depending on the sport. Risks of serious injuries are especially high in such contact sports as football, rugby, and boxing, mountain climbing, and extreme sports. People who practice mixed martial arts and mountain climbers frequently face grave dangers to life and limb. Children may be pushed too hard to excel in youth sports before their bodies have developed enough to handle the strain. So balancing the rewards of participation against risks often is necessary, but complicated, as we will see in discussion later in this chapter.

*Should people be encouraged, persuaded, or even required to exercise on grounds of promoting public health? Do parents have a duty to make sure children get sufficient exercise, perhaps through participation in sports?*

Interference with the choices of competent adults in order to promote their own good is called paternalism. Acts of paternalism on behalf of a state or system, which we will discuss more fully in the next section, pose a threat to personal liberty and, sometimes with good reason, face substantial opposition. Who would like to be constantly required to eat what is healthy, do only what is considered safe, and never make choices that involve risk? A paternalistic society looks to many like a society of obnoxious interfering busybodies.

Of course, there may be exceptions, such as requiring motorcyclists to wear helmets and drivers of automobiles to wear seat belts. Be that as it may, the burden of proof surely is on those who want to interfere with the choices of informed competent adults, not to prevent harm to others, but to protect them from themselves. (An exception may be so-called soft paternalism, where we interfere just long enough to make sure the people in question are truly competent and informed about the consequences of their decision.)

However, preventing people from acting on their choices is one thing, especially if done through laws that impose penalties for the behavior is question, but persuading people to avoid certain behaviors is quite another. Thus, smoking cigarettes is not prohibited by law, although restrictions may be required to protect others from secondhand smoke. But while smoking is not prohibited, all sorts of arguably noncoercive devices can be used to persuade people not to smoke. These range from warnings on packages of tobacco products to advertisements graphically illustrating the effects of smoking on health.

Similarly, although requiring people under threat of legal sanction to get proper exercise is indefensible, various techniques of persuasion arguably are legitimate. After all, a sedentary lifestyle can be as dangerous, or nearly as dangerous, to health as smoking. Even spending public money on advertisements or other forms of public education on the benefits of exercise seems warranted if it is likely to prevent future illnesses and their associated costs and to contribute to public health.

The case of children surely is a different story. Because children are not yet competent adults, the antipaternalistic defense of liberty and personal autonomy does not fully apply to them, especially to younger children, including young teens. Children in school already are required to study many subjects, including mathematics, science, literature, and social studies, even if they would prefer not to. Although physical education classes sometimes are considered a frill, they may actually be necessary not only for reasons of health. Sedentary children who grow into unhealthy adults not only impose costs on the rest of society but may lack the fitness necessary to participate fully in public discourse and dialogue. Moreover, as will be argued more fully in Chapter 5, lessons learned through involvement in sports, even if not at varsity levels of competition, can promote such values as the ability to get along with a diverse group of people, and teamwork in pursuit of a common cause.

If such a view is sound, parents may well have an obligation to at least introduce their children to the benefits of exercise and perhaps to strongly encourage them to participate in sport as well. Coercing children to participate in organized sport surely is going too far, but getting them to at least try participation, much as they might be urged to at least try to enjoy new and healthy foods, seems highly desirable. Allowing young children to act like couch potatoes, spending all their free time engaged with their electronic devices, should be as open to criticism as feeding children only unhealthy food or constantly exposing them to secondhand smoke.

If these remarks are sound, we need to consider whether there is a public responsibility to provide facilities for exercise, and for play involving physical activity, including recreational sport. These might include playgrounds, regular physical education classes in school, and perhaps provision for participation in sports appropriate for various age and skill levels through recreation centers. Although this would involve some costs, parents may not have the time or access to facilities for active play otherwise, especially in cities. Moreover, neglecting the health of children by not encouraging active play also will have dire costs down the road that may be more significant than the cost of providing such resources.

### Does watching sports turn us into couch potatoes?

What detrimental health effects may result from our spending too much time watching sports rather than participating? This question is largely a factual or empirical one, not a philosophical one. No matter how intense the game or sporting event that we're watching, after all, we can't reap physical benefits from other people's exertion!

However, it also is plausible to think that the performances of great athletes may inspire many of us, especially young people, to go out and play and even to try to imitate the techniques of the great stars. Kids all over the world practice the soccer moves of star players, while children and teens on American basketball courts do the same with their own collegiate or professional idols. Perhaps emphasis on elite sports increases participation and thus is a net positive.[2]

Moreover, as cultural critic Christopher Lasch once argued, sports fans are often knowledgeable and debate issues of strategy and technique endlessly.[3] They are no more passive sloths than audiences in other areas such as the arts—they may not be burning calories as they watch, but they are reaping intellectual rewards, especially when they participate in the micro-analysis in which many sports fans delight. Many fans also have learned to appreciate the internal goods of sports—the excellences created through outstanding athletic performances that one needs some knowledge of the game to appreciate, such as the perfectly run fast break in basketball, the expertly executed double play in baseball, the strategic crossing pass in soccer, and the cut shot that fades gently to the pin in golf.

### Are the risks involved in playing sports worth taking?

Active play and recreational sports may not only be enjoyable activities in themselves but, as suggested earlier, they provide important benefits for public health. However, the more athletes become involved in competitive athletics, the more they risk injury.

In a class I recently taught on ethical issues in sport, a visiting lecturer noted that several of the students who were athletes on college teams were recovering from injuries. One was on crutches, another was visibly limping, and when the speaker asked the class about concussions, another student acknowledged she was recovering from one suffered during basketball practice.

The speaker then asked the student-athletes why they played, given the risk of injuries. (My institution, Hamilton College, competes in Division III of the NCAA, and there are no athletic scholarships. Student-athletes compete primarily because they love their sport and have no financial incentive to continue playing.) One young female athlete replied that it was a matter of cost–benefit analysis; the gains of playing outweigh the risks.

The risks for participating in sports are real and often significant. Recent data have shown that concussions are frequent in many sports with rugby, football, and soccer players being among those at special risk. The Centers for Disease Control and Prevention estimates that 1.6 million to 3.8 million concussions occur each season with 5%–10% of participants receiving concussions in higher risk sports in the United States. Some research indicates that professional football players may receive well over 900 blows to the head in a particular season. Research now makes it clear that concussions, especially multiple concussions, can have long-term effects both on cognitive abilities and general health.[4]

Indeed, the risk of concussion is causing researchers in a variety of areas as well as athletes, coaches, and parents of student-athletes, to reassess the value of contact sports. Awareness of the issue has led to such reevaluation even at the highest levels of professional athletics. For example, San Francisco 49ers linebacker Chris Borland, after completing a successful rookie football season and looking at millions of dollars in future earnings as a professional athlete, walked away from the game announcing his retirement in 2015 due to fears of long-term serious effects of repeated blows to the head. A $765 million settlement reached in 2015 between the NFL and former players is widely regarded as a form of compensation for injuries to the athletes' long-term health due to their long-term participation in professional football. The settlement provides compensation for diagnoses of various illnesses, including dementia and certain cases of chronic traumatic encephalopathy or CTE (a neuropathological finding diagnosed after death often caused by repeated blows to the head). The movie *Concussion*, starring actor Will Smith and released in 2015, explores the story of the doctor who discovered CTE and the alleged resistance of the NFL to having the truth about the risks of playing professional football made public.

### How should we weigh the benefits of participation in sports against the costs? What other methods might we use to assess risk in sports in addition to cost–benefit analysis?

There probably is no general answer to this question. For one thing, cost–benefit analysis itself can be understood in multiple ways that may point in different directions when performed differently.

For example, are we calculating the costs and benefits for an individual athlete deciding whether she should play rugby? Or are we calculating overall costs and benefits across society if rugby is made an interscholastic and intercollegiate varsity sport? In other words, are we looking at costs and benefits for everyone or just an individual?

Second, do we accept each individual's subjective evaluation of the consequences of playing—say the weight each individual assigns to meeting the challenge of the sport? If so, do we consider their actual preferences or the ones they would have if fully informed and objective? Is there an objective weight—a standard that applies to everyone—for identifying and weighing costs and benefits?

Finally, should we discount the benefits of playing rugby, such as friendships formed, that might be obtained by playing less dangerous sports or through activities having nothing to do with athletics at all? What weight should be assigned to what might be called the internal benefits of playing the sport, such as the excellences exhibited in play and the skill in meeting the special challenges of the sport?

Surely the value of participating in sport normally is far broader than that of exercise and the benefits for health that follow, although those surely are important. Most people find that playing a sport is more interesting than simply exercising, in part because of their interest in meeting the challenges implicit in the sport they are playing. (Some forms of physical activity, such as yoga, dance, and long-distance running, may also create a similar form of intense interest, although I would suggest that all three differ from simply running on a treadmill or using an exercise bike. In particular, long-distance running can be far closer to a sport than say simply running on a treadmill.) Even professionals, whose motive for playing may sometimes simply be financial gain, have to overcome those obstacles. In doing so, they not only create drama and excitement for the rest of us but also demonstrate the internal goods or excellences of the sport, such as executing a perfect play or especially difficult move in a highly competitive situation.

Our discussion of cost–benefit analysis supports a number of significant conclusions. First, there is no one favored conception of such analysis; different forms of cost–benefit analysis may even yield conflicting results. For example, an individual rugby player, considering only her own ranking of her own subjective preferences, might find it rational to play, but an overall cost–benefit analysis of the social costs of making rugby an intercollegiate or interscholastic sport may turn out quite differently. Although the very name—cost–benefit analysis—suggests an objective formula for making decisions, we have seen that, on the contrary, actual application of cost–benefit analysis raises many issues that are not easily resolved.

Suppose we conclude, as I do, that cost–benefit analysis raises too many complex issues to yield an uncontroversial solution, or indeed any solution at all, to the assessment of risk in sports. I suggest we take another approach and try to more clearly focus on the values involved in playing risky and even dangerous sports. Then, if we start out with the assumption that competent adults have the right to choose their plan of life, at least absent especially weighty considerations to the contrary such as whether their choices impose an unreasonable risk of harm to others, we can see whether the values involved in especially risky sports make the choice to participate in them reasonable, or at least intelligible. If so, such a conclusion may help us assess such sports without delving into the complexities of cost–benefit analysis. Let us turn, then, to the analysis of especially risky or dangerous sports.

*Can we justify the risks that we incur in dangerous sports such as mountain climbing or boxing? Should they be permitted?*
If most of the benefits of participation can be obtained by playing safer sports, what if anything justifies participation in the most dangerous ones? Would we be justified in prohibiting or regulating dangerous sports in order to protect participants from serious injury or even death?

We should distinguish two separate questions here. First, would we be justified in prohibiting individuals from participation in dangerous sports for their own good? Second, does participation in such sports have a special value of its own, over and above the general values such as exercise and the meeting of challenges that can be obtained through playing less dangerous sports? If so, do such values support not only allowing but even admiring or endorsing participation in dangerous sports?

As we have seen, limiting the freedom of individuals to promote their own good or protect them from harm is controversial. In his classic defense of individual freedom, *On Liberty* (1849) the nineteenth-century British philosopher John Stuart Mill defended what has come to be called the harm principle. According to this principle, the only ground for restricting the liberty of the individual is to prevent harm to others. If we adopted the harm principle, we would not only be prohibited from interfering with individuals for their own good, but we would also be prohibited from interfering with individuals in order to prevent them from offending others or acting in ways that the majority deems immoral. Mill made clear that the principle was to apply only to competent adults, not to children or to any other persons not competent to make decisions for themselves. He also allowed what has come to be called soft paternalism, which we referred to earlier: temporarily limiting the freedom of individuals to make sure their choice is free and informed. Thus, we might be justified in restricting an individual's choice to box until but only until we were sure he was aware of the very real risks of brain injury that can result from repeated blows to the head.

Prohibiting some dangerous sports such as mountain climbing simply to protect the climbers from injury violates the harm principle, at least where competent adults are concerned. Moreover, we have good grounds for supporting that principle. Our freedom to choose our way of life surely is one of our fundamental goods, only to be outweighed by conflicting values of the most significant kind, if it is to be outweighed at all.

If we journey down the path of paternalism, Mill's supporters would ask, just where would we stop? What other sports might be too dangerous to allow? Should we make moderate exercise and a healthy diet mandatory, because a sedentary lifestyle and poor diet also are significant threats to health?

Even if we do not slide down this slippery slope, we still need to be careful about restricting people's ability to take part in dangerous activities. The freedom to take risks is an important one in itself.

In addition, there may be special values to be found through participation in dangerous sports. These special values may include opportunities to exhibit a degree of courage not found in safer pursuits and to meet special challenges, such as that presented by natural obstacles found in mountain climbing. They also especially include the opportunity for growth, self-understanding, and self-affirmation found by placing oneself in the extreme contexts of dangerous sport.[5] On this view, such sports extend us by pushing us up to and sometimes beyond our limits to a degree well beyond that found in less dangerous pursuits. Moreover, such sports may generate a significant sense of trust in others, such as among members of a team of mountain climbers whose very lives may depend on all the team members doing their part.[6]

Indeed, the book *Touching the Void* by Joe Simpson, and the documentary movie based upon it, detail all the dangers that Simpson and his companion Simon Yates faced when they descended Siula Grande in the Peruvian Andes in 1985.[7] Struggling to make an already challenging descent that was worsened by extreme weather conditions, Yates fell into a deep crevice and injured himself. Simpson believed his partner had died and cut the rope tying them together. Miraculously, both survived. Their story illustrates the trust and teamwork required by climbers and the excruciating moral dilemmas they face when things go terribly wrong.

Although many of us may not find such values at all compelling, or worth the risk involved, do we have the right to impose our conception of what matters in life on others? Proponents of individual freedom and the harm principle maintain we do not. As we have seen, there are at least two significant reasons for allowing participation in dangerous sports. The first is the curtailment of personal autonomy that paternalistic interference would entail. The second is the value that arguably may be found in the dangerous activity itself. Putting the two together, we can conclude, however provisionally, that participation in many dangerous sports is not irrational and indeed involves positive values of genuine significance. Surely, prohibiting participation in such sports as mountain climbing, auto racing, and some highly risky extreme sports would be unwarranted.

This does not mean, however, that such sports are beyond the pale of all outside regulation. Mountain climbing, for example, can threaten the environment, as the refuse from base camps mounts up and clutters what have been pristine mountainsides. The Nepali government, for example, has taken steps to require climbers to bring back their trash as Everest itself increasingly becomes covered with debris, although there is some doubt how these measures might be enforced.

Similarly, sports authorities legitimately might require protective equipment in many sports to reduce the risk of injury. This latter move sometimes may be controversial, however, when participants argue that the addition of such gear as helmets and pads simply makes players more aggressive, thereby increasing the risk of injury rather than lowering it. Thus, requiring helmets in women's lacrosse, both at the high school and college level, seems a no-brainer because speedy athletes wielding sticks seems to present a danger of severe head injuries to the participants. Yet many players and coaches resist any regulation requiring helmets on the grounds that the addition of protective equipment will weaken existing constraints on contact already in place and actually make the game more dangerous.

Whatever the merits of that particular argument, however, regulations requiring the use of protective equipment in dangerous sports often do seem legitimate. At the very least, they pose a much less significant violation of personal autonomy than prohibiting participation in such sports altogether.

### Should children be allowed to engage in dangerous sports?

In the United States, about 30 million children participate in sports and, among these, there are about 3.5 million injuries each year, the majority of which are sprains and strains. More serious injuries such as brain injuries result most often from such activities as bicycling, skating, and skateboarding. Many, perhaps most, injuries result from such factors as falls and collisions, often in unorganized or informal play. As noted earlier, some sports are much more dangerous than others, but young athletes in any sport face some risk of injury.[8] But should children be encouraged, or even allowed, to participate in more dangerous sports?

It is difficult to provide a definitive answer to this question. For one thing, there is no sharp line separating dangerous from safe sports. Rather, there is a continuum of sports going from relatively safe, to less safe, to dangerous, to extremely dangerous. In any given case, it may be difficult to say where on the spectrum a given sport applies. Secondly, and probably more important, prohibitions on children engaging in activities would clash with parental discretion, and so would involve balancing concerns for safety of children with respect for the autonomy of the family.

The issue is complicated further by doubts about whether children are good at assessing risk or appreciating what a serious injury may involve. Indeed, some research suggests that the centers of the brain we employ in assessing risk remain relatively undeveloped often until our early 20s. Thus, the enthusiasm children may express for risky extreme sports must be taken with a grain of salt.

On the positive side, participation in dangerous sports can help children gain confidence and develop more maturely than otherwise. In one study, Norwegian children with drug problems were less prone to commit drug offenses or engage in vandalism after being introduced to and participating in a program of skydiving. On the other hand, other children suffer multiple injuries but with parental support return to risky sports. Such parents often claim, as in the Norwegian study, that their children are better students and better people as a result.[9]

Although I have no knock-down argument to support my own conclusions, I think we need to question whether similar positive results could be achieved through involvement in other sports that are safer than skydiving or extreme skateboarding. But I understand that we cannot protect children from all risk, and to overemphasize freedom from injury may deprive children of important goods that come through taking chances and accepting some risk.

Perhaps balancing all these conflicting values requires judicious parents and coaches who can balance competing costs and benefits in a balanced way (by finding Aristotle's Golden Mean, which was mentioned earlier). What might be prohibited, or at least discouraged, however, is allowing children to participate in highly dangerous sports with only the supervision of parents who may have no real expertise in the sport in question. Perhaps the best compromise here is to allow participation in highly dangerous sports only under the supervision of and training by experts. Education about the dangers of concussion and proper protocols for treatment also ought to be widespread, not just for dangerous sports but more broadly throughout the world of children's athletics. The more dangerous the sport, the greater burden of proof on adults to provide a strong justification for allowing their children to participate.

### Boxing is particularly dangerous to participants who risk serious brain injury and even death. Should boxing be prohibited?

Boxing surely has many of the virtues of participation in dangerous sports. Boxers exhibit physical courage, persistence, and dedication in preparation for matches and in the fighting itself. Moreover, boxers may test themselves to their limits and beyond and so develop in the self-affirming ways suggested earlier. Both the lure and the dangers of boxing were captured in the award-winning movie *Million Dollar Baby* (2004), in which a top female boxer, played beautifully by Hilary Swank, finds self-affirmation and self-worth through success in the ring but (spoiler alert!) suffers a tragic injury in the ring as well. However, boxing raises a number of special problems that deserve consideration.

First, it may be unclear that boxers actually give informed consent to risking the dangers of their sport. Second, boxing raises moral issues because the intent of the participants is to injure or harm their opponents. The phenomenon of the punch-drunk boxer, well known in popular lore, is now thought to often be the result of cumulative blows to the head that, while they can result in death in the ring, generally lead to cognitive deficiencies such as dementia over the course of a lifetime. The great fighter and cultural icon Mohammad Ali suffers from Parkinson's disease and is a widely cited example of the dangers faced by boxers due to the cumulative effect of blows to the head.[10]

The force transmitted by the punch of a skilled boxer has been estimated to be equivalent to being hit by a 15-pound bowling ball traveling at 15 miles per hour. Estimates suggest that 90% of boxers will experience at least one brain injury during their career and, in some studies, a significant percentage of ex-boxers, ranging from 15% to 40%, have been found to have symptoms of chronic brain injury.[11]

Striking as these statistics may be, professional boxers today fight fewer matches than in the past and have better medical supervision, so if the degree of injury to the brain is proportional to the number of fights an individual engages in, rates of injury may improve. Nevertheless, there is virtually no doubt that boxers, especially professional boxers, face a significant risk of serious brain damage due to blows to the head that they receive in the course of bouts.

What are the ethical issues raised by these considerations? Should boxing be prohibited on paternalistic grounds to protect boxers from themselves? Advocates of the harm principle would argue that as long as boxers make free and informed decisions, and do not harm others, we have no more right to interfere with their decision to fight professionally than we have to interfere with participation in other dangerous sports, or to protect us generally from taking significant risks outside of sport.

But do boxers make free and informed choices? Many would argue that most fighters come from economically disadvantaged backgrounds and are drawn to professional boxing because it offers them what might be the only opportunity to lift themselves out of poverty and even gain great wealth. But does this mean their choice is the result of coercion? In other words, are they forced into boxing by their socioeconomic circumstances?

If coercion were involved, boxers would not be exercising free choice. We could suggest that boxing should be prohibited without being labeled paternalistic or violating the harm principle. However, the implications of such a position are not all attractive. Would the argument that boxers were coerced into their sport by poverty imply that anyone from a disadvantaged background working in a dangerous job also has been coerced? What about coal miners, for example, who might be regarded by many as coerced? But then, what about construction workers or others who work at dangerous jobs? How far would we go in dismissing the choices of others because their economic status allegedly makes them unfree? While the idea that economic deprivation limits the range of choices people have may apply is more circumstances than generally thought and shouldn't just be dismissed without considering the specifics of any given situation, applying it indiscriminately risks depriving the economically disadvantaged of autonomy, of the dignity of being competent persons, and reducing their status when we are trying to look out for them? Wouldn't we, therefore, be working against ourselves?

It should be clear, then, that we ought to be cautious about denying the capacity of boxers to make autonomous choices. Of course, soft paternalism allows us to interfere temporarily with their choices to make sure they are informed. In some cases we may find specific reasons to say that some boxers are coerced into fighting. But a general denial of the competency of boxers who seek to escape poverty through becoming fighters seems too broad to be justifiable.

A second concern focuses on the ethics of boxing itself. Boxing, along with other sports involving combat such as mixed martial arts, involves the intentional infliction of harm on the opponent. Professional boxers aim to knock out their opponent if possible.

Other sports that involve the use of significant force, such as football, do not require that players intend to harm opponents and indeed when there is evidence of such intent, severe penalties may be applied. For example, in 2012 the NFL released the findings of an investigation showing that from 2009, the year in which the New Orleans Saints won the Super Bowl, to 2011, numerous Saints players led by their defensive coordinator participated in a bounty system in which players received bonuses for not only delivering especially hard hits but also for deliberately injuring opponents. Head Coach Sean Payton, who did not participate in the system but is said to have known about it, was suspended for a year; defensive coordinator Gregg Williams, then with the Rams, was suspended indefinitely; and various other individuals, including some front office personnel, also received suspensions. Clearly, the NFL regards deliberate attempts to injure opponents as prohibited activity, well beyond the limits of ethical play.

Now consider a hypothetical, borrowed from an example employed by the social commentator, the late Irving Kristol.[12] Suppose a group of investors started a gladiatorial league, in which participants fight sometimes to the death for financial rewards, using weapons like swords, spears, and clubs. In these gladiatorial games, called Mayhem, potential players are fully informed of the dangers of competition and are only accepted into the games if they are not socially or economically disadvantaged. Because they have the informed consent of all the players, the investors argue, the harm principle has not been violated and the state has no business prohibiting the "game."

Is Mayhem acceptable? Can we find grounds for prohibiting it without violating the harm principle or, as Kristol suggests, do we need a justification different from Mill's brand of liberalism for doing so?

Proponents of the harm principle can argue, surely with some plausibility, that it is reasonable to doubt whether potential participants are truly giving informed consent. Are the potential gladiators truly competent? After all, the risks of death, loss of limbs, and other serious injuries are high, and these harms surely are basic evils that no reasonable person wants to suffer without an overriding reason.[13] On the other hand, the thrill of combat and the kind of self-affirmation discussed earlier in connection with dangerous sports may be offered as goods outweighing the risk, to say nothing of the fame and fortune that might be involved.

Mayhem, however, also involves the willingness to deliberately inflict such injuries on others, which is the very point of the contest. We may reasonably doubt whether any mentally stable individual would really want to do that, especially since the benefits of dangerous sports can be obtained through other means, such as mountain climbing or auto racing, that do not involve the deliberate infliction of harm to others.

Although such considerations may reconcile prohibiting Mayhem with the harm principle, some readers may find them thin. Perhaps participants would argue there are internal goods of Mayhem that cannot be obtained elsewhere, such as certain skills of combat, or that their choice is free and informed after all.

Another set of grounds for prohibiting Mayhem, and perhaps boxing as well, goes beyond Mill's version of liberalism to appeal to the impact on the values and nature of the community itself. If Mayhem were to become a popular sport, would the community become even more insensitive to violence than at present, become cruder and coarser, and result in more children growing up with questionable values? Imagine, for example, children collecting cards featuring top gladiators, just as children used to collect baseball cards when I was growing up. A typical card might read as follows: "Alex Mills is skilled with sword and ax, has survived six straight contests without serious injury, and has killed 12% of his opponents and maimed 20% to rank in the top ten in league last year in the mortality statistics." Is this what we want for a role model?

A similar case might be made that boxing, at least at the professional level, also coarsens and desensitizes the community in which it takes place. Boxing, along with other combat sports, involves the intentional infliction of injury to opponents, and so it differs from other sports, such as American football, that involve the use of physical force directly against opponents but that do not by their very nature involve an intent to injure.

The argument that boxing corrupts society appeals not to the autonomy of the individual but to the nature of the good community. It suggests that protecting community standards provides a reason independent of prevention of harm to others to limit the freedom of choice of individuals. After all, the kind of community in which one grows up can significantly influence the kind of person one turns out to be and so is perhaps more fundamental a concern than the choices of individuals, which are not independent of the context in which they grow and develop.

Liberals of all kinds, as well as libertarians who share a belief in the primacy of choice with liberals, are suspicious of this argument. Once we open the door to the state prohibiting activities in the name of community values, where do we stop? Oppressive communities might enforce racial segregation, deny various legal protections on the basis of sexual orientation, or impose religious values on dissenters. As one liberal philosopher pointed out, "the communitarians want us to live in Salem . . . but not believe in witches."[14]

### So should we prohibit boxing? Can we allow boxing but prohibit Mayhem without contradicting ourselves?

There do seem to be relatively clear grounds for prohibiting Mayhem. First, there is good reason to question the mental state of individuals who consent to be gladiators. Although we cannot rule out all who allegedly consent to participate as incompetent, the general difficulty of distinguishing them from others whose mental states are more questionable at least partially supports prohibition. Moreover, communitarians and proponents of the harm principle might agree that children might be harmed by the adoption of top gladiators as role models.

Second, although full-fledged versions of the communitarian argument might risk the oppressive imposition of questionable "community values" on others, perhaps a more minimal form of what might be called "civic communitarianism" is acceptable. According to this view, the state does have a legitimate interest in promoting such values as civility, open discourse, and respect for others that seem to be fundamental to the operations of political democracy. Mayhem, were it to become a popular spectator "sport," might threaten such values and so could be prohibited on such minimalist communitarian grounds.

Would the same reasoning apply to boxing and perhaps such other practices as actual combat in mixed martial arts? Perhaps not. As noted earlier, soft paternalism allows temporary intervention only to ensure that boxers are making free and informed choices to participate but does not support full prohibition. Moreover, the civic communitarian case, while it applies to boxing, seems to do so with less force than it applies to Mayhem. After all, boxing is regulated by rules that limit the kind of violence that can be employed, serious injury is not as immediate or generally not as devastating as in Mayhem, and one-sided fights are stopped by referees to protect the losing fighter from further injury.

My own view is that the case for prohibiting boxing, while not lacking in some force, is not strong enough to justify total prohibition, especially legal prohibition. However, boxing might legitimately be reformed, for, as noted earlier, sports organizations may permissibly use their authority to reduce the chances of serious injury to participants. The suggestion by some observers that the rules be modified to prohibit blows to the head, just as boxers are now prohibited from hitting below the belt, or requiring the use of protective head gear in professional boxing, are justifiable.[15] These reforms might preserve many of the values associated with boxing as a combat sport but reduce the force of many of the criticisms of the sport. They need not be imposed upon the sport by the state but through moral pressure based on legitimate concerns about boxing as it is presently practiced.

Risks of participation in sport encompass much more than injuries suffered in the normal course of play. Such injuries are a risk of participation in sports all along the spectrum of risk, although of course the risk is far less on one end of the spectrum than the other. Let us turn now to the ethical issues raised by technological developments and enhancement in sport that not only do carry risks for the participants but also may have the potential to radically transform the very character of sport itself, for example performance-enhancing drugs.

# 4

# ENHANCEMENT, TECHNOLOGY, AND FAIRNESS IN COMPETITIVE SPORT

*What are the key issues raised by advances in technology and pharmacology in sports? What other areas raise issues about safety in sports, and how should they be addressed?*

In the 2008 Olympics and Short Course Championships, as well as the 2009 World Championships, the use of special full-body-fitting swimsuits helped athletes set multiple records. Shortly after, the use of certain of these swimsuits was prohibited by sports organizations basically on the grounds that they significantly reduced the challenge of competitive swimming.

In the 1970s, a golf ball known as the "Polara straight" with a dimple pattern and other features that made it easier for the ball to go straight instead of curving away from the target was marketed primarily to help less skilled players master the challenges of the game. However, the ball was later prohibited for use in competitions by the United States Golf Association (USGA), presumably for making the game too easy.[1]

Oscar Pistorius was famously allowed to use prosthetic blades, called Cheetah blades, in the 2012 Olympic Games in London. Did the blades give him an unfair advantage over other runners?

To what extent should we allow technological developments to affect athletic performance? What justifies prohibiting skin-fitting full-body swimsuits while, on the other hand, we allow runners to train with hypoxic oxygen chambers, which duplicate the advantages of training at high altitude? Immersion in these chambers increases the number of oxygen-bearing red blood cells significantly and as a result increases long-distance runners' endurance.

These cases suggest a conundrum; namely, where should we draw the line when assessing the impact of technology on sport? Which developments are permissible advances and which are not? The issue has become prominent due to the alleged use of performance-enhancing drugs (PEDs) by prominent athletes in many sports, including Major League Baseball and cycling. The cyclist Lance Armstrong's use of such drugs drew international attention and undermined the respect in which he was held by millions of fans, in part because of his battle with testicular cancer. In fact, there seem to be two related but not identical sets of issues, one of which concerns the use of PEDs and the other raises broader concerns about the effect of technology on performance. Issues raised by the use of anabolic steroids, a synthetic drug regarded as performance enhancing when taken in sufficiently high doses, falls under the first heading while use of the streamlined swimsuits falls under the second.

One of the best ways of exploring these issues is by examining the issues raised by PEDs, so it is with an inquiry into the ethics of their use that we will begin.

### Can we define what counts as a performance-enhancing drug?

Unfortunately, providing a definition in terms of essential qualities possessed by all PEDs is surprisingly difficult. Indeed, the attempt to do so may be fruitless. Major League Baseball provides a list of prohibited substances but no real definition. FIFA, which regulates soccer around the world, states that doping, which refers to the use of drugs to get ahead in sports is defined "as any attempt either by the player, or at the instigation of another person such as manager, coach, trainer, doctor, physiotherapist or masseur, to enhance mental and physical performance physiologically or to treat ailments or injury—when this is medically unjustified—for the sole purpose of taking part in a competition." This account does emphasize that PEDs employed in doping are not used as medicines to treat an ailment but are taken simply to enhance athletic performance. However, this definition might even include a healthy Mediterranean diet that an athlete adopts only on the basis of her opinion that it will enhance performance, although many would find such an extension of the definition of PEDs to be exaggerated if they considered this kind of example.

Many different kinds of substances, not just anabolic steroids, can be classified as performance enhancers, which of course complicates the attempt to find any neat definition. For example, erythropoietin, commonly called EPO, increases the number of oxygen-carrying cells (red blood cells) in the bodies of users, which can be desirable in that it typically increases their endurance. Such thickening of the blood can be dangerous, however, because it raises the risk of strokes and heart problems, and it may be responsible for the deaths of a number of elite cyclists who are believed to have used the drug. The use of beta-blockers, which slow the heart rate and are commonly prescribed to control cardiac arrhythmias, may reduce the effects of nervousness during competition. Even moderate use of alcohol, which can slow the heart rate, counts as a banned substance in some sports, such as riflery, where competitors shoot between heartbeats in order to keep steady when firing.

The distinction between drugs that restore ability, much the same way that medicines do, and those that enhance abilities, while it may look like a promising tool for identifying PEDs, is unlikely to be helpful. There is simply no clear line distinguishing restoration from enhancement. Does the Mediterranean diet, mentioned earlier, restore or enhance? Do steroids, which enable athletes to recover more quickly from harder workouts, enhance performance or restore the body to good shape and help athletes to overcome the tendency to fatigue just as the diet overcomes metabolic deficiencies that may hinder performance? Does Lasik eye surgery restore vision to normal or does it enhance it?

It also may be difficult to classify cases where a drug has a medical or restorative function in one context but may act as a performance enhancer in another.[2] For example, the drug Ritalin is used to treat attention-deficit/hyperactivity disorder (ADHD) in children, but it might also enhance performance in sports that require concentration or sudden bursts of energy. The use of Ritalin when prescribed by a doctor for a medical condition is legitimate but becomes questionable when used simply to enhance performance. The difficulty in hard cases is that this line can sometimes be blurred, making evaluation of such borderline cases difficult. Our concerns do not mean that the restorative-enhancement distinction is useless, but they do suggest that this distinction is unlikely to be helpful in resolving difficult cases.

Is it any more helpful to think about PEDs as resources athletes use that are unnatural? Unfortunately, the natural-unnatural distinction also is unlikely to prove helpful. Are medicines always natural? Are steroids, which are an artificial form of the human hormone testosterone, unnatural? If they are, so what? Why should something unnatural in some sense be regarded as wrong or prohibited? Are artificial hips or knees natural or unnatural? If the latter, should they be prohibited?

Rather than attempt to define what counts as a PED, it may prove wiser to follow a suggestion that I presented elsewhere: that we first try to find reasons why certain substances should be prohibited and then label any substance to which those reasons apply as a PED.[3] In other words, instead of trying to define "PED" and then see if the use of substances falling under our definition is morally wrong, let's first find out why using certain substances is morally wrong (if it is) and then call those drugs PEDs.

*Isn't it obvious that the use of drugs to enhance athletic performance is unethical? Aren't fans right to regard such known users as Lance Armstrong in cycling and Alex Rodriguez in Major League Baseball as cheaters, or at least in violation of the ethics that should govern competitive athletics?*

When I first started writing about the ethics of using PEDs in sports, I thought, foolishly as it turned out, that the issue was relatively easy to resolve. So, when I was asked to participate on a panel at the Scientific Olympic Congress to be held in Eugene, Oregon, in the summer of 1984 on the topic of the use of PEDs by athletes, I jumped at the chance. (The Congress is a forum held before Olympic Games for academics, coaches, and athletes to discuss ethical issues in sports, especially those involving the Olympic movement.) I presented a paper that I thought clearly showed why the use of performance enhancers in athletics was wrong and should be prohibited. Much to my surprise, many of the other panelists disagreed with me. Even worse, some found my arguments flawed, and with reason! Afterward I realized I was lucky to learn that the use of PEDs, and even the definition of PEDs, as we just saw, was much more complex than I had appreciated.

Despite this complexity, there are some plain facts we can establish. To begin with, if there is a rule in place forbidding the use of certain PEDs that applies to competitions in a sport, to deliberately use the drug to gain an advantage over others seems clearly wrong and, in many cases, fits our paradigm of cheating discussed in Chapter 2. Just like carrying the ball in basketball, or cutting a corner in a marathon, this is a clear case of breaking the rules, and therefore isn't fair to other athletes. The fact that drug use is the specific type of rule breaking one engages in doesn't make it a special case, in this example. Breaking the existing rules, with no good reason for making an exception of oneself, is cheating. In such cases, drug users are treating fellow competitors who follow the rules and do not use PEDs as mere obstacles to success, not as persons engaged in a mutually acceptable activity designed to test each other through a challenge defined by the rules and principles applying to the sport in question.

However, the more significant issue, as numerous writers on the subject have pointed out, is whether the use of PEDs should be prohibited in the first place. Why not change the rules in order to allow athletes to use such drugs as they see fit since so many do it anyway? What, if anything, justifies restricting their freedom to experiment in their quest to achieve excellence?

In responding to this question, it is important to keep a number of different issues distinct. For example, is the prohibition of the use of PEDs based on the belief they give users an unfair advantage over athletes who are "clean?" Or is it that users harm other athletes by in effect coercing them to also become users in order to avoid being disadvantaged? Is prohibition based on the view that use of PEDs violates some ideal that sports ought to fit? Is our primary concern to protect young athletes from starting to use PEDs either because they want to emulate the elite athletes who use, or because they believe they must become users to achieve elite status themselves? On the other hand, does prohibiting PEDs unjustly interfere with the freedom of athletes to decide for themselves what risks they want to take? Isn't this what they do anyway when they decide whether to participate in dangerous sports in the first place? To seek some answers to these challenging questions, let's start with the question of athletes' freedom to choose.

### Shouldn't athletes be free to choose for themselves whether to use PEDs?

What has come to be called the harm principle, defended by nineteenth-century philosopher John Stuart Mill and discussed earlier in our examination of dangerous sports, will help us answer this question. According to this principle, the only ground for restricting the liberty of the individual is to prevent harm to others.

If we adopted the harm principle, restrictions on PEDs would be justified only if we could demonstrate that their use by some harms others or has the clear potential to do so. Moreover, we would have to show that the harm in question is one that drug users have no right to impose on others. For example, if I apply for a job that someone else wants and I am the more qualified candidate, I may harm my competitor because he or she will be unemployed if I am the successful applicant. Similarly, if I am in business and my shrewd marketing leads to a decrease in my competitor's sales, the competitor may be harmed. This does not mean that I should be prohibited from applying for the job or marketing my business aggressively, however. The harm principle does not imply that all potentially harmful behavior may be prohibited, but only that if we do prohibit behavior, it must be in order to prevent harm to others.

Paternalism, limiting the freedom of others for their own good, seems to be ruled out by the harm principle, but, in *On Liberty*, Mill himself made an exception for what has come to be called "soft paternalism." Soft paternalism, as we noted earlier, refers to temporary restriction of individual liberty to make sure that persons about to take risky action that might harm them understand and appreciate the likely consequences. Mill uses the example of an individual who is stopped from trying to cross over a washed-out bridge in order to make sure the driver knows just what he is doing. Similarly, a bystander may interfere with an attempt at suicide in order to ensure that the decision is informed, not made in the grip of an overpowering and perhaps irrational emotion, and that the agent is truly competent.

Political liberals and libertarians generally each give great weight to the harm principle. Libertarians believe that an individual's choices should not be restricted by the state except to prevent some people from using force on others. Libertarians of sport, then, would favor granting athletes the widest latitude to experiment, including experimentation with PEDs, unless the risk of harm to others could be demonstrated. Liberals also give great weight to individual freedom, but they do not construe liberty as broadly as do the libertarians. Although liberals generally agree with libertarians about the dangers of some groups imposing their ideals of the good life, say a religious ideal, on others, they believe the state does have an obligation to provide a just social structure in which individuals have a fair opportunity to pursue their own personal visions of the good life. Nevertheless, in many domains, liberals, like libertarians, tend to be wary of paternalistic interference with the liberty of competent adults. If we regard liberty to choose how we live our daily lives (so long as we aren't harming others) as among our fundamental rights, restricting the freedom of athletes to use PEDs for their own good is likely to be an unattractive strategy to pursue.

### What arguments often are cited for prohibiting the use of PEDs that we should consider? How strong are they?

In addition to paternalistic reasons for wanting to prevent athletes from using PEDs, for example wanting to spare them from the health risks that come with many PEDs, as we discussed, there also may be grounds for prohibiting the use of PEDs. As we noted earlier, they may provide some competitors who use with an unfair advantage over those who refrain from using. In fact, that often is the very reason why athletes use them. By doing so, they may undermine an ideal of sport we think worth preserving. Although liberals and libertarians are wary of the state imposing an ideal of to how to live on its citizens, perhaps a different set of norms apply to sports organizations than to the state.

Just how do political theories such as liberalism and libertarianism apply to the debate over PEDs? It is important to remember during our discussion that one can be a libertarian of sport, arguing for example that athletes should be able to use PEDs on the basis of personal freedom, without being a full-fledged political libertarian. That is, one may consistently believe both that athletes in particular should be free to decide for themselves whether to use PEDs but also hold characteristically liberal political views, for example that the state may tax us even against our will, in order to provide basic services such as free public education or food and shelter to those who cannot provide such basic necessities for themselves. A person can reasonably hold one set of views when it comes to sports and another when it comes to politics. Indeed, to invoke the key concept in the debates we have been discussing, we are free to do so.

### Aren't we justified in prohibiting PEDs to protect athletes from harming themselves?

Some PEDs, especially anabolic steroids, are considered to be dangerous to the user. Thus, it is frequently claimed that frequent and prolonged use of steroids can increase the risk of serious illness, including cardiac arrest, kidney disease, and liver cancer. Unfortunately, there is no well-designed clinical study that supports this conclusion, in part because it is illegal to give subjects steroids in the strengths and combinations said to be used by athletes. Accordingly, much of the evidence for the harms caused by steroids is based on reports of specific cases, on side effects of steroids used for medical purposes, and knowledge of the chemistry of steroid use but not on the kind of peer-reviewed double-blind studies that are the gold standard for claims about the side effects of drug use. Indeed, some athletes engaged in particularly grueling sports, such as long-distance cycling, sometimes claim that the use of steroids may even make their sport safer by allowing them to recover more quickly from the kind of exertion involved in their sport. Nevertheless, the case for the dangers of steroid use to enhance athletic performance generally is very plausible based on the considerations cited and the expected effects of prolonged heavy use. Unfortunately, the dangers are too often ignored by users.

In any case, let us stipulate for the sake of argument that the use of anabolic steroids, as well as use of other PEDs such as human growth hormone, does carry with it serious risks to the health of the user. Libertarians argue that even if they grant this stipulation, the case for prohibiting the use of such drugs remains weak.

First, libertarians point that out we already allow athletes to risk their health in many ways. Some sports, such as mountain climbing, are inherently dangerous. We are becoming increasingly aware of the dangers of playing football, especially in the NFL, and the long-term effects of frequent blows to the head. Professional boxing is not prohibited despite the well-known phenomenon of the punch drunk, that is, brain-damaged, ex-fighter. Injuries, including concussions, are not infrequent in sports such as soccer, basketball, and especially rugby. Back pain, often chronic and sometimes temporarily disabling, is frequent among avid golfers. But despite the danger to participants, we don't prohibit any of these activities. Therefore, libertarians conclude, it would be arbitrary to prohibit the use of PEDs on the grounds of dangers to the user when we allow athletes to risk serious dangers in pursuing their sport in so many other areas. (As noted above, some athletes such as long-distance cyclists argue that the use of some PEDs makes their sport safer by allowing for faster recovery from their grueling days on the race course.)

Second, as we have seen, libertarians point out the dangers of paternalism in interfering with the choices of competent athletes allegedly for their own good. Mill's harm principle, remember, allows us to prevent the children or the mentally disabled from acting on their choices for their own good, but it is quite another thing to interfere with the choices of a competent adult. Many of us would be outraged if what might be called the Nanny State prohibited us from having unhealthy meals or penalized us for failing to exercise. Competent adults, on this view, should be at liberty to make bad choices so long as they do not violate Mill's principle by harming others. Libertarians of sport, then, argue for the freedom of competent and informed adults to make their own choices. To allow us to choose only what someone else thinks is good for us is to treat us as children and not respect us as autonomous persons, as what Kant called ends-in-ourselves.

### Aren't we justified in prohibiting PEDs to protect athletes from harming other athletes?

Many of us, including many in favor of prohibiting PEDs in organized athletic competition, would agree with the antipaternalist view sketched earlier. But what about harm to *others*? Don't the athletes who use PEDs in effect force others to use them in order to be competitive? And if those athletes who would rather play drug-free sports are coerced into doping, aren't they in effect being forced to harm themselves, or at least run the risk of serious harm due to the side effects of the substances they are using? Mill's harm principle allows us to restrict the actions of some to prevent harm to others. Doesn't the use of risky PEDs fall under the heading of harm to others?

This argument relies on two assumptions: that the use of PEDs by some athletes coerces others into using and that use harms them or risks harming them in a morally impermissible way. Critics, however, question both assumptions, sometimes with good reason.

Consider the claim about coercion. If we are to be consistent, and regard users as coercing other athletes to use PEDs in order to remain competitive, we may be led into accepting much too broad a view of coercion. For example, if I work harder at weight training to be more competitive in my sport, am I coercing my fellow competitors into working harder as well? When Tiger Woods burst on the golfing scene, his success demonstrated the effectiveness of athleticism and fitness in elite golf. Did he literally force other players to get fitter, or did they choose to do so in order to have a chance to beat Woods? It seems a stretch to classify either of these as examples of coercion. So then why are athletes who dope seen as coercing others to do the same? If competing athletes don't want to dope, they can choose not to and work harder on some other dimension of their games or leave the sport altogether.

Of course, dopers, by their own use of PEDs, assuming it was known to other athletes, might be putting pressure on others to use PEDs as well. But putting pressure on others—in effect providing them with an incentive to become users in order to rise to the dopers' level of performance—is quite different from coercing them. Many things we do put pressure on others, both in sports and in other domains of everyday life. If one of my students works especially hard on an assignment, rewriting it numerous times until it is especially well crafted, that might put pressure on other ambitious students to do the same, but few would go so far as to say that they are being forced to work harder.

These criticisms of the argument from coercion have force but may not be decisive. The notion of "coercion" itself can be understood in a variety of ways, and some defensible conceptions of coercion may be much broader and apply to a wider range of cases than others.[4] For example, if some workers need to take a low-paying job to support their family, on some understandings of "coercion," the workers are coerced out of economic necessity, but, on other notions, they are making a free choice reacting to the incentives to which they give the most weight.

Perhaps, then, contrary to opposing arguments, it is plausible to think that in some, perhaps many cases, athletes are coerced (on a broader understanding of "coercion") into using sometimes dangerous PEDs. Think of the aging professional who thinks he may get cut from the team if he does not use drugs to help him keep up with younger competitors. Think of the young athlete who thinks he will never reach elite levels without becoming a user. Although on some views of "coercion, it may be too much of a stretch to say such individuals are "coerced" (after all, they can just work harder without taking drugs or simply change their goals), on other views of coercion it is not a stretch at all.

My own conclusion is that while the coercion argument probably is not decisive, since the concept of coercion is itself contested territory, it also is not worthless. Perhaps, even if the coercion argument is not decisive by itself, it has force when supported by other arguments for the same conclusion. Perhaps a case can be made in favor of prohibiting the use of PEDs through the combination of many arguments that is stronger than the case that can be made by any one argument alone.

In any case, the second assumption of the coercion argument we identified earlier is that if some athletes do harm others by using PEDs, they do so *unjustly* or in a *morally impermissible* way. But can we just assume that when athletes choose to dope, they are *unjustly* raising the risk of harm to fellow competitors? Why is what they are doing any more unjust than what the student is doing who works harder than her peers in order to produce excellent work? Without a strong reply to such questions, critics of the prohibition on PEDs argue that the coercion argument fails. So to strengthen the argument from coercion, we need a further reason for thinking that users pressure nonusers in a way that can plausibly be regarded as unfair or unjust.

### Don't users of PEDs in sports have an unfair advantage over competitors who are drug-free?

Even if the use of PEDs does not reduce the challenge of many sports to an unacceptable level, perhaps users have an unfair advantage over nonusers. After all, why would anyone dope in the first place if not to gain an advantage over the opposition?

But what makes the advantage unfair? Athletes often start out with advantages over other competitors. For example, some have better coaching, better facilities for training, or significantly more financial support than others. Some are taller or faster than others due only to the luck of the genetic draw. Are all these advantages unfair? If not, what distinguishes those that are unfair from others?

I am inclined to say that precompetitive inequalities that arise from social and economic conditions beyond the athletes' control are presumptively unfair. If a wealthy country's Olympic team has access to enormous resources and a less developed country's team has significantly less financial support, the precompetition playing field is not level. In such cases, fairness may even call for redistribution from the better-off team to the worse-off team. (At present, we sometimes see a "muscle drain" when athletes from less developed countries, especially in soccer, decide to play in the developed world, where pay for professional athletes is higher.)

On the other hand, differences in coaching arguably are less questionable from the moral point of view. Coaching itself requires a skill set that can be regarded as part of the competition, just as are the abilities and strategic skills of the athletes themselves, which are not necessarily anywhere near equal. (Of course, there might be an overlap where only the richest teams have access to the best coaches.)

So are the advantages dopers have over "clean" athletes fair or unfair? Are they any different from other advantages we accept, such as superior natural talent?

Although there may be no uncontroversial answer to this question, I suggest that the unfairness argument does have some weight. The greatest advantage for an athlete is to be the only one in the competition using PEDs. But if everyone was allowed to use, the advantage would generally be cancelled out by benefits gained by the other users and there would then be no real point in using, especially if the drug in question had dangerous side effects.

Thus, it is unlikely reasonable athletes could consent to a policy allowing drug use for all, since no individual athlete would be likely to gain a significant advantage over others and all would be exposed to risks. If this point is sound, a reasonable social contract among athletes would not contain a rule allowing the use of PEDs (at least those with risky side effects). This explains why many identify the use of PEDs with cheating—it only makes sense if a few use and the great majority do not. Users arbitrarily exempt themselves from what would be a system of rules to which all could assent, and so arguably fall under our account of cheating developed in Chapter 2.

Although this sort of argument needs further development and exposure to critical scrutiny before it can be regarded as determinative, perhaps the sketch developed earlier adds weight to the prohibitionist position, especially when conjoined with the other reasons supporting such a view.

### Does the use of PEDs make sports too easy?

Advocates of prohibiting PEDs also may argue that the use of PEDs reduces the challenge of sports by making success too easy to achieve. For evidence, they can point to the plethora of home runs, especially by older ball players such as Bobby Bonds, who should have been past their prime, during the so-called steroid era in baseball. Star player Jose Canesco's book, *Juiced: Wild Times, Rampant 'Roids, Smash Hits and How Baseball Got Big*, while greeted with initial skepticism, exposed the use of PEDs in Major League Baseball. His stories were followed by an investigation into the use of performance enhancers in the Major Leagues that was summarized in the thorough Mitchell Report, written by former Senator George Mitchell. In elite cycling, Lance Armstrong's success is often attributed to his use of performance-enhancing technology, including the drug EPO and "blood doping," or the injection of his own red blood cells, both of which raise the individual's oxygen-carrying capacity and presumably endurance. Revelations such as these diminished many fans' respect for the professional athletes they idolized and made cynics out of some who once had deep admiration and awe for these athletes' feats.

But despite the strong emotions that these doping scandals evoked in fans, and the questions about fairness that they raise, the argument for prohibiting PEDs is not decisive. After all, we could say, for example, that batters during the steroid era may have faced pitchers who also were "juiced," perhaps evening out the playing field. And although Armstrong was among the most famous cyclists to have been caught in such a scandal, he was hardly the only one doping.

More important, the use of equipment that enhances performance is often permitted, despite the fact that it too may make the sport in question easier. For example, before the introduction of multilayered golf balls around the 2000 season, elite players had to choose between distance balls that flew far but lacked the spin to provide control around the greens or high-spin balls that didn't go as far as their distance counterparts. The new multilayered balls provided both distance and control. According to many observers, they made the game easier by allowing players to drive prodigious distances and still control their balls landing on the green, reducing the need for controlled shot making. The replacement of wooden tennis racquets with graphite racquets may have played a similar role. Thus, when told that an older professional, Bjorn Borg, would use a wooden racket when making a comeback in a major tournament, a fellow competitor replied, "If he plays a wooden racquet, he'll be holding splinters." Isn't it arbitrary, then, to allow advances in equipment that may reduce the challenge of a sport but then prohibit PEDs that only do the same thing?[5]

Although the charge of arbitrariness is important, the argument that the use of PEDs significantly reduces the challenge of many sports is not worthless either. Sports authorities often prohibit equipment that makes a sport too easy, such as the streamlined swimsuits we referred to earlier or the golf ball that goes straight even if it is hit badly. What we need, however, is some principle that allows us to make reasonable decisions about which technological advances are permissible and which are not. Perhaps we can defend a position such as this: If a specific PED provides an athlete with an advantage in sport that would be impermissible if it were provided by new, technologically advanced equipment, then the PED that provides the same advantage also ought to be prohibited.

### Is there an ideal of sport that the use of PEDs undermines? What considerations support such an ideal and how might it be defined?

The sort of argument I presented at the Olympic Scientific Congress that I mentioned earlier appealed to what I now see was an ideal of sport. In particular, I argued that because different athletes react differently to the same PED, and because the way in which one's body reacts to the PED is not a skill sports are designed to test, the use of PEDs makes who wins and loses in significant part the result of something other than the skill of the athletes. This violates the skills thesis that maintains that athletic contests (at least at their best) should be decided by the skill of the competitors. More broadly, competition in sport ideally should be between people—beings capable of making choices who decide what skills to develop, what strategies to employ, and how to react to moves by opponents. The use of PEDs, according to this argument, changes sport into a competition among scientists to produce the best athletes through the use of drugs, and hence violates the ideal of what we called mutualism: sports as a mutual quest for excellence among people.

Don't sports organizations act properly, then, in prohibiting the use of substances that tie the outcome of competitions to athletically irrelevant qualities of athletes, such as how well their bodies metabolize a drug? A PED then can be roughly characterized as any digestible substance that has a significant role in determining the outcome of athletic contests in a way other than by the skill of the athletes, and which is neither medically necessary, part of a normal or healthy diet, or equipment sanctioned for use by sports authorities.[6]

At the time I presented that argument, I regarded it as quite strong. However, discussion has convinced me that it has many weaknesses, although perhaps not decisive ones. For example, different athletes react differently to similar programs of weight training. Some become stronger than others, even though they are going through the same regimen of resistance training. Isn't how one's body reacts to resistance training, which arguably is not under the individual's control, as athletically irrelevant as how one's body reacts to a PED?

Wouldn't the same be true for special diets that may be healthy but affect different athletes differently? If so, isn't it arbitrary to restrict the use of drugs on the grounds I suggest when we allow many other practices, such as resistance training and special diets, which are open to the same criticism?

Clearly, these objections have force. My original argument was not as strong as I had hoped. But was it worthless? Perhaps not. Granted, there is no perfect line separating what substances affect athletic performance legitimately and which do so illegitimately. But perhaps it is reasonable to distinguish between PEDs, on one hand, and healthy diets and resistance or strength training, on the other. One difference is that PEDs may adversely affect health and arguably can be downright dangerous in specific cases, whereas strength training, when done under proper supervision, can enhance general health and fitness, as does the Mediterranean and similar diets associated with enhanced well-being. Moreover, the degree to which one benefits from strength training may be more athletically relevant than how one's body utilizes a drug. That is, it seems more plausible to say that how one reacts to weight training is part of what makes one a good athlete, at least more so than how one reacts to a drug. Given that, it may be reasonable for sports authorities to protect sports as an area of healthy competition, rather than let the quest for "faster, higher, stronger" make participation in athletics far riskier than otherwise would be the case.

If we view sports organizations as guardians of certain ideals of sport, other arguments against allowing the use of PEDs also are worth attention. Let us consider two and then see if we can come to any sort of conclusion, however tentative.

### Are the proponents of prohibition rejecting good policies because they are not perfect?

This is an excellent question. Recall the admonition not to let the perfect be the enemy of the good. Libertarians of sport argue—correctly, in my view—that there is no perfect place to draw the line between which tools that enhance performance should be allowed and which prohibited. Their point here is a strong one. But even if there is no *perfect* place to draw a clear bright line in the sand, there may be *reasonable* places to draw perhaps not a line but a boundary that is clear enough to be useful.

In fact, this is what we do in other areas. There is no perfect age, for example, to allow young people to drive automobiles. Some 22-year-olds surely are more dangerous drivers than some mature and careful 14-year-olds. Nevertheless, most of us would agree that it is reasonable to set an age around 18 for issuing of full driver licenses. Similarly, some 15-year-old voters would be better informed and more judicious than many much older citizens, yet we have to draw a line somewhere and 18 seems a reasonable if not perfect place to do it. Might the same approach apply to PEDs?

The suggestion we are considering, then, is whether sports organizations act reasonably in prohibiting the use of PEDs. Isn't this just what happens with advancements in equipment, which such authorities already regulate? What would make prohibitions on the use of PEDs reasonable? Would drawing a reasonable line unjustly interfere with the liberty of athletes to make their own choices about whether to use or not?

### Is prohibiting the use of PEDs more reasonable than allowing it?

First of all, think of all the problems that would arise if athletes were allowed to choose for themselves not only whether to use PEDs but which combinations of drugs they should use as well. What would an open policy look like?[7] First, presumably athletes would keep their favorite formula secret to prevent others from using it as well. If so, other players and spectators would be in the dark about just who was using what. Under such conditions, there surely would be even more huge questions about how much of an athlete's achievements were due to the drugs than if PEDs were taken openly due to uncertainty about just what drugs were being used by which athletes.

Furthermore, if no one knew what drugs each athlete was using, opportunities for research on the effects of the PEDs would be minimal at best. Presumably we would know little more about which drugs were being used by which athlete, which were harmful, and which actually enhanced performance than we know at present. Safety concerns would be warranted since secrecy would inhibit our ability to learn just which drugs were especially harmful and to what extent.

Indeed, the point I suggested earlier that athletic success might be attributed more to athletically irrelevant characteristics of athletes, such as how their body reacted to a specific combination of drugs, or which chemists and physicians they used as advisers might have special force in this context.

Although different regimens of strength training and different diets also might have different effects on different athletes, these normally would not be secret. In addition, we might deny with plausibility that a healthy diet enhanced normal function (although as noted earlier "enhancement" itself is not a clear term) and maintain that how one utilizes weight training is an athletically relevant quality. Moreover, if various combinations of drugs were taken in secret, it is likely that risk to the health of users would be magnified due to lack of research on or regulation of the dose taken.

It is perhaps for this reason that advocates of allowing the use of PEDs might want the drugs administered openly under the supervision of physicians. However, if the physicians were employed by the teams for which the athletes played, conflicts of interest might be prevalent. Does the physician advise the player to take a drug because it might help the team win or protect the athlete from a drug that carries a level of risk the athlete might not want to take? Moreover, pressures on nonusers to take PEDs might become quite significant since teammates would use drugs openly. In professional sports in particular, coaches, owners, and teammates might accuse nonusers of letting them down, and might even threaten their place on the team if they continued to refrain from drug use. (This consideration would bring the coercion argument back into play.)

So one reason sports organizations might have reasonable grounds not to open the door to the use of PEDs is the practical difficulty of formulating a policy for doing so. Still another reason might concern what we can call the conjunction of considerations already considered. That is, if I am right to think that while the arguments from coercion, unfairness, an ideal of sport, and advantage over the sport by themselves are not decisive, when taken individually their weight when aggregated nevertheless may be sufficient to tip the scales in favor of prohibition.

This latter argument becomes even stronger if we add the requirement that the athletes reason *impartially*, for example without knowing whether the drugs will help them more than anyone else. Reasoning impartially rather than selfishly requires athletes to take a moral point of view. From that perspective, allowing everyone to use, as we have seen in discussing fairness, only exposes athletes to risks while remaining ignorant of whether they as individuals are likely to gain.

Keeping these points in mind, consider the issue from the perspective of the organizations regulating athletic competition, such as the NCAA, which regulates intercollegiate sport in the United States, or the International Olympic Committee. We already noted that they would have a difficult time designing a fair and open policy permitting drug use. Which drugs would be allowed? Would use be regulated by public rules applying to all or done privately and in secret by individuals and teams? Would the effects minimize the challenges of the sports in question?

In addition, some have argued that sports organizations would have the right to protect an ideal of drug-free sports if it was widely shared by the athletic community. In other words, they not only do no wrong by prohibiting the use of PEDs but express the wishes of a significant element, probably the majority, of the athletic community.[8] The argument from the collective interest of athletes suggests we can go even further. If unrestricted use of PEDs is not in the collective interest of athletes, sports organizations may have a duty (or at least a very good reason) to protect that interest from being undermined.

For some athletes, gaining competitive advantage is not the highest priority. Their goal is not simply to beat others, but to perform at higher and higher levels, setting new record over new record on the way. If all athletes performed with these kinds of goals in mind, they would be happy as individuals regardless of whether they won medals because their goal would be to advance the levels of human achievement—to go where no athlete has ever gone before. They would be relatively unmoved by argument to the effect that drug use gives some athletes an unfair competitive advantage over others because their goal would be to set records and raise the level of achievement, and therefore maintaining competitive equity would not be such an important consideration.

However, the principal function of sports organizations is to regulate competition, not necessarily to provide an arena for setting records. Protecting the collective competitive interest of athletes, then, should be a higher priority for them than concern for record breaking. Indeed, as Norwegian philosopher Sigmund Loland has pointed out, in such sports as swimming, track, and skiing, new records may surpass the old by such a small margin that the instruments for detecting the difference may not even have existed even a relatively short time ago. Loland suggests, rightly, in my view, that a more significant test of athletic excellence in such sports is finishing ahead of competitors over a series of events, for example, winning the World Cup, winning most of the races of a certain length over a season, or winning the World Series, rather than breaking a record by an almost indiscernible margin.[9] In any case, the fact that in many sports, new records eclipse old ones by only barely detectable levels suggests that at least in such sports, the goal of setting new records should take a back seat to enduring that legitimacy of competition is protected.

The opposing views on the use of PEDs are supported by arguments worthy of consideration, so the debate will continue to rage. My own conclusion is that the arguments for prohibition make the stronger case. Prohibition not only preserves the challenge of our sports and makes participation less dangerous, it is unclear what would be gained if all athletes were permitted to use performance enhancers. Although the overall level of performance might be raised, achievement may also be cheapened—consider the devaluing of the home run in Major League Baseball during the steroid era—so it is doubtful if competition itself would be any better.

Perhaps the desire of some athletes to use PEDs assigns too high a priority to setting records and performing better and better—what Aristotle might call an excess or vice rather than the Golden Mean. I myself place significant weight on the collective interest argument. If athletic competition should conform to the ideal of mutualism, it is difficult to see why a policy to which it would be unreasonable for all athletes to consent should be implemented.

Those who favor allowing the use of PEDs sometimes argue that since we allow new technologies that enhance athletic performance, it would be arbitrary not to allow the use of drugs that do the same. But, in fact, the introduction of new technologies is regulated by sports authorities. Let us see if our discussion of PEDs sheds light on issues raised by other technological innovations in sport.

### What principles apply to the regulation of technological innovation in sport?

As technology develops, improvements in equipment often have a significant effect on performance in sports. New materials or technology used in golf clubs and balls, tennis racquets, poles for vaulting, swimsuits, and perhaps even wax (applied to skis to reduce friction) for cross country skiing arguably have contributed to better performance by athletes, especially at the elite level but perhaps for amateur athletes as well. At what point do improved running shoes or full-body swimsuits or improved golf clubs enhance performance to an unacceptable degree? What makes improvement in equipment allowable but not PEDs or genetic enhancement? Both arguably are forms of enhancement. So aren't our rules and attitudes toward each inconsistent?

Maybe so, but as we have seen, changes in equipment due to technological advances are not always approved. Sports authorities have the duty to protect the integrity of their sport by prohibiting innovations that in their view significantly reduce the challenge of the sport. In the 2009 World Swimming Championships at Rome, numerous world records were set by swimmers wearing full-body seamless polyurethane swimsuits. In fact, some brands seemed to perform better than others, but swimmers were not able to switch to the most efficient brand because of contractual relationships with other companies. The suits basically reduced drag in the water, enabling wearers to post significantly better times in their events without necessarily swimming any better than before. Not surprisingly, use of the suits in major competitions was banned in 2010.

In fact, if sports organizations did not set limits on the implementation of new technologies in equipment, sports might devolve into a state with parallels to Hobbes's state of nature, which we discussed in Chapter 1. That is, in the absence of regulation, companies and competitors might work to come up with technological advantages that were kept secret. Everyone would be looking for a technological edge over everyone else. Eventually, it might be doubtful whether competitors were even playing the same sport. Similarly, if everyone used their own secret formula of PEDs, wouldn't the idea of a level playing field be in jeopardy?

So sports authorities do impose limits on technology to preserve the integrity of their sport. Their decisions are not always uncontroversial, however, and questions may arise about the standard used to evaluate them. I suggest that those making the decisions at least implicitly rely on a theory of the key skills and challenges of their sport (what the broad internalists discussed in Chapter 1 might call an interpretation of the sport) and ask whether according to that theory the introduction of the new technology improves the game or reduces its challenges in an unacceptable manner. Although some decisions will be controversial or even mistaken, they are legitimate (even if corrected in the future) if reasonable and arrived at only after consultation with affected parties, such as athletes, officials, and manufacturers involved in the sport in question. (We suggested earlier, in a similar vein, that if the use of a drug reduces the challenge of the sport to a degree that if the same effect was achieved by new technology the technology would be banned, then there is good reason to label that drug a PED and prohibit its use in the sport at issue.)

### How should we assess technology that allows athletes with a disability to compete with other athletes at the highest levels of competition?

The classic case may well be the use of Cheetah Blades by Oscar Pistorius in the 2012 Olympics in London. These prosthetic devices allowed Pistorius, a double amputee below the knee, to become the first amputee sprinter to compete in the Olympics after an official body, the Court of Arbitration, ruled they did not give him any advantage over able-bodied sprinters.

A more controversial case, involving the golfer Casey Martin, was settled by the Supreme Court of the United States in *PGA Tour Inc. vs. Casey Martin* (2001). The case arose because Martin, who had a circulatory ailment in his legs, was unable to walk as required by the rules in a late-stage qualifying tournament for membership on the Professional Golfers Association (PGA) Tour, the highest level of professional golf in the United States and possibly the world.

The Tour, supported by some golf stars, argued that walking the course was an integral part of the game, possibly because of the endurance required to do so. The opposing view, of course, is that the key skill of the game is striking the ball in such a way as to control one's shots and the distance they fly, and that walking is not a fundamental skill of golf. The Court ruled 7-2 in favor of Martin and he was allowed to use a golf cart in the qualifying event and later on the PGA Tour itself. In a humorous dissent, drawing in part on author Kurt Vonnegut's satire of extreme egalitarianism in the short story

"Harrison Bergeron" in which Vonnegut postulates a society in which, for example, people must wear masks so they can gain no advantage from being attractive, Justice Anthony Scalia wrote that the main issue in the case was defining what was essential to golf. "The Court ultimately concludes, and it will henceforth be the Law of the Land, that walking is not a 'fundamental' aspect of golf."

Whether or not the decision was correct, it seems that the Court must rely on an interpretation or theory of golf that provides an account of just what skills are fundamental to the sport. My own view is that walking and endurance can be relevant to who wins a tournament, for example if one has to walk 36 holes on an extremely hot day in a major competition. However, I also think that riding a cart under some conditions also can be a disadvantage, for example on a cold day when walking helps a player to keep warm. If riding did not give Martin a significant advantage over other players, and I suggest it did not, then the ruling is correct. After all, all the players who do use carts, sometimes in competition, surely are still playing golf, regardless of their method of locomotion.

Regardless of particular decisions, however, our discussion indicates there is a principled framework for discussing whether technological innovations, or adjustments for disabilities, are permissible at various levels of competition. That is, those charged with making the decision should, however informally, follow the broad internalist strategy outlined in Chapter 1. That is, they need at least a rough theory of the sport at issue and the skills fundamental to it. A major consideration in their decision about the technology, then, will be the extent to which it undermines or reduces the fundamental skills of the game, as defined by the interpretation, and whether, if it does, it reduces them to an unacceptable extent. Although the framework itself only gives us a way of proceeding, it sets the ground rules for making reasonable decisions about technological innovation in sports.

PEDs' and accommodation for disability and technological innovations in equipment are only parts of the debate about using technology to enhance performance. As our knowledge of the human genome increases and it becomes more possible for us to manipulate behavior through modifications at the genetic level, new issues concerning technological enhancement also need to be considered. Is what might be called "gene doping" any more acceptable than the use of PEDs, and does it raise new issues not yet considered in the enhancement debate?

### What does genetic enhancement involve?

Manipulating genes for purposes either of therapy or of enhancement can be broken down into two basic categories. *Somatic* treatment for therapeutic goals involves replacing genetic material in nonreproductive or somatic cells so as to remedy a medical condition with a genetic basis. For example, if extreme muscle weakness is caused by a gene mutation, in theory the faulty genetic material can be replaced and the weakness alleviated. However, it is possible that the same technique could be used to enhance the strength of healthy athletes, significantly improving their performance in their sport. Because reproductive cells (sperm and egg cells) are not affected in this kind of treatment, changes from somatic gene therapy will not be passed on to offspring.

On the other hand, genetic changes in reproductive cells, known as genetic changes in the germline, do get passed on to one's children. Theoretically at least, given technological developments in the techniques of germline manipulation, we could, on one hand, eliminate certain genetic diseases and, on the other hand, produce "designer" children with enhanced abilities or characteristics, not only of a kind that would affect their performance in sports, but perhaps in appearance, musical talent, mathematical ability, and even in longevity.

Many writers distinguish genetic manipulation used for therapeutic purposes, such as curing or preventing debilitating diseases with a genetic origin, from enhancement. Although this distinction is not necessarily useless, we have already seen that it is often difficult to distinguish the two in difficult cases. For example, is it therapeutic or enhancing if you replace genetic material that limits a patient's previously limited oxygen-carrying capacity to the extent that the recipient now can run 5K races?

Most of us support the use of new genetic technologies to cure diseases and perhaps free us from some of the disabilities and frailties associated with old age. But opinion is much more divided when we move toward genetic enhancement, especially enhancements that involve significant changes in various human characteristics, including abilities and radical extension of the human life span. Although our focus will be on enhancement of athletes, the issues cannot help but transcend the world of sports and apply in varying degrees to a much wider range of subjects.

### What ethical issues arise from the prospect of genetically enhancing athletes?

Genetic enhancement has an understandably bad name in many quarters because of its association with the eugenic movement, a program advanced in several countries, including early twentieth-century America, and later adopted by the Nazis. The goal of the movement was to eliminate "defectives." One wonders what the proponents of eugenics would have made of the diversity of individuals from various circumstances and varied genetic endowments who have contributed to the benefit of humanity.

Most contemporary thinkers who argue for genetic enhancement are concerned with the more benign goal of improving human existence. In some versions, human nature as it now exists is seen as a developing project that has not yet come to fruition. If we can improve human abilities, extend life to a significant extent, and make us stronger, smarter, and healthier, isn't there close to a moral imperative to do so? In an extreme version, sometimes called transhumanism, the ultimate goal may be to transform humans into genetically superior beings who might be called posthumans. In less controversial and much more widely accepted versions, the goal is to improve the overall health of human beings by eliminating, alleviating, or curing diseases that are largely genetic in origin.

Of course, more extreme genetic technologies, such as those defended by the transhumanists, are simply not yet available. However, research is ongoing on somatic therapy for genetically based diseases with pharmaceutical companies investing hundreds of millions of dollars in developing new treatments and with some treatments already available to patients with specific disorders. Although the ethical issues raised by genetic enhancement are not in the headlines to the same extent as scandals involving the use of PEDs, a discussion of them might not only shed light on the ethics of pursuing perfection in sports but on concrete problems that may arise in the not-so-distant future as well.

For the sake of argument, let us assume that the risks of genetic enhancement are minimal so we can focus on the moral issues at stake from a different perspective. Indeed, where germline (inheritable) modification is at stake, it could be argued that there is no individual to be harmed, since the enhanced individual arguably will not even be the same person who would otherwise have been born. To keep our discussion within manageable limits, we will pay special attention to three significant arguments against genetic enhancement of athletes. These are the argument from the right to an open future, the inequality argument, and the communitarian critique of enhancement.

The principal overall perspective from which proponents of genetic enhancement argue will be based on autonomy and the right of people to exercise free choice and experiment with genetic enhancement, or, in other words, a version of libertarianism of sport. As we have seen in the debate over PEDs, however, such an approach may have its limits.

### If parents could design their children's genetic heritage to promote specific abilities, wouldn't this undermine the autonomy of the affected children themselves?

This question suggests that those who defend a right to enhancement as an expression of autonomy contradict themselves, since in cases in which germline enhancements are implemented before the child is born, clearly the child has no say in the decision. Even worse, the parent may expect designer children to pursue their enhanced talents and excel in the area to which the enhancement applies, be it sports or music or mathematics. Some argue this deprives the designer children of what has been called the right to an open future, the right to choose their own path in life. In other words, the result of germline genetic enhancement is not to promote autonomy but to destroy it.[10]

Libertarians of sport do have some important replies to this sort of criticism. First, they might point out that people already are born with different genetic endowments through luck of the draw in what has been called the genetic lottery. Some genetic endowments may allow the bearer to do better in some activities than others. When I was in middle school, I struggled to learn to play a musical instrument, but my neighbor, Linda, could immediately play any popular tune she had heard on the piano "by ear" without being able to read sheet music or having any formal instruction.

Moreover, many parents today already put pressure on their children to excel in certain areas, sometimes to the extent that this pressure causes burnout, which results in the children simply dropping out or quitting the activity in question, and this kind of parental pressure is permitted (although sometimes criticized in extreme cases). Why are the pressures on designer children any greater than what we already allow? Of course, wise parents of all children, designed or not, can continue to introduce their kids to activities and encourage them to persevere without behaving in an excessive or fanatical manner. An Aristotlean might maintain that there is a Golden Mean, relative to each child, between indifference to the youngster's development and fanaticism in excessively pushing the child to excel. Parents who use good judgment could find that balanced approach, whether or not their offspring were genetically enhanced.

Many of us may believe, plausibly in my view, that the pressures on designer children are likely to be of a higher order of magnitude than on the unenhanced. To cite a possibility I discussed elsewhere, a parent of a designer child could say, "Look, I went to a lot of expense to design you to be an athlete and now you want to go play in the band!"[11] Nevertheless, the libertarian response is not without force, so we need to consider the other two arguments against enhancement before coming to any conclusion.

### Would genetic enhancement of designer offspring create a genetic elite and contribute to inequality between genetic superiors and inferiors?

This is a serious worry, especially if opportunity for enhancement was more available to the very affluent than to anyone else because of its expense. Of course, one might hope that the enhanced would use their gifts to benefit everyone, for example in science, medicine, and the arts, thereby achieving utilitarian goals of promoting the best results for society as a whole. This may not be the most likely outcome, however. Moreover, the genetic differences might give the enhanced such an advantage that even if the unenhanced were made better off in some ways, they would lose self-respect and perhaps no longer be regarded as equal citizens with the same fundamental rights as the posthumans.

Suppose, however, that opportunities for enhancement were distributed in some equitable manner and the fundamental rights of all somehow were protected. At least one writer, Claudio Tamburrini, has argued this might be a good thing, at least for competitive athletics. If all athletes in a sport had equal access to enhancement, he argues, outcomes would no longer be influenced by the luck of the draw in the natural genetic lottery. Rather, success would be determined more by psychological characteristics such as dedication, the will to win, coolness under pressure, and strategic skills rather than physical ones. In other words, winning and virtue would align, or at least be more aligned than at present. Thus, sports would be more tests of moral virtue than of natural talents arising from accidents of birth.[12]

However, this proposal faces some major difficulties, even assuming we could distribute opportunities for enhancement in some equitable manner. First, the mental capacities that contribute to athletic success (or success elsewhere for that matter) may themselves have a genetic basis. This does not imply genetic determinism, since genes have different effects in different environments and our own values may help dictate outcomes, but it is at least possible that genetic manipulation could enhance our capacity to exercise virtues or exert effort as much as it might enhance our capacity to exercise physical skills.

In addition, many regard the ability of people with different physical and mental endowments to succeed in athletics as one of its great charms. Although most basketball players are tall, many shorter players have excelled at the high school, college, and even professional levels. People with different body types have been stars in golf, soccer, and various events in track and field. Often, players and fans cheer for the underdog, especially the player who overcomes physical deficiencies through effort and intelligent play. One of the tests of competitive sports is for athletes to use whatever package of gifts they have, both physical and mental, most effectively. If all athletes were enhanced, the value of such diversity in athletics would be lost, or at least diminished, because the kind of diversity at issue would be significantly reduced.

Finally, of special importance for athletics, the value of meeting the challenge set by the constitutive rules of each sport might be diminished. Enhanced athletes might find the challenges of some sports too easy to overcome. Of course, if our present sports did become too easy for enhanced athletes, we could invent new, more challenging ones, but why would that be any better than what we already have? This point needs to be pursued further by considering not just the effect of enhancement on individual athletes but on the community of athletes as well.

### Why shouldn't "faster, higher, stronger" be the principal aim of athletics? Doesn't genetic enhancement help us achieve that goal?

This question seems crucial since our discussion suggests a conflict between two different ideals of athletic competition. On one, the goal is to reach higher and higher levels of athletic competition. From what might be called a *perfectionist* perspective, not only should athletes be free to choose whether to pursue such a goal, the ideal of perfecting humans in a variety of ways through genetic enhancement is a worthy goal in itself.

On the second ideal (or set of related ideals), which resemble what I have called mutualism, athletic competition is valuable because it enables athletes under a mutually acceptable set of rules and principles to test themselves against the challenges central to their sport. On this view, setting new records and performing at ever higher levels are at best secondary goals; the major goal is to meet the challenge of sport. Setting new records often is not of paramount importance because, as we have seen, many records in many sports such as track and swimming, to cite two examples, break old ones by almost infinitesimal gaps that can be detected only by the latest technology. Should setting such records by perhaps trivial amounts be a major goal of athletic competition?[13]

The mutualist approach may not be totally incompatible with all forms of enhancement, but it is more open to the idea that the burden of proof falls on those who favor enhancement. Those sympathetic to mutualism tend to believe, as suggested by our discussion of PEDs, that the freedom of athletes to choose can be limited by values central to the idea of sport as mutually acceptable challenge as well as concerns about equity and equal opportunity. Of course, those more sympathetic to aspects of the transhumanist agenda can retort that enhancement would not eliminate the challenge of competition but only bring it to a new level. Before we try to weigh all these competing considerations, however, one more set of arguments needs to be considered.

### How do communitarian considerations apply to the enhancement debate?

Earlier, we distinguished between two general approaches to the proper role of government and regulation. Liberalism emphasizes both liberty, understood primarily as protections for political and civil freedoms, and also provision of fair opportunities, sometimes to be achieved by redistributive programs to provide education, health care, and other basic goods for all. Libertarians, on the other hand, emphasize liberty, broadly understood as any interference with autonomous individual action. On the strict libertarian view, liberty is so important that it can only be interfered with to protect individuals from assault, coercion, or fraud. Taxation for redistributive purposes, even to provide public education for all, is considered by strict libertarians to be an infringement on liberty and so is morally prohibited according to the their position. To be clear, libertarians may encourage individuals to voluntarily support good causes: it is required taxation to which they object.

Note, however, that both positions agree on one major point; namely, it is not the business of the state to impose an ideal of the good life on its citizens. Citizens should be left free to choose their own way of life. Thus, liberals who favor redistribution generally do so to provide fair opportunities for all to choose for themselves how to live, not to dictate how others should live.[14]

But isn't there a case for the state imposing some values on its citizens, or at least supporting some substantive conceptions of one way of life over others? Does liberalism lead to a society of autonomous but rootless individuals with no common social ties, isolated from each other due to lack of common values?

Communitarians, reacting to the liberal-libertarian emphasis on individual choice, argue that individuals are often shaped by their communities. Our identities may at least in part be constituted by our religious affiliations, cultural background, ethnicity and race, gender and sexual orientation, political values, and even allegiance to sports teams.

Following Aristotle, communitarians regard the character of the communities to which we belong as vital to ethics. Whether or not it takes a community to raise a child, surely the kind of community a child is raised in significantly influences the kind of person that child will become.

For example, Michael Sandel, a leading contemporary communitarian, has argued in his book *What Money Can't Buy* that the intrusion of markets into sports has distorted values that should be central to the activity.[15] For example, some elite college basketball teams in the United States, in the pursuit of profits, have moved their games from on-campus venues to larger off-campus arenas, making it much more difficult for students, with all their enthusiasm for their teams, to attend.

Elsewhere, in a similar vein, Sandel argues that enhancement is dangerous to the kind of sporting community we should seek to promote because it corrupts values that should be central in a community that promotes a good life for its citizens.[16] What is his argument?

Although Sandel's argument on this topic is complex, and sometimes difficult to interpret, the basic point seems to be that in sports and beyond, striving for perfection through enhancement threatens to undermine certain fundamental values. In our pursuit of perfection, Sandel worries, we strive so much for mastery of the world that, for example, we lose humility and perhaps develop reduced compassion for the misfortune of others who are regarded as more and more responsible for their fate. If the genetic lottery were replaced by designed posthumans, we would no longer feel sympathy for the disadvantaged. Instead, we would start to believe that their plight was not our concern, and instead, perhaps, the result of poor decisions about their own enhancements made either by themselves or by their parents.

Sandel's argument is much more complex than the earlier sketch suggests, but for our purposes I want to focus just on one of his worries: the diminishment of achievement in sports. We should note, however, that his argument has been subject to various criticisms, for example that enhancement would not reduce our sense of humility or make us feel we were masters of the universe because many other factors ranging from vulnerability to accident to the possibility of failure due to the efforts of equally enhanced competitors would be sufficient to keep us humble. Let us focus on the effects of enhancement on our conception of achievement, and how it might affect our sporting communities.

## Would enhancement diminish the significance of achievement in sports (and elsewhere)?

Should we worry, for example, that the value of achievement in baseball might be diminished if genetically enhanced sluggers routinely hit home runs? The value of the home run as the result of an act of skill would be lowered, perhaps almost to the breaking point. (Perhaps this has up to a point already happened due to the multitude of home runs hit during Major League Baseball's "steroid era.")

This specific worry about batting in baseball may be exaggerated because presumably the pitchers also would be enhanced, perhaps to an extent to be on a level playing field with the batters. However, if the balance between batter and pitcher were preserved, why would the game be any better than it already is? The struggle between pitcher and batter, perhaps the heart and soul of baseball, would remain the same.

A key issue raised by this discussion is whether genetic enhancement would lower the value of achievement is many different areas, not just sports. In the TV series "Dark Angel" (2000–2002), Jessica Alba played a genetically enhanced soldier named Max who escaped from a government program as a child and who makes her way as best she can in a dysfunctional America, the victim of an electronic pulse that turned the United States into a technologically, economically, and culturally backward country. Max, due to her genetic enhancements, is physically superior to normal humans and is able to perform physical feats well beyond the abilities of the unenhanced. But does she deserve credit for them? Many would argue she does not because her abilities are not due to anything she has done but rather to how she was designed.

Consider as well a future in which people are enhanced for musical ability and many of the enhanced become truly superior pianists. Would it make sense to praise these musicians for their achievements or regard their performances as achievements at all? Would their "achievement" be devalued because it was in great part the result of enhancement for which they may not be responsible—that is, if they were designed to be great musicians just as Max was designed to be a superior soldier?

These are legitimate questions that are difficult to answer. It might well be that germline enhancement in particular, if it became a principal form of enhancement, might alter our common views of achievement and might undermine the value we assign to individuals for making the best of whatever package of genetic assets they receive from the genetic lottery. This might not be all to the good. As noted earlier, we certainly admire athletes who succeed at high levels of sport by making the best of what they have, even though they may lack the natural assets of many other competitors.

Unfortunately, these concerns are far from decisive. For one thing, we already have different genetic endowments as a result of the natural lottery. Accordingly, our achievements may already be due in some part, perhaps in some cases in significant part, to our genetic inheritance. Why should enhancement lower the value of our achievements any more than different natural genetic endowment, which in effect provides some of us with a headstart, already does?

Moreover, as discussed earlier, if genetic endowments were more equal, success in athletics might be more due to mental qualities such as coolness under pressure and determination that reflect well on the character of the athletes than mere physical ability. Instead of admiring star athletes for their physical attributes, we would admire them for their character.

In response to the earlier objection that mental characteristics might be as subject to enhancement as physical ones, one might reply that genes alone do not determine outcomes but only provide behavioral tendencies so that there is still plenty of room for character to make a difference. After all, in *Dark Angel*, Max was a morally laudable character not because of the enhancements for which she was not responsible but for her compassion and sense of right or wrong, for which she was responsible.

Finally, consider a last point on behalf of enhancement. Why should we give preference to an ideal of achievement that makes it dependent on the genetic lottery?[17] Why not adopt an ideal that either dismisses the idea that we deserve credit for our achievements at all, or develop a new conception of achievement that does not depend on admiration for what we do with our natural genetic inheritance? Isn't allowing the natural genetic lottery to affect outcomes less ethical than equalizing genetic endowments and then allowing character to make the major difference in whether we succeed or fail?

## What should we conclude about the morality of enhancement?

Our discussion suggests that the issue is not only a very complicated one but also one on which reasonable people may end up disagreeing. I myself think that four opposing positions are worthy of consideration. Although they resemble views we have already explored in our consideration of PEDs, the cases are not strictly parallel if we assume, at least for the sake of argument, that genetic enhancement of both the somatic and germline varieties can be done safely. (Of course, if we assume the opposite, many of the arguments against the use of PEDs that appeal to the collective safety of athletes also apply to enhancement as well.)

The first position worth considering is the libertarian one conjoined with the assumption that designer athletes are not harmed by germline modification because they would not even exist if a different person with a different genetic heritage had been born instead. This position appeals to the value of human freedom, but it is vulnerable to many of the criticisms of genetic enhancement already discussed, and in addition it may lead to an arms race in which genetic engineers compete to design superior athletes who may eventually morph into posthumans. Although some may consider this a virtue, going where humanity has never gone before, others may fear the unanticipated consequences of such a transformation—and with good reason.

A second position, which we can call the perfectionist view, argues that we should strive for an ideal of human perfection, even through genetic enhancement if possible. At its transhumanist extreme, this view accepts the possibility that humans as we know them ideally might be replaced by enhanced posthumans, a new and arguably superior variant of the human race. Although this turn of events may sound to us now like the plot of a science-fiction novel, the perfectionists remind us not to be uncritically committed to the status quo and not to oppose radical change just because it is radical.

A third position, sometimes called liberal eugenics, favors enhancement if limited by certain moral requirements. Opportunities for enhancements must be either available to all or fairly distributed and be general in character, making it difficult for ambitious parents to design children for success at specific tasks. Like the libertarians, liberals reject the idea of a government-sponsored program of genetic enhancement, as both believe government should not impose a conception of the good life on its citizens. So whether to enhance or not would be a choice of individuals rather than the state.

Finally, a fourth position, perhaps influenced by the sorts of communitarian concerns raised by Sandel, while allowing for genetic modification to prevent illness and disease, would either prohibit genetic enhancement or proceed cautiously at best. Indeed, the prohibitionists, as we can call them, might point out that sports played by genetically enhanced athletes may be no more of a test of excellence than what is already available, may undermine such important values as achievement, and have consequences, such as exacerbating existing inequalities, that may be unfair or unjust. This position urges caution, because if we go where no human has ever gone before, we may not like what we find once we arrive!

Although it would be wonderful to be more decisive, the argument so far suggests that the debate needs to be continued and key points thought out more fully before we come to any final conclusion. My own view aligns with the fourth position, which is skeptical of allowing genetic enhancement, although further discussion may lead to more decisive reasoning in favor of one of the other contending views.

*What are some of the main themes that emerge from*
*the discussion in this chapter?*

Our discussion has illustrated how major approaches to political thought—liberalism, libertarianism, communitarianism, and even perfectionism—might apply to issues involving fairness, enhancement, and technology in competitive sport. It also indicates that although debate in these areas is quite complex, reason is not paralyzed by complexity. Some responses to the issues we have considered, while not decisive, seem strong enough to put the burden of proof on opponents.

Of course, further critical discussion might require revision of some of the suggested resolutions made earlier. Perhaps, however, the approaches suggested for examining issues of PEDs, genetic enhancement, and technological advances in equipment are themselves reasonable. They may create a framework for further inquiry, and I hope that they are also of sufficient merit to withstand the critical examination and debate central to philosophic inquiry itself.

# 5

# COMPETITIVE SPORT

## EDUCATION OR MIS-EDUCATION?

*Is there an historical connection between sport and education?*

In the West at least, organized competitive sport goes back beyond the founding of the Olympic Games in ancient Greece, probably around 776 B.C.E. Athletic contests surely are likely to be even older. As philosopher Heather Reid points out, there are important parallels between athletic contests in ancient Greece and the much later rise of philosophy in that culture. Reid argues that both sports and philosophy employed methods for sorting out claims to athletic or intellectual superiority without appeal to the gods, neither were restricted to aristocrats, and both were relatively cosmopolitan in exposing participants to new ideas emanating from different cultures or different segments of Greek society from different city states.[1] Indeed, contests of skill and athleticism were celebrated in such classic works as Homer's *Iliad*. Although sports, such as archery in China, played significant roles outside the West, and sometimes served functions from selecting the best soldiers to deciding who should be sacrificed, the connection between sports and education was developed and defended in important ways by thinkers in ancient Greece.

We can see evidence of the deep connection between philosophy and sports in the work of Plato; athletics played a major role in the ideal education for leaders of the state that he proposed in *The Republic*. Although Plato surely understood the value of athletic training for military preparedness, he also thought it important for teaching wisdom and love of excellence. In Plato's dialogues, Socrates, Plato's teacher and the principal character in these works, uses his signature methods of questioning and debate to help arrive at more justified belief or to discredit ideas that cannot stand up to critical examination, as in the dialogue *Euthyphro* where Socrates raises acute questions that a self-proclaimed expert on piety cannot effectively answer. Socratic dialogue resembles in this respect what we have called mutualism in sports; both parties freely enter the contest or debate and although only one normally comes out on top as a winner or makes the better case in argument, both benefit from being tested by the other in the pursuit of a common goal.

Many educators in nineteenth-century England took a somewhat different but related approach. They believed that competition in sports promoted the development of important virtues in the participants, virtues that were important not just for educational purposes but as a way to develop skills in leadership that could be brought to bear in the broader society. The claim that "the battle of Waterloo was won on the playing fields of Eton," traditionally but perhaps incorrectly attributed to the Duke of Wellington, illustrates this perspective. Although elite sport in England at the time was generally reserved for the upper classes and the ideal of "amateurism" was often used to exclude the working class, athletics were seen as an important training ground for leadership and for the building of character.

Many defenders of competitive sports today, both inside and outside of educational systems, also speak of their role in building character and promoting a love of fair play. If sports affect character, do they promote virtue alone or also vice? As we will see, significant challenges have been presented to the view that participation in sports is a force for good.

***Isn't the vast amount of time and money poured
into interscholastic and intercollegiate athletic programs in
the United States highly problematic?***

The extensive role of athletic programs within American high
schools and colleges sets the United States apart from most
other countries. Although other countries also have extensive
sports programs, these are frequently conducted by clubs associated with towns, cities, and regions, and they compete at
various levels of skill and experience. Schools in the United
Kingdom and Canada do field teams, but at least in the United
Kingdom, institutional support is much less extensive than in
the United States and is generally eclipsed in the public mind
by competitions at the club and professional levels.

It also is important to realize that there are many levels of competition in intercollegiate sport in the United States. The largest
division of the National Collegiate Athletic Association (NCAA),
the body that regulates intercollegiate sport, is Division III, in
which schools do not award athletic scholarships, play more restricted schedules than the athletically elite major powers, and
are charged with integrating athletics into the overall life of
the campus. Yet it is the major Division I programs, especially
in high-visibility sports like football and men's and sometimes
women's basketball, that get the lion's share of publicity.

Recently, what we can call big-time or elite intercollegiate
sport in the United States has come under increasing critical fire.
Although major football games and the so-called March Madness
involved with the NCAA Division I national basketball tournament captivate sports fans and dominate the sporting news
in America, elite intercollegiate sport clearly faces a number of
truly significant problems. Let's consider these issues in detail.

***What are some of the major problems with intercollegiate sports
in the United States?***

Although many athletically elite universities and the NCAA
refer to "student-athletes," a series of academic scandals going

back many years have called the integrity of big-time college sports into question. One of the latest and perhaps the most egregious occurred over a period of decades at the academically prestigious University of North Carolina at Chapel Hill, where, over time, a great many students, including but not restricted to college athletes, took what were basically fake courses allegedly offered by a professor and an assistant in the African American Studies Department.[2] These "courses," which required little or no work and often were not even held, were used to keep academically weak athletes eligible to play on university teams. It is unclear the degree to which coaches in major sports were aware of the fraud. It is particularly significant that it took place at an institution like North Carolina, which had prided itself on doing intercollegiate sports properly, and which was the home of legendary basketball coach, the late Dean Smith (who was not involved in the scandal), known not only for his winning record but also for his integrity and his role in promoting racial integration in Chapel Hill.

Unfortunately, the scandal at North Carolina, while especially egregious, is only one on a long list that goes back decades. Recently, schools such as Syracuse University, Oklahoma, and Florida State have been implicated for a number of offenses ranging from violations of NCAA rules on illegal payment to athletes to academic fraud. In another scandal involving lack of academic integrity, an NCAA investigation found that from 1994 to1998, an employee in the University of Minnesota's athletic department's counseling office helped prepare hundreds of assignments for men's basketball players, allegedly with the knowledge of the coaching staff.

There is also the scandal at Penn State University in which former assistant football coach Jerry Sandusky, hiding behind the prestige of his former association with the renowned football program, was able to sexually molest children over a period of years. Although the team itself was not involved in Sandusky's predatory activities, many observers felt the desire to protect the reputation of the football program may have helped prevent earlier detection of Sandusky's behavior. The reputation of legendary football coach Joe Paterno was tarnished, perhaps to an unfair extent, and the university suffered severe penalties imposed by the NCAA.

In addition to such scandals, which have captured the public mind, there are deeper and perhaps more significant concerns as well. For example, intercollegiate sport, especially at the most elite Division I level, takes up a tremendous amount of time, not only in practices but also in games that often involve national travel. Contests between elite teams in high-visibility sports often are scheduled to attract the largest television audience rather than to accommodate the academic schedule of the athletes themselves. Even in less visible sports, the time commitment can be enormous and arguably conflict with academic responsibilities. Some college baseball teams play 50 to over 60 games a season, many of which involve travel and missed classes, plus the intense play can lead to fatigue that can affect athletes' ability to study.

Winning, especially in national championship tournaments, is the major goal of elite athletic programs. Winning is essential to bringing in revenue, and losing coaches often find their jobs in jeopardy. The heavy weight assigned to winning creates pressures to recruit the very best athletes, even if they are at best marginal students or are of questionable moral character. Many of the cases of academic fraud noted earlier reflect the effort to keep those poorly prepared athletes academically eligible to play. In view of these issues, it should be no surprise that elite intercollegiate athletics increasingly has come under critical fire.

Many observers have noted as well that some intercollegiate sports, particularly football and basketball, have become proving grounds for direct jumps to professional sports. The "one and done" phenomenon, in which top prospects play one year of Division I basketball and then jump to professional teams, calls into further question whether such players are "student-athletes" or just athletes using their university as a jumping-off point to the National Basketball Association.

*Don't major intercollegiate sports make money that supports the rest of the athletic program and even the university itself? Don't these benefits justify big-time college sports?*

These questions make two assumptions, both of which are highly questionable. The first of these is that big-time college sports, mainly men's football and basketball but in some cases women's basketball as well, make enough money to support and perhaps secure a profit for the entire athletic program and potentially the university.

The research on the subject, however, does not support this assumption. Statistics published by the NCAA, for example, indicate that in 2012, only 23 athletic programs at institutions in the Football Bowl Series division (a division of American intercollegiate football that plays at the most elite level) actually made a profit.[3] Consider also the report of the Knight Commission on Intercollegiate Athletics, a group of college and university presidents and administrators that monitor college sports, entitled "Restoring the Balance." The report pointed out that most elite athletic programs are supported by increasing amounts taken from student fees and general funds.[4] For every Joe Paterno at Penn State who used profits from his successful football program to support an extensive new library benefitting the whole campus, there are many more programs draining funds that might have been put to use supporting other priorities.

In addition, at the athletically elite institutions, spending per student-athlete far exceeds that per student at large. Thus, the Knight Commission reports that for 2010, in the athletically prestigious Southeast Conference, median athletic spending per athlete was $163, 000 and some change, whereas median spending per student was $13,390. Although the gap was not as great in some other major conferences, even Division

I schools with no football program spent slightly over three times as much per student-athlete as per student.[5] Some difference in the spending ratio might be expected, as the equipment required by an athletic team may exceed in cost that required by, say, the Philosophy Department. This being said, critics of intercollegiate athletics surely have a point when they maintain the extent of the gap in expenditures reported by the Knight Commission is extremely difficult for supporters of intercollegiate sport to justify, especially in the athletically elite intercollegiate conferences.

So not only do most athletic programs at athletically elite universities in the United States not make money, their relative spending on athletes arguably is out of proportion and getting more and more so as time goes on.

### What can be said in defense of intercollegiate sport? Is the criticism the whole story?

Criticism along these lines is not the whole story. For one thing, the men's basketball and football programs at athletically elite Division I institutions are the tip of a much bigger iceberg. Criticism that applies to then may not apply, at least not with equal force, to other kinds or levels of intercollegiate athletics. Intercollegiate sport encompasses not just the highly visible elite Division I men's football and basketball programs. In addition, it includes women's sports, some of which, like the University of Connecticut women's basketball team, are highly visible, but many of which are less visible than men's sports and which often are less prone to the problems that afflict high-visibility men's programs. Of course, Division I itself includes the Ivy League, which also does not offer athletic scholarships and whose teams only rarely compete for national championships at the most elite levels of Division I sports. There also many Division III institutions that field highly competitive teams without offering athletic scholarships and whose students are rarely selected to play professional sports. Indeed, Division III is the largest division of the NCAA. As the NCCA says in its television advertising campaign, almost all intercollegiate athletes will have a career outside professional sports. Issues that apply to highly visible men's sports, such as huge expenses needed to maintain such programs, may not apply to less visible sports, to women's sports, and to less athletically elite conferences or lower divisions of the NCAA where intercollegiate athletics is not expected to produce revenue.

It is true that some teams, especially in the men's basketball and football programs in Division I, have dismal graduation rates. According to the NCAA, only one in five players in the 2002 national championship basketball game between Maryland and Oklahoma met graduation requirements. In the 1990s a number of key programs did not graduate a single African American basketball player.

However, if we look at the larger picture, we find that NCAA athletes graduate at higher rates than students at large. African American athletes also graduate at higher rates than African American students at large. Moreover, reforms instituted by the NCAA under former President Myles Brand now deprive major programs of athletic scholarships if their graduation rates are unreasonably low. (Critics might maintain, with some justice, that this just creates pressures to get athletes through courses with little academic content in order to promote a high graduation rate. Although this is a danger, other stipulations on core course requirements plus effective faculty supervision can sometimes serve as a reasonable check on such abuses.)

Even if there are bright spots, however, the problems of intercollegiate athletics at the Division I level remain significant. Time spent practicing and traveling—in addition to the race to recruit even better athletes, who are lured in part by even better facilities, which arguably take revenue from other areas of education—raises the prospect of significant conflict with academic goals.

*Shouldn't major athletic programs be seen as entertainment*
*provided by the university to the larger community and not*
*as part of their overall academic program?*

Some writers have made the case that college sports provide entertainment for spectators and should be embraced for this reason, and not assessed as part of academic institutions or based on how they fit into the overall aims of colleges and universities.[6] They argue that universities today have many functions and, like the artistic performances they support, athletics also represent a form of entertainment for the larger community. Indeed, the charters of many large state universities talk about their obligation to the culture of the larger surrounding community. Why not be honest and acknowledge that athletics is not part of the academic program? Rather, some argue, it is a way of fulfilling the university's cultural obligations to the larger community, and, especially in the case of state universities, getting support from that community in return.

Thus, North Carolina and Duke men's basketball programs are the center of communities of fans in the Chapel Hill and Durham areas, and as a former resident, I can attest that other activities practically come to a stop when the Tarheels take to the court. The prestige of and loyalty to the basketball program surely contributed to the success of legendary Carolina coach Dean Smith's efforts to promote racial integration in Chapel Hill when he brought African American students and a local minister with him to a popular restaurant in the area in order to make a political statement. He also recruited Charlie Scott, the first African American to star in the elite Atlantic Coast Conference in which Carolina competed.[7] Had the coach and his team not held a respected position in the community, this act would not have gained such attention nor would it have been so meaningful and impactful.

Sports teams may well help garner support for universities in indirect ways, perhaps by creating communities of fans broader than the campus community itself, and by increasing their visibility. For these reasons, perhaps providing entertainment to the wider community is a legitimate function of some educational institutions. However, this utilitarian benefit provided by institutions should not be at the expense of injustice to or exploitation of the athletes in high-visibility sports. If they are not provided a legitimate chance to get an education, or are if they accepted without the academic skills to succeed in the classroom, the benefit to the community is provided at the expense of injustice to the very people who provide the overall gain to the university.

### Are college athletes exploited? Would professionalization of college sports remove any exploitation that takes place?

Some argue that we should shed the pretense that student-athletes, at least in elite, highly visible sports such as men's football and basketball, are students. Why not treat them as professionals? Such a change in their status would be honest and would unburden college athletes of academic duties when they view their college experience as training for the pros. Let's consider this proposal further.

When one looks at the huge expenditures on intercollegiate athletics, the revenues brought in by some successful programs, and the salaries paid to star coaches and other sports administrators, one might consider that the players themselves are being taken advantage of or even being exploited. Scholar Billy Hawkins refers to much of elite Division I athletics as "the new plantation" in which athletes at the elite Division I level, who are disproportionately African American, are exploited at predominantly white institutions.[8]

Hawkins's critique certainly is understandable. Top coaches make enormous salaries and obtain extra income that can go into the millions and are often the highest paid individuals on campus. For example, the highest paid college football coach in 2014, Nick Saben of Alabama, reportedly made nearly $7 million in base salary, whereas number 30 in the salary rankings, Mark Helfrich of Oregon, reportedly made over $3 million.[9] Meanwhile, the players, who arguably are responsible for much of the success of the coaches, are not paid at all.

Nevertheless, the claim that college athletes are exploited, or even taken advantage of, may be too strong, at least in some circumstances. The concept of exploitation itself is problematic, and scholars differ on how the concept is best understood.[10] Although a full analysis cannot be offered here, exploitation does seem to always involve taking unfair advantage of another, but disagreement may also arise over just when some particular transaction actually is unfair. For our purposes, exploitation can be considered as also involving taking advantage of limited opportunities available to the victim in such a way as to harm the victim in the long run. Exploiters may give the victim a choice, but because of the situation the victim is in, the victim is essentially forced to do what the exploiter wants him or her to do.

For example, if I desperately need a life-saving medicine, and an individual who possesses the only supply available to me and knows I am in dire straits charges me hundreds of times the market price, then that person is treating me unfairly and in fact exploiting my difficult circumstances. I am unable to travel or obtain the medicine at the market price, and I will be harmed by losing so much money. Of course, the medicine may also save my life, and so this example may be a case of what has been called mutually beneficial exploitation, but I am being taken unfair advantage of nevertheless.[11]

Are Division I college athletes in highly visible sports in elite athletic programs actually being exploited? I suggest the answer depends on at least two major considerations. First, the value of an athletic scholarship and the opportunities for education it provides may be a valuable form of compensation for the scholarship athlete. Much depends here on whether the educational opportunity is genuine, however. Is the athlete academically prepared for college work, or has the institution offered a scholarship to a young man or woman unprepared to do work at the college level? Former Minnesota Vikings lineman Alan Page recalls that his teammates, who all attended college but couldn't read a playbook, "were never expected to read and write. They floated through ... because they were talented athletes."[12] Moreover, even if an athlete is motivated to learn, the extensive commitments to athletics required of many Division I athletes just might not leave enough time for effective study. Thus, they aren't reaping the full benefits of the academic scholarship and in a sense they are being cheated out of their education.

It is true that since the 1970s, when Page played, the NCAA has passed legislation limiting the number of hours students can be required to devote to athletics while in season, although it is debatable whether informal off-season, allegedly voluntary training, as well as in-season requirements not clearly covered by the legislation, have allowed that legislation to make as much difference as was intended. However, as we noted earlier, graduation rates for all NCAA athletes exceed those of other students. And one study, conducted at highly selective colleges and universities, indicated that after graduation, athletes tend to have higher incomes than other students, perhaps because, as the authors of the study suggest, they are more focused on economic success than others (due maybe to differences in their own financial background from that of students at large) or even in part because participation in athletics gives them an edge in applying for jobs because it is valued by employers.[13] This may not testify to the quality of their education but might indicate that they are not necessarily being taken advantage of economically; the rewards simply are not immediate.

Accordingly, the claim of exploitation is weakened, perhaps to the vanishing point, if educational opportunities offered by the university are genuine. Of course, the players themselves must also be motivated to work hard on their academics and not view themselves as only at the school for sports.

### What are the problems with full professionalization? Why not treat college athletes in athletically elite, highly visible programs as professionals?

To focus first on practical reasons, there is the cost. It is unclear now whether big-time college sports are financially sustainable. The situation would be even worse if college athletes became paid employees of their university. In an attempt to save money, institutions may be tempted to eliminate many sports that do not produce revenue, ranging from men's swimming, to tennis, to volleyball, to golf. (Women's sports most likely would not be cut due to the requirements of Title IX that we will discuss in Chapter 6.) More likely, many universities would drop out of big-time college sports to avoid the costs, which might not be a bad thing if they moved to the Ivy or Division III level rather than abandoning intercollegiate sport altogether.

Such a change would be messy, however. Which athletes would be paid? Would they be only participants in men's revenue-producing programs, in women's high-visibility programs such as basketball, or across all sports? Would the salaries reflect market competition, or would they be set at a certain level, perhaps by the NCAA, and would that be illegal restraint of trade? Also, wouldn't there be backlash from faculty and staff whose salaries must come out of the same university or college budget, but who, unlike most student-athletes, have to worry about supporting families? Wouldn't this lead to having a far larger piece of the budgetary pie of a given school go toward athletics, which critics would worry would cut into funding other important programs? In addition, wouldn't much of the spirit and excitement of college sports be lost if teams were openly part of a professional minor league?[14]

Perhaps the most serious cost of professionalizing athletically elite college sports is that it would mean fully abandoning the view—some would say the "pretense"—that athletics can be part of a student-athlete's educational experience. Perhaps Plato's belief that athletics can and should be a major part of one's education is no longer viable at the athletically elite levels of Division I. However, it may still apply to other divisions of college sports, high school athletics, and youth sports as well.

### What is the O'Bannon lawsuit, and how does it apply to professionalization of college athletes?

Ed O'Bannon was a star basketball player on UCLA's 1995 national championship team. Years later, he was startled to see his image used in a commercial video game and agreed to be the plaintiff in a class action suit against the NCAA on behalf of Division I men's football and basketball players. The suit, joined by such former NBA greats as Oscar Robertson and Bill Russell, claimed they should be allowed to receive compensation for the use of their images for commercial purposes. The NCAA argued that such compensation would violate its conception of amateurism.

In a complex decision made in August 2014, judge Claudia Wilken ruled in favor of O'Bannon and against the NCAA. The judge held that the NCAA's bylaws regarding amateurism constituted an unreasonable restraint of trade, arguing that colleges and universities be prohibited "from enforcing any rules or bylaws that would prohibit its member schools and conferences from offering their FBS football or Division I basketball recruits a limited share of the revenues generated from the use of their names, images, and likenesses in addition to a full grant-in-aid." Although the judge limited the amount that might be put in trust for players for their use after graduation, her ruling opened the door for further payments.

A more recent decision in October 2015 by a US Court of Appeals upheld the claim that the NCAA was violating antitrust provisions but then, perhaps surprisingly in view of that finding, denied that educational institutions were required to set aside funds to pay athletes for the use of their likenesses. Undoubtedly, further adjudication will be needed to resolve this issue. Not only legally but morally, it is plausible to think, given the antitrust finding, that athletes should be compensated to some extent as Judge Wilken first ruled.

In fact, in 2015, the NCAA Division I Board of Directors granted autonomy to the most athletically elite conferences, enabling them to adopt legislation allowing them to cover the full costs of a player's education, not just the tuition and books now covered by athletic scholarships. For example, travel home and a stipend to cover cost of living and some recreational expenses would be made available.

The idea of covering all expenses for athletes seems justifiable in part because in- season and even off-season demands on athletes' time for practice and fitness training leave them far fewer opportunities to earn income through employment at their institution compared to other students. A perhaps unintended consequence of this change, however, is that the higher cost of such scholarships may adversely affect recruiting for those schools unable or unwilling to spend even more on athletics than they already do. Thus, the result may be to put so called "mid-major" universities at a competitive disadvantage against their more affluent competitors.

In any case, the steps, allowed by the O'Bannon lawsuit and the proposal to expand coverage by athletic scholarships, fall short of full professionalization.

*It has been claimed that participation in sports can build character or be a form of moral education, but who decides what character to build or what values should be taught?*

The claims that sports build character or that they are a form of moral education are problematic for a variety of reasons. What kind of character should we aim to build? Should educational institutions make moral decisions of this kind, in effect imposing values on their students? What about empirical studies that suggest that playing sports does have an effect on character but often a negative one?[15] What is and what ought to be the connection between playing sports and building character or virtue?

One view is that there are certain values, perhaps those which mutualists would call internal to or intrinsic to sports, that are of great ethical importance and that are promoted by participation in sports and especially competitive athletics. These include, but are not restricted to, teamwork, understood broadly as the ability to work with others in pursuit of a common goal; perseverance; discipline; and coolness under pressure. But does participation actually promote those values? Even if it does, might such values be distorted in ethically undesirable directions by players and coaches? For example, might the idea of teamwork be transformed through sports, so that it morphs into the attitude, "me and my team, right or wrong?" Might such distortion lead to unsportsmanlike behavior as the opponent comes to be viewed as an obstacle or the enemy rather than a facilitator in a mutual quest for excellence?

Let's explore these concerns, starting with the issue of what values sports should promote. Many people might fear, quite reasonably, that coaches or institutions, rather than emphasizing what we called internal values of sport, such as sportsmanship, teamwork, and discipline, impose values upon players that the athletes themselves may not hold. For example, athletes may be required to join in a Christian prayer before a game even if they are not Christians themselves. What about partisan political values? Should coaches, supported by their institution, proselytize for gun control or be against it, fight for climate change or deny it, support a specific political party or not? What character traits are regarded as desirable for coaches to promote? Do we want to teach obedience to the orders of authority such as the coach, or do we want to encourage critical thinking by athletes instead? Should we teach athletes to equate success with winning? Should we make an effort to balance the values of competitive success and respect for the game and its traditions?

One response is that teaching ethics and building character is the responsibility of parents and families. Schools, even colleges and universities, should not take over that task and impose values on athletes that at least potentially might run counter to what they have learned at home. On an extreme version of this view, schools should be value-free, and so should athletic programs, by extension. Others believe schools should if not impose at least support major values, whether religious ideals based perhaps on the Ten Commandments or some political agenda regarded as virtually self-evident by its adherents. So if sports are to be a form of education, including moral education, what values should be promoted?

It looks as if adherents of sport as a form of moral education are faced with a dilemma. Coaches and institutions either stand for and try to impose a partisan set of values on athletes, in which case the autonomy of the athletes themselves is threatened, or they are totally value neutral, which seems impossible. After all, schools by their very nature stand for certain values, such as literacy over illiteracy, critical thinking over blind acceptance of ideas, and respect for others rather than intolerance and bullying.

Perhaps we can go between the horns of this dilemma by adopting what I have called elsewhere the stance of *critical institutional neutrality*.[16] This view is a form of neutrality because it does not require the institution to take official stands on hot-button or highly partisan issues (although in colleges and universities, academic freedom rightly protects the freedom of faculty and students to do so as individuals). It does, however, allow educational institutions to support those values presupposed by the nature of education and intellectual inquiry itself, both formally and informally. These include the freedom to inquire, adherence to tools of critical thinking such as logic and standards of good reasoning, willingness to hear the arguments of others as well as the liberty to respond, and the value of civil critical discourse.

By supporting these fundamental civic and educational virtues and trying to promote them in the student body, the institution promotes personal autonomy rather than undermines it. Without the tools for critical thinking and inquiry, students lack the ability to engage in reasoned discourse and to examine not only the views of others but also to form their own in a reasonable and thoughtful manner. Because these fundamental values are central to good education, schools cannot be value-free but that does not mean that as institutions they need to or ought to go further to promote values more partisan in nature.

What about educational institutions that claim to have a partisan mission, such as religious schools, or those organized around a particular theme, like environmental studies? Perhaps the best response is that if these institutions allow critical discussion of their own core values, the education that they offer is compatible with critical institutional neutrality, but if inquiry into certain areas is not permitted, the autonomy of the students in those areas is compromised.

### What is the significance of institutional critical neutrality for athletics?

We have seen that in view of the problems of high-visibility elite Division I sports, many believe intercollegiate athletics has no place in the university. Many others argue, sometimes with reason, that even high school sports have been overemphasized and that they may even undermine the primary educational mission of our schools. However, our discussion of critical neutrality and the civic virtues suggests that, on the contrary, athletics *properly conducted* can serve academic purposes and not only be compatible with educational goals but even reinforce them.

We already have seen that competitive sports embody challenges created by their constitutive rules. The constitutive rules make what might be an easy task, such as placing a small ball in a hole in the ground, extremely difficult. Meeting interesting challenges seems to be an activity that many find valuable for its own sake. As we noted in Section I, people prefer more complex and demanding challenges to easy ones, and these turn out to not only be more engaging and rewarding for us than easier challenges but also more objectively valuable.

Beyond the intrinsic value of sports, sports are valuable in their capacity to promote core educational values. That is, athletic programs can foster values central or internal to sport, like teamwork and willingness to analyze and criticize play, which are related to the core educational values we spoke of earlier. For example, through seeking to excel at the challenges intrinsic to specific sports, athletes learn more broadly applicable skills, such as learning to improve through appreciating criticism and analysis of their play. On this view, athletic programs, if carried out in appropriate ways, can promote central values relevant to education rather than undoing any of the positive effects of academic programs. It should be added, however, that this can only be true when teams are encouraged to focus on team members and opponents alike as people, not as means to an end, when winning is not the only goal but emphasis also is placed on what athletes can learn by engaging in critical reflection about their performances and their values in competition.

### Are there reasons for thinking that sports, especially intercollegiate sports, are a bad influence on athletes who participate?

Critics of sports as a form of moral education sometimes claim that participation (or even watching) sports can affect values negatively. They maintain that, although, under ideal conditions, sports might promote important virtues related to academic growth as suggested earlier, they hardly play such a role in the real world.

First, some critics charge that rather than promoting critical thinking or developing inquiring minds, sports teach blind obedience to the coach.[17] Players learn offenses and defenses decided upon by coaches, and in sports such as football, they often run plays that simply are dictated by the coaches. Where in this picture is there room for critical thinking?

Critics also charge that even if athletes do exhibit positive values, such as teamwork, these either do not carry over outside of sports (the compartmentalization thesis) or athletes already possess such values before playing athletics at a high level. Indeed, they claim athletes are successful because they are already team players rather than learning through sports to become team players in order to be successful (the preselection thesis).[18]

Although the objections considered here need to be taken seriously, they themselves are open to major objection. For example, the first criticism, that sports teach blind obedience to the coach, seems to be overstated at best. After all, how would we apply this critique to individual sports such as golf, squash, skiing, and tennis in which players constantly have to make decisions about what sort of shots and strokes or moves to employ and to assess the strategic options open to them? Golfers such as Tiger Woods and especially the late Seve Ballesteros are known not only for their power but for their creativity in extricating themselves from trouble and for manufacturing shots that best fit the situation they are in. My own best teams, sometimes nationally ranked in Division III, were not always the best ball strikers but often had the good judgment to be able to consistently shoot good scores even when not striking the ball at their best. Similarly, soccer and basketball players often run offenses and play defenses that call upon them to exercise good judgment in the course of play and not simply run rigid plays designed by the coach. Some sports ranging from intercollegiate tennis to track and cross country either prohibit communication with the coach during play or include features of the contest itself, such as the speed of runners in a sprint, that preclude communication.

What about football, which best seems to fit the paradigm of players mechanically running plays designed by the coaching staff? Of course, some coaches can be very controlling and attempt to minimize decision making by players. Other coaches, however, listen to strategic suggestions from players and design plays that give players discretion in how to carry out their assignments. Moreover, football is a reactive game and players need to constantly make decisions about how best to counter unexpected moves by opponents. According to one story I heard when I first joined the Hamilton College faculty in 1968, the football team was losing at halftime to a physically superior opponent. At the half-time team meeting, the players asked the coach, Don Jones, what they should do to change the momentum of the game. He replied, "You are supposed to be smart, so figure it out!" and left the room. Hamilton won the game.

Not only is the charge that athletes are taught blind subservience to authority at best overstated, the contrast with academics that encourage critical thinking arguably is overdrawn. After all, professors decide the syllabus for their course, determine points of emphasis in their lectures, dictate assignments, and design tests often without significant input from students. Some, I hope a small minority, of professors may be overly controlling, discouraging rather than encouraging critical responses to their own views. But let us keep in mind that students are not equal partners, then, either in athletics or academics. There is an underlying relationship of unequal authority on which the teacher-student and likewise the coach-athlete hinges, based on experience and perspective. Good professors encourage critical thinking and good coaches may often do so as well, but both also have to structure the activity they are engaged in based on their experience and expertise. Thus, the objection fails. There is good reason to believe that both academics and athletics when properly conducted can contribute to critical thinking, although both coaches and teachers are in a different position than athletes or students in directing the learning that takes place in each activity. We will discuss the role of the coach as educator more fully later in this section.

What about the compartmentalization and preselection theses? As we saw earlier, some critics claim that even if athletes learn some positive values through sports, they do not carry over to other areas of life and in any case success in athletics reflects values the athletes already possess, not those they have learned on the field of play.

Compartmentalization may sometimes be a real phenomenon, but surely life is not generally divided up into totally separate containers with no interaction among them. Professors assume, for example, that what is learned in a class on logic or expository writing carries over to critical analysis and better writing outside of class. Likewise, if parents are cruel to their young children, the children may in turn be cruel when they grow up. If another family is kind and compassionate to its members, that too is likely to be reflected in the behavior of the children raised there.

Thus, although the compartmentalization thesis may well have force in some contexts, it seems doubtful that athletics in particular has little effect outside its immediate sphere of influence. For serious athletes, sports are not just a hobby but often also a passion, which in turn helps shape their own identity. Their relationships with teammates and coaches are often intense and lasting. If athletes are taught or helped to cultivate virtues through their involvement in sports, it would be surprising, to say the least, if they did not express these virtues in other areas of their lives.

Similarly, the students accepted by more selective colleges have already demonstrated they have sound academic skills, but those colleges don't attribute the success of their students solely to qualities the students possessed before enrolling. The most plausible position is that students enter these colleges prepared to do academic work, but their skills are developed and honed by their college experience. Why wouldn't the same be true for athletes, especially at the college level? Prospective college athletes already are skilled; otherwise they wouldn't be recruited in the first place. But just as good professors can help students develop and learn, good coaches can also help athletes develop existing skills and values, learn new ones, and make better strategic decisions during contests. Rather than following the critics in attributing all success to preselection, whether in academics or athletics, the default position is interaction, where participants bring a partially formed character to the table but that character can be enhanced by the intense education to which they are exposed.

### What about the research that suggests that athletics can change athletes' characters for the worse?

Actual empirical studies by writers who argue against the value-instilling power of sports certainly need to be taken seriously. It would be a mistake, however, to simply draw the conclusion that participation in sports teaches bad values. In fact, two of the top researchers in the field, Brenda Bredemeier and David Shields, caution us that "generalizations about sport involvement and moral character are not warranted," and they also note note that "The influence that sport has for its participants depends on a complex set of factors tied to the specific sport, and the social interactions that are present."[19]

For example, in one study, Bredemeier and Shields found that their sample of Division I college basketball players was less morally sensitive than a control group of nonathletes, but when swimmers were added to the mix, the difference disappeared.[20] Perhaps different sports socialize participants differently. Golf, in which principles of etiquette are even part of the rulebook, may have a very different ethos and very different effect on character than rugby. Gender may also make a difference; some scholars suggest that women tend to engage in a kind of moral reasoning more sympathetic to the individual circumstances of those they deal, whereas men tend to appeal to more abstract notions of fairness and justice.

Most important, I would suggest, is the influence of the coach. If athletes are coached from a very young age to give the highest priority to winning, to see opponents as mere obstacles in their path, and to put their team first, right or wrong, they are likely to develop a different moral stance than athletes who are coached to respect opponents, use critical judgment, and to value other factors such as excellence in performance over a poorly played victory. Just as authoritarian teachers may influence students differently than those who encourage independence of thought, authoritarian coaches promote different values in their players than more compassionate and cooperative coaches would.

Perhaps the most important issue facing studies of the moral development of athletes is what counts as good character, what distinguishes moral from immoral judgment, or what counts as an acceptable justification for moral decisions. These are questions in ethics, not science, and although responses to them may well have an empirical component, the investigators themselves are making a sometimes unacknowledged moral judgment as to what counts as ethically more acceptable and ethically less acceptable responses to their questions.

For example, some researchers may tend to regard reasoning from abstract universal principles that can be impartially upheld as perhaps the most sophisticated form of ethical reasoning, perhaps showing that they are influenced by the Kantian notions of respect for persons or John Rawls's emphasis on evaluating principles of justice from behind a veil of ignorance that obscures how they would affect us personally. However, this would surely be contested not only by sophisticated utilitarian theorists but by communitarians, virtue ethicists, and proponents of an ethic of care who stress good judgment in concrete instances rather than abstract reasoning.

As a result, some researchers may emphasize social values such as teamwork and its contribution to community, as well as the capacity to set aside differences and work with diverse others toward a common end, whereas others may focus on how good athletes are in responding logically from an abstract position of impartiality to moral dilemmas posed by the investigator. In other words, different researchers may understand notions like moral character, virtue, and moral maturity quite differently and so come to different results because of a difference in the standards of moral maturity they employ. For example, should we view teamwork and loyalty to one's teammates as largely positive, morally speaking, or should teamwork be downgraded as leading to a partisan or biased concern with one's own team at the expense of opponents who are also persons in their own right?

Be that as it may, we need to keep two points in mind. First, the convergence of studies that suggest that the moral development of athletes is to some degree stunted when compared to nonathletes is troubling, but the findings also are open to criticism. Second, and more important, what effects participation in athletics has on the moral development and character of participants may depend to a very large extent on *how athletics are conducted*. This point will be developed more extensively in the responses to several questions that follow.

### Are there positive values that athletics might promote, at least when athletics are conducted properly? Are these values compatible with academics?

We need to develop a rough distinction alluded to earlier between three sorts of values in order to develop a response to these questions. On one hand, there are what we have called core intellectual values that plausibly can be regarded as presuppositions of education itself. These include respect for truth, willingness to engage in critical inquiry (including examining criticisms of one's own beliefs), honesty about one's ability and in one's work, and adherence to key elements of reasonable debate such as standards of good reasoning and factual accuracy.

A second set of values, which we called civic values, include ability to function as part of a community, respect for reasonable dissent from one's own view, the ability to work with others from different backgrounds than ourselves, and respect toward those who reasonably disagree with our own views. As the name suggests, these values are essential to the proper workings of democracy.

A third set of values might be called partisan political values, such as support for a more equal distribution of wealth, opposition to regulation of the economic market, support or opposition to strict laws protecting the environment, and allegiance to a particular political party. The core intellectual and civic values must be presupposed if we are to have productive discourse about these issues—discourse that can help lead us to justifiable conclusions.

Although these distinctions between the three kinds of values are rough, far from exhaustive, and allow for all sorts of intermediate cases, they nevertheless are useful and will enhance the discussion that follows.

A major argument for the compatibility and even mutual support of academic and athletics is that athletics also promote not only civic values but also the core educational or intellectual values themselves, or at least close analogs of them. The claim is not that organized athletics always do this, but that they do so when properly conducted. That is, if athletics are conducted with educational goals given significant priority, as the ideal of mutualism in sports suggests, they have significant educational value.

Thus, the value of truth and of honesty can be as important in athletics as in academics. Competitors who make false assumptions about their own abilities or those of their opponents or who are not honest about their own strengths and weaknesses are all too likely to be unpleasantly surprised in actual competition. If they are to improve, athletes need to be able to accept criticism and put critiques to use. Competition itself can be compared to a dialogue in which each side tries to anticipate and respond to strategies of the opponent.[21]

Coaches, if they function as educators, should be willing to engage in reasonable dialogue with their teams about why they prefer one strategy or technique to another. They should be truthful, but tactful, about telling the truth about the strengths and weaknesses of their own team and of opponents, and help their players absorb and learn from criticism.

Just as coaches can encourage and support core intellectual values, they also can support the civic values specified earlier. For example, they can encourage teammates with different political views, from different social and economic backgrounds, and of different races and ethnicities to work together for a common goal.

One of my colleagues in the Hamilton philosophy department was giving a talk on major issues involving race. He was asked by a student in the audience how best to prepare for often difficult conversations that might occur on campus on controversial topics involving race. He replied, "Make friends!"

Although it is true that friends can often engage in difficult discussions more honestly than strangers, there also are other at least equally significant factors that can promote understanding across a variety of ethnic, racial, gender, and cultural differences. These might include learning to listen to others, reflecting on obvious cases of injustice, and critically examining our own stereotypes.

Nevertheless, sports and athletics provide a special venue outside of the classroom where friendships can be forged, and these in turn can make difficult conversations far easier to carry out. Indeed, the noted social scientist James Q. Wilson has identified athletic teams, along with churches and the military, as three major areas where racially and ethnically diverse individuals have learned to get along and cooperate to a degree rarely found elsewhere in society.[22]

Of course, sports are not unique in these respects. Debate teams, cooperative classroom projects, social service organizations, and discussion in class surely are among the most significant venues for promoting the core educational and civic values, including respect for difference. The claim for athletics is not that they are unique in the respects suggested earlier but that they too can be a significant source of reinforcement for educational and civic values.

Moreover, athletics in educational institutions may reinforce core educational and civic values not only for the participants. They can also illustrate or express these values in the wider community. For example, players working harmoniously on the soccer field can demonstrate the value of teamwork. Conversely, selfish players who care more about their own statistics than their team can illustrate the opposite. Players who start the season slowly but work hard to improve and learn from their coaches can illustrate the value of taking criticism seriously and working hard to get better. Thus, the idea that athletics and academics can be mutually reinforcing applies both to participants and spectators alike.

*You describe an ideal that is fine in theory, but does it actually apply to organized athletics in educational institutions? What practical things can we do to help make sure that athletics and academics reinforce each other?*

The rhetoric of many colleges and universities implicitly endorses the ideal of mutual reinforcement between athletics and academics. For example, the mission statement of the New England Small College Athletic Conference (NESCAC), a group of highly selective liberal arts colleges that compete in Division III, to which my institution belongs, states that "members are committed first and foremost to academic excellence and believe that our athletic programs must always support our educational mission."

The mission statement of academically and athletically elite Duke University, the home of many Division I championship teams, strikes a similar note. "The guiding principle behind Duke's participation in Division I athletics is our belief in its educational value for our students. Intercollegiate athletics promotes character traits of high value to personal development and success in later life." Similar statements are found in the mission statements of most intercollegiate athletic programs, ranging from institutions in Division III that do not award athletic scholarships and make institutional commitments to integrate athletics and academics, to those encompassing highly visible Division I programs in large state universities.

Is the rhetoric actually applied in action? In my view conferences like the NESCAC at the very least come close to making good on their word in this regard and represent perhaps the purest form of intercollegiate sport. As we noted earlier, there are significant difficulties with high-visibility Division I programs that make it difficult to integrate sports and academics. There certainly are problems in Division III as well. For example, one study suggests that even at academically very selective institutions, the academic performance of male athletes in particular may fall below that of male students at large, even at those academically strong schools included in the study. This can be quite significant because athletes may constitute as much as one-third of the student body at smaller colleges. On the other hand, the same study suggests that female athletes at the institutions in question perform as well or perhaps better than female students at large at the schools in question.[23]

Whatever the level of competition, if an athlete is unprepared for college work or if teams are on the road so often that a great many classes are missed, athletics and academics may indeed conflict. Later in this section I will suggest some specific kinds of reforms of Division I athletics that may help to better integrate athletics and academics.

The idea of compatibility can be applied well beyond the college level. Many critics bemoan the emphasis placed on high school sports in the United States, but if these sports are conducted in the manner sketched earlier, they can reinforce educational values perhaps even more so than at the college level. In some instances, they may even sustain and create the incentive for many young people to stay in school rather than drop out. They can be the hook that eventually leads apparently disinterested young people to develop and internalize the core educational and civic values we already have explored.

In this regard, participation in sports may be particularly beneficial for young girls and young women. In a complex study, Betsy Stevenson, then of the Wharton School, found a causal relationship between participation in sports and rises in women's educational attainments and employment. Her study suggests that "It's not just that the people who are going to do well in life play sports, but that sports help people do better in life."[24] It is reasonable to assume that acceptance by participants of some of the core values we have been discussing contributed to the effects of participation in athletics on improving their lives.

Youth sports, of course, are especially important. Although competition can be overemphasized at this level and parental involvement sometimes is excessive, a topic we also will discuss later, a reasonable emphasis on competition can help children to internalize values such as dedication, acceptance of criticism as a tool for improvement, respect for opponents, and many of the other values we have already considered.

How sports are coached has a major influence on whether they serve educational functions or are treated as a win-at-all-costs endeavor. The role of the coach is crucial if sports are to be compatible with or even reinforce education.

### What are some of the ethical responsibilities of coaches at various levels of competition?

The role of the coach often does and to an extent should differ depending upon the level of sport at which the coaching takes place. In elite Division I intercollegiate sport, the Division

I coach of a high visibility sport, as we have already seen, will often be the highest paid person on campus, with an even higher income than the governor of the state or in some cases even the President of the United States.[25] It also is important to remember that top coaches often are icons not only in their university community but also regionally and even nationally, and sometimes they are more the center of attention and publicity than their players. Some observers fear that, as a result, such star coaches may have too much influence on other areas of the university, sometimes creating an atmosphere of tolerance of meddling with academics and even creating incentives for the scandals involving academic fraud cited earlier. Of course, this is not true of the vast majority of coaches in Division I, especially those coaching less visible sports, but critics surely are right to worry whether the phenomenon of the star coach raises the potential of conflicts with athletics to a level that is questionable at best.

On the other end of the scale, coaches in youth sports almost always are volunteers but may have a very special role in the educational process. Coaches at this level do not, or at least should not, be individuals who simply instruct about technique but rather have the task of introducing young athletes into a social practice and teaching them to appreciate the excellences internal to it.[26]

It is difficult, therefore, to generalize across all layers in which coaching in sport takes place. For that reason, let us bracket for the moment issues of coaching in professional sports and perhaps also elite levels of amateur sports as well, and see if we can arrive at some ethical guidelines for coaching in both youth sports, interscholastic sports, most intercollegiate athletics, and club sports outside the United States. We can then see how such principles might apply when professional and big-time college sports are at issue. Our focus here is on coaching a team or individual in broad facets of a sport, and not serving only as a technical instructor, as a golf professional might do when giving lessons to aspiring players or even stars on the PGA Tour.

Why not make the ethics of coaching simple? Why not just say that the main job of the coach is to win? Teaching skills is a means to that end. So why not judge coaches on their record of wins and losses alone? Reflection will show, I suggest, that such a view is much too simple. For example, teaching skills can conflict with winning when a coach in youth sport plays less experienced players at meaningful points in the game so they can gain experience and learn to perform in game conditions. Should a coach ever lie to players to help them perform better as, for example, when a coach falsely tells a player she has a chance to make the starting lineup only to get her to play harder and challenge the first-stringers more in practice?[27] Should a coach at a competitive level play only the best players in meaningful game situations, or is there also a duty to promote participation? If the latter, does it apply only to youth sports (where rules sometimes mandate significant playing time for all on the team), to high school sports, and even intercollegiate competition? Is a coach who has a losing record but whose team improves significantly a worse coach than one who wins but whose team stays at the same level of play? Is a coach who stresses respect for opponents a better coach than one who wins more but creates enmity toward the opposition to motivate his team?

These questions are leading ones in that they are meant to suggest that the role of the coach should be much broader and ethically more significant than just trying to win games.

### If the coach's role has an ethical component, as you suggest, how is that component best understood?

One writer, philosopher Heather Reid, drawing on the role of athletics in Plato's Academy, suggests that we should view the coach in most contexts broadly as a teacher of virtue.[28] The coach, particularly in youth sports but also in educational institutions, should teach players to internalize and act according to key civic virtues such as fairness, respect for others, courage under pressure, and the exercise of good judgment. On this view, the coach is primarily an educator and is directly engaged in moral education designed to help athletes live a life of excellence and good citizenship.

This is an attractive view. It suggests that athletics ought not to emphasize what might be called external goods, such as the fame and sometimes fortune that come with athletic success, as often is the case in contemporary sports, but instead should provide training on how to become a good person, a good citizen, and live a good life. The best coach, on this view, need not be a logician applying ethical principles in a rigid manner but rather be a person of good judgment, ethical enough to model the virtues by his or her own behavior and sensible enough to use good judgment in treating players appropriately in various sporting contexts.

The view that the coach should be primarily an educator is a strong one, but it may go too far to say that the coach is primarily a teacher of virtue. Coaches also need to be more than judicious individuals who exercise good judgment in specific situations. In addition, they often need to be able to articulate the reasons for their decisions—especially controversial judgments about how to treat players—to parents, players, spectators, and sometimes the broader community as well. For example, if a starting basketball player is benched for missing practice, the coach needs to be able to explain both the importance of attendance and how the team might be affected if a key player misses important adjustments made in team strategy to adjust to the next opponent.

In an important essay on the ethics of coaching, Jeffrey Fry has argued that coaches ought to follow the injunction, famously defended by Kant, as we have now discussed several times, that we should never treat others as mere means or tools but as persons in their own right or what

Kant calls ends in themselves. Fry gives the example, mentioned earlier in this chapter, of a coach who during preseason lies to a candidate for a starting position in order to get him to work harder to challenge a teammate whom the coach has already decided will start at the position in question. The coach's hope is that the challenge will elevate the play of both players, but at least one of the players has been manipulated by the coach's lie. Not only might this manipulation lead the player who is lied to to pass up such options as deciding not to play or to transfer to another school, it treats the athlete as a mere thing or means to an end—a cog in the process of winning games.[29]

The idea that players should not be manipulated or used as mere means surely provides a moral baseline for coaches. Of course, the way this Kantian principle is applied is age relative; young athletes may not yet be sufficiently mature to be treated as fully autonomous agents. Nevertheless, children are not mere means to competitive success either, so their welfare must always be a primary concern. They or their parents should be informed about team policies, and coaches should take advantage of opportunities to teach good decision making in competition and basics of strategy as appropriate for the age of the children involved.

Why regard the Kantian injunction to treat others as persons or ends and never as mere means only as a baseline for ethical coaching? Many issues in coaching are so complex that coaches need a broader range of moral resources to apply, not just this single principle, or at least they need concrete guidelines as to how the Kantian formula might be applied in different contexts. The abstract injunction not to treat others as mere means does not tell coaches how far they can go in laying down restrictions on the behavior of their athletes off the field, which in many cases may be none of their business, or whether to show loyalty to senior payers in the distribution of playing time or bench them in favor of younger players who are potentially more talented.

The account of the coach as a teacher of virtue would be sharpened if narrowed down to the specific work of coaching sports, while the Kantian injunction not to treat others as mere means provides a baseline but may not cover all issues that coaches face. My own suggestion is that we narrow the virtue account and broaden the Kantian baseline by turning back to those values we have already found central to competitive sport. These include what we have called the intellectual virtues—such as truthfulness, learning to accept and benefit from criticism, and appreciation of excellence—as well as civic values such as taking responsibility and working well with others.

Perhaps we can illustrate how these approaches apply by considering the kind of case sketched earlier. A coach has several senior starters, but as the season ends, the team seems likely to lose a majority of its games overall and has little chance of qualifying for postseason playoffs. Should the coach continue to start the seniors, perhaps out of loyalty due to their contributions in the past, or start the younger players who may be more talented and need game experience to be prepared for the next season? If the coach makes the latter decision, are the seniors being treated as mere means to the team's success in the future—a future in which they will play no role? If the younger players stay on the bench for the most part, are their talents and aspirations being ignored? Are they being used as mere means to make the seniors feel good?[30]

This scenario suggests first that there probably is no mechanical way to simply take an abstract ethical principle, apply it to the facts of the case, and then read off an easy answer. Ethical principles may function more like guidelines demarcating the parameters of ethical decision making than as strict rules for making decisions without the need for good sense, just as the virtue theory suggests. What the coach can do is approach the case in a variety of ways, none of which just treat players as less than persons, and which involve application of the core intellectual and civic virtues.

For example, the coach might discuss the situation with the players, keeping them informed, and then suggest that the seniors act as assistant coaches to help the younger players develop and to willingly share playing time to that end. Although a team is no more a democracy than a classroom, where the professor often must make the final call about such things as assignments and how long to let discussion continue, the coach also needs to decide how best to handle the situation. But by including the players in the discussion and considering their views, and by encouraging all of them to think about the consequences of various approaches for others as well as themselves, the coach has applied core values such as truthfulness, respect for all, and teamwork to achieve an acceptable result.

If coaches are thought of and expected to act as educators, instilling respect for the core intellectual and civic values as a part of teaching respect for the game and its values, many of the problems associated with competitive athletics can be minimized, if not eliminated. Winning, while a major goal of any competition, would not be overemphasized and athletics would better complement academic pursuits through emphasis on shared values than often is the case at present.

*This approach sounds good when applied to youth sports and perhaps even to intermediate-level competition, such as interscholastic sports in the United States. But is it at all applicable to elite sports, whether at the intercollegiate, Olympic, or professional levels?*

As athletic competition approaches elite levels, the emphasis on winning and competitive success normally increases. However, this is a descriptive point, telling us what is the case, and it does not settle the ethical question of what the role of the coach should be even at those levels. In fact, in elite intercollegiate sport, where athletes face the pressures of competition, travel, and adjustment to a college environment for which some are not academically well prepared, the guidance of the coach or coaching staff may be especially important. Coaches can encourage academically weak athletes to develop the writing, speaking, and other academic skills they need to succeed in the classroom, or they can encourage their players to take the easy way out by selecting minimally challenging courses or focusing on athletics to the virtual exclusion of academics. In the most egregious cases, we end up with the kind of academic fraud allegedly found at North Carolina, Minnesota, and other institutions, where keeping athletes eligible to play often seemed to have been a higher priority than helping them to acquire the academic skills necessary for achievement in the classroom. In addition, young college athletes may need guidance from older ethical role models on how to act maturely and ethically themselves.

Eric Taylor, the fictional high school coach portrayed in the dramatic television series *Friday Night Lights*, is perhaps a model of what an ethical coach might be. Although tough with and demanding of his players, while also trying to be a good father and husband, he helps his players to face the personal crises in their lives and to grow up as better people. Although flawed in some respects, Coach Taylor puts the welfare of his players over winning but also stresses the core values of dedication, commitment to excellence, honesty, and respect that we have argued are inextricably tied to ethical competition itself.

Many coaches throughout the sports world try to act as educators, in youth sports through high school and in the different divisions of the NCAA in US intercollegiate sports. Nevertheless, the pressures to win, to generate revenue, and to put an entertaining "product" on the field surely can conflict with the broader responsibilities of the coach to players. Ethical obligations do not vanish at the professional level either. Surely European soccer coaches have a moral duty to prohibit their players from making racist comments to opponents and to discourage fans from engaging in the racist and increasingly anti-Semitic chants that have raised serious issues about behavior in the European soccer community. For example, soccer officials in Holland had to apologize when fans expressed such sentiments shouted from the stands as "Hamas, Hamas, Jews to the gas" and "Jews burn the best!"[31]

Moreover, even professional coaches surely have the duty to treat their players with respect and not as mere means to victory. For example, coaches need to show concern for the health of injured players and not rush them back into action even to win an important contest without proper medical clearance. This is why medical personnel connected with teams ought to be independent of coaching staffs or management of professional teams so that their first concern is the health of the athletes themselves. Indeed, sometimes athletes may want to return to action too soon after an injury, so the coach will need to step in, especially with younger players and even college students, to protect players from themselves.[32]

It might be argued that the players consent to be used as pawns in the quest for competitive success by becoming professionals, yet this cannot be the case because professional athletes, like all of us, want to be treated as persons, not just bodies to be employed for the success of the professional organization for which they compete.

Players who commit heinous acts, such as assaulting women, surely need to be suspended or otherwise punished through the legal system. But no person should be treated as a mere means or thing, hence the right we all have to due process. In any case, those athletes who demonstrate perseverance, skill, dedication, and respect for the game and for others surely should not be regarded just as things or only as mere property of the teams to which they contract. Indeed, consider developments in professional sports such as the legal overthrow of the reserve clause, which legally bound Major League Baseball players to the team that "owned" them, in 1975, following an unsuccessful 1969 lawsuit by player Curt Flood. Subsequently the development of what is called free agency, which allows players to move from team to team once their contractual obligations to their present team are fulfilled, has given professional athletes in the United States much more control over the course of their careers than was previously the case. This commitment to securing more autonomy for professional athletes goes to show that the athletes themselves do not regard themselves as mere property nor do they believe that by becoming professionals, they have consented to any such thing. By upholding their freedom to negotiate new contracts and affiliate with new teams, players have rejected the view that they are simply property of the team that originally signs or employs them.

Although winning and breaking records undoubtedly are the major goals of elite sports, ethical requirements, as we have seen, do not vanish even at that level. Professional coaches are and should be held to some ethical standards. As noted earlier, the penalties handed down to coaches by the NFL for the bounty system employed by the New Orleans Saints are one example illustrating that sports organizations themselves endorse (or at least have accepted) such a view.

*Coaches have the authority to distribute playing time among the athletes on their teams. What criteria should they follow in making decisions about who plays, when they play, and who sits on the bench?*

The answer to this question depends in great part on the level of sport we are considering. Perhaps the conventional wisdom is that in youth sport, playing time should be distributed nearly equally but that as the competitive level of play increases and players grow older, playing time should more and more be distributed by ability. In the United States, many would say that by the time athletes are playing at the high school varsity level, winning becomes a major goal of competition. The way to win is by playing the best players, or those most suited to produce a victory in the game situation at hand.

That conventional wisdom, however, is open to challenge based on the very premises about the potential educational value of sport defended earlier. In one version of this argument, adherents maintain that if we do view the educational benefits of participation in sport as important and we respect all our players as equal autonomous persons, there is a presumptive case for giving each player on a team meaningful playing time—that is, time in a game when the outcome is still in doubt—in contests so they can all benefit accordingly.[33] Proponents of this view may acknowledges that at higher levels of competition, coaches are justified in assigning winning much greater weight than at lower levels; they would deny that the value of winning automatically trumps other goals, such as promoting the development and education of the athletes involved.

This approach has special force in youth sport. Children and early adolescents are learning basic skills and strategies, are eager to have fun by participating, and learn early to internalize and act upon the core intellectual and civic values we have already considered. At that level, there seems to be a compelling argument for participation for all.

Meaningful participation, moreover, is not necessarily equal participation. I almost learned this the hard way in my very first baseball game as a coach in our local Little League. The more experienced head coach, a colleague of mine in the philosophy department, had to leave early, but our team had a large lead and he told me I would do just fine taking over for him for the final few innings. Because we had a substantial lead, I thought I would implement my egalitarian leanings by giving players with only minimal experience in pitching a chance to pitch. As opposing batters one after the other walked or hit safely, our lead shrank nearly to the vanishing point. Finally, with two out in the last inning, the opposition had the bases loaded, and we had only a one-run lead. Fortunately, the next batter struck out on a pitch over his head, and we escaped with a narrow victory. When the head coach asked me the next day how we did, all I could say was, "Just fine!"

Clearly the idea of equal playing time can be carried too far. In baseball, it is even dangerous to ask a child who is just learning to catch to play first base because the hard throws that come into that base may be too much for that child to handle. There is even the danger of the child getting hit in the face and being seriously injured. Asking someone to pitch who can't throw strikes leaves all the other players on the field standing around watching opponent after opponent draw walks, and losing the opportunity to field batted balls.

Even if strict equality of playing time is not a reasonable requirement for most youth sports, providing meaningful playing time at positions appropriate to the skill level of the player should be a prime consideration for coaches in youth sport. Just how this should be accomplished depends on context and cannot be reduced to a formula. Instead, it simply requires the good judgment and common sense of the coaches.

What about at more competitive levels of sport for older athletes, ranging from high school to college? One view is that while winning gains importance at those levels, the educational case for meaningful playing time still carries weight. Don't dedicated reserves often deserve meaningful time on the court or field based on their contributions to the team in practice and the effort they have exerted on its behalf?[34]

The argument that values playing time over winning does have some force in many contexts, but there are considerations that diminish its strength, even if they do not completely undermine it. In particular, isn't there moral value to earning playing time rather than having it given?[35] The coach may be treating players as persons by reacting to how well each does in practice and in previous games and allotting playing time according to not only hard work but how the bench plyers actually improve in exhibiting the skills of their sport. The educational benefit of improving enough to deserve being played can be impressive, as earning playing time may require perseverance, dedication, cooperation, and the ability to learn from criticism. Hard work serves as a basis for a claim to playing time, but other factors such as learning to make good strategic decisions or actually developing skills rather than staying at the same level of play also might justify claims to playing time.

I suggest then that although the conventional wisdom might go too far in totally dismissing the claims of bench players to meaningful time in the game, there is nevertheless a strong case to be made arguing that once we arrive at higher levels of competition than youth sport, time in the game is something to be earned through good play and hard work in practice.[36]

It is true that some coaches go too far in the other direction, playing the most talented players absolutely as much as possible, perhaps trying to win by the widest margin or fearing giving the opponents a chance to mount a rally against the second string. Once again, we need judicious coaches who can make good decisions in game situations about how to balance the conflicting goals of victory and meaningful participation appropriately.

*Is there any hope that an approach prioritizing core educational values can apply to high-visibility sports in the major conferences of Division I of the NCAA, where winning national championships, revenue, and visibility seem to be the major goals?*

Perhaps we should abandon the idea that elite high-visibility intercollegiate sports have anything to do with education; rather, they are concerned with winning and the revenue that flows from winning. Perhaps they constitute a legitimate form of entertainment that large universities provide for the public. But, on this view, they are divorced from the educational mission of the university.

In some earlier publications, I myself was perhaps more optimistic about the prospects for reconciling academics and athletics at the Division I level than I should have been.[37] Given recent developments, especially the kind of academic fraud we have seen at even educationally highly regarded institutions, that optimism certainly has been tempered.

Nevertheless, the picture may not be as bleak as we might think. First, as we already noted, graduation rates for Division I athletes as a group are improving and higher than those of students at large. Many players even in high-visibility Division I sports do graduate and receive an education that would otherwise be out of their reach and may learn important moral lessons from some outstanding coaches. Good teams also can illustrate to a wide audience important values such as the importance of teamwork, dedication to excellence, and the value of getting along together despite many sorts of differences among the athletes themselves.

But although there undoubtedly are bright spots, as well as a significant number of thoughtful and dedicated coaches and administrators in Division I top-tier athletics, the structural problems and market incentives to win remain. Despite honorable exceptions, the highly critical assessment of Division I men's football and basketball quoted earlier largely rings true. Even if we assign elite intercollegiate athletics to the realm of entertainment and not education, there nevertheless is still an obligation not to exploit the scholarship athletes who actually take the field or court. Unless we are to go the route of full professionalization, with all the problems outlined earlier that such a move would entail, some significant reforms are needed so that educational institutions provide genuine opportunities for their scholarship athletes to acquire a meaningful education.

I would suggest at least the following changes. If ever implemented as a body, which is highly unlikely, they would move Division I in the direction of the Ivy League and Division III, but not so much, I suggest, as to abolish elite Division I competition, which at this point is not a realistic option.

First, restrict the number of games played, especially contests that conflict with classes (weekday contests), and restrict national travel largely to vacation periods, breaks in the academic calendar, and postseason competition. For example, to pick just one program that is not atypical for its sport, the University of Iowa's women's softball team plays over 50 games, not counting postseason competition, many of which fall on weekdays. Players may have team tutors and special academic support, but it would be naive to believe that such an extensive schedule does not place a burden on their class attendance and hence their academic performance. Schedules for all sports emphasizing more weekend contests, less national travel, and extensive scheduling of contests only during breaks would go a long away in allowing athletes to take full advantage of the academic opportunities open to them.

Second, restrict the length of seasons. When I became a college basketball fan in the 1960s and 1970s, the college basketball season typically began around Thanksgiving, but now it starts in early November for many Division I teams.

Critics might reply that restricting the length of seasons would compress the time allowed for contests, meaning players would get shorter breaks between games, but this would not be case if the number of contests allowed also was reduced.

Third, first-year students in Division I should be made ineligible for varsity competition until they complete a full year's worth of courses with acceptable grades. They could compete on freshman teams that play limited schedules and still receive coaching from the varsity staff in order to develop the fundamentals they need to succeed at high levels of competition. This would allow recruited athletes to adjust to college before being thrown into high-pressure competition. It would also make more room for individuals who have not been recruited to walk on the freshman teams, creating opportunities for participation that do not now exist.

As a side effect, those athletes interested in the "one and done" route in which players compete for their university for only their first year and then, if they are highly successful, depart for the professional leagues would no longer have an incentive to attend. Some might be better off demonstrating their abilities in minor leagues that professional leagues should sponsor, the NBA "D or developmental league" being a case in point. Although it is completely understandable why athletes from economically struggling backgrounds might want to turn professional as soon as possible, there is no reason why intercollegiate athletes ought to be the main route for doing so.

Fourth, only athletes capable of and prepared for doing college-level academic work should be admitted. Colleges and universities should be permitted to offer programs for students not yet ready for the academic load, but enrollment in such programs should not be for athletes alone. Schools also ought to establish rigorous academic standards for students to meet in order to be considered eligible to participate in athletics.

Finally, coaches should be evaluated not only by athletic administrators but also by faculty so that their contribution to the education of their students is weighted heavily in the appointment and reappointment process. (Ideally, I would like to see coaches be members of the faculty, paid on the faculty scale, as is normally the case at my own institution. But once when I suggested this to the chancellor of a major university competing in a major conference, he replied. "That's a great idea, but if I ever tried to implement it, I would be fired within a week.")

Practically speaking, it is extremely unlikely that all of these reforms would be instituted. In any case, they are only listed as examples of what might be done to promote the compatibility of big-time intercollegiate athletics with academics. Perhaps the suggestion that might have the most significant immediate effect is removing freshman eligibility for varsity play because it would provide recruited student-athletes with a breather period to adjust to the academic load of college and, perhaps as a side effect, reduce prevalence of the "one-and-done" athletic star who would be more likely to turn professional rather than go to college in the first place.

Should we switch to a club sports model for various levels of proficiency? Wouldn't this help ensure that sports didn't detract from the education schools provide?

The idea of local and regional clubs and teams is attractive and is hardly nonexistent in America. Local softball teams, soccer clubs, tennis organizations, golf organizations, and in some regions lesser known sports such as curling thrive throughout the country. The advantages of a club system, or of organizing competitive sport apart from educational institutions, are significant. Athletes need not give up their sport when they graduate, institutions need not spend substantial sums on athletic programs, and students would understand they are in school to do academic work, not to play sports. Nevertheless, although sports organized around local and regional clubs, unaffiliated with educational institutions, certainly can and should coexist with interscholastic and intercollegiate athletics, the advantages of tying athletics and academics together also are significant.

For one thing, eliminating competition at the middle and high school level might contribute to a more sedentary generation of young people, which of course would have implications from a public health perspective as well as for their overall well-being. (It is possible, however, that this problem might be remedied by imposing more demanding physical education requirements for all students, not just varsity athletes.) More important, athletics can function as a hook keeping many kids in school who otherwise might drop out. As noted earlier, research also indicates that participation in competitive athletics has special benefits for females.

However, the most important argument we have considered is that when properly conducted, athletic and academic programs can be mutually reinforcing. Success in both fields requires emphasis on the core values, both intellectual and civic, which are presupposed by the pursuit of excellence in each area. This does not mean that coaches (or classroom teachers) need be preachers but rather that they can, on appropriate occasions, illustrate that core values in one area can, when implemented, promote success in the other. For example, students who accept criticism on their written work and try to learn from it but who resent criticism from coaches can be made to see the importance of honest critical scrutiny of their own performance in each area.

Core values would also be presupposed by *properly run* athletic programs outside of schools and colleges such as local and regional clubs or athletic associations. However, the opportunity for mutual reinforcement between properly run athletics and academic would be lost. Contrary to what many critics of high school and college athletics may believe, participation in athletics can complement and reinforce an institution's academic program.

The likelihood of such cohesiveness can be enhanced by a variety of factors. Coaches should, above all, be thought of and treated as educators. Although failure to win over a number of seasons may be a sign that a coach is a poor teacher, winning, while important, is not the only criterion by which the coach-as-educator should be evaluated. Support for core civic and intellectual values, including teaching respect for opponents and respect for the game, also are highly relevant.

Students-athletes and students who don't participate in varsity athletics should all have the opportunity to explore the cultural phenomenon of sport in a variety of ways, including in the classroom. Classes on sociological, ethical, and social issues in sport would help students to better understand the issues raised by competitive athletics and make student-athletes much more conscious of the ethical and social issues raised by participation.

Several years ago, I visited the University of Wisconsin to speak to students, including athletes and students at large, who participated in just such a pilot project. They were enrolled in sections of a literature course that gave special attention to works dealing with athletics. I was impressed by their awareness of issues in athletics, and by their presentation. These reports integrated athletes with other areas by tying issues in sports to studies in literature, history, and other disciplines. The program was a terrific example of how athletics and academic might be integrated at the classroom level.

As we have seen, Plato's emphasis on athletics in his Academy may often be misapplied today, especially at the highest levels of intercollegiate competition. Winning, while important, is not everything, and the educational value of sport can be compromised by the pursuit of revenue and success in the market.

Nevertheless, our discussion suggests that athletics and academics in the right context can be, and sometimes are, mutually reinforcing. Although mutual reinforcement is to some degree an ideal we should strive to attain, we sometimes can come close, as athletic programs in colleges and universities that compete outside the arena of truly big-time college sports, as well as those at many secondary schools, all illustrate. Perhaps I am naïve or influenced too much by my own experience at an academically oriented but athletically competitive Division III institution. Be that as it may, I hope you, the reader, agree that if we promote the proper values in sport, including educational and civic values, athletic competition can be and sometimes is an important contributor to the educational experience.

# 6

# SPORTS, EQUITY, AND SOCIETY

*Should sports be independent of politics? Shouldn't politics be kept out of sports?*

If sport is an activity involved with what we have called a mutual quest for excellence, shouldn't it occupy its own world in which, as in the arts, we focus on its internal goals, whether they be the achievement of excellence or beauty? On this view, politics threaten to pollute sport and thereby corrupt something that many hold almost sacred. Avery Brundage, who later became chairman of the International Olympic Committee from 1952 to 1972, expressed such a view when he opposed a proposed American boycott of the 1936 Olympics to be held in Nazi Germany. But is that view justified?

What does it mean to claim that sports should be independent or apart from politics? First of all, we need to distinguish the normative thesis that politics *should be* kept out of sport from the descriptive thesis that politics and sport *are in fact* separate. The descriptive thesis clearly seems to be false. The political storm over participation in the 1936 "Hitler" Olympics in Berlin, the exclusion of South African teams from the Olympics from 1964 through 1988 because of protests against apartheid, the massacre of Israeli athletes by the Palestinian group Black September at the 1972 Munich Olympics, and the recent expressions of support from prominent professional athletes in the United States for the Black Lives Matter movement, which arose in response to police shootings of young unarmed African American males in 2014 and 2015, all go to show that in reality sports and politics frequently intersect. For further proof we can look to the famous Soccer War (or Football War as it is called outside the United States), also known as the Hundred Hour War, fought in 1969 by El Salvador and Honduras over immigration, from the former to the latter, and attempts at land reform that adversely affected immigrants from El Salvador. Although causes of the conflict were political and quite complex, some suggest that fighting was triggered by rioting during a qualifying round of the FIFA World Cup.

I suggest that we should reject the descriptive thesis that sports and politics are in fact separate. But how should we understand the normative thesis that they should be kept separate? If it is taken to mean that sports should be totally value neutral, it runs into the difficulties raised by our own discussion of ethics and sports. On most conceptions of sport, athletes are encouraged to be dedicated, to accept criticism, and to work to overcome deficiencies in their performance, to pursue excellence, and to make good strategic decisions under pressure. These are all values virtually impossible to separate from competitive sport. Similarly, in youth sport, coaches should try to help their charges improve and to love or at least respect and understand the game they are playing. These too are all values. In particular, if athletic competition is understood as something like a mutual quest for excellence through meeting challenges, the values of excellence and of meeting challenges are presupposed. Clearly, sports are not value-free.

Perhaps the most plausible way of understanding the normative thesis is that partisan values, those that are highly controversial politically, should be kept out of sport. Thus, we should not have professional sports teams endorsing presidential candidates in the United States or taking stands on issues that go well beyond the boundaries of sport, such as how much of a nation's budget should be allocated to foreign aid versus expenditures at home.

However, the line between partisan and nonpartisan values is likely to be a blurred one. Although a sports team endorsing a political party would be partisan, and so be prohibited on the view being considered, what about the NCAA and some professional sport teams such as the Indiana Pacers professional basketball team sharply criticizing a 2015 Indiana statute that granted certain exemptions from government interference when such government action substantially burdened an individual's religious freedom? The statute was widely regarded as allowing businesses to refuse to serve gays, as when a bakery might be asked to bake a cake for a reception at a gay marriage. Sports teams and athletes, as well as the business community of Indianapolis and indeed around the country, spoke out against the statute on the grounds that it could be used to justify discrimination against their gay employees, gay athletes, fans, and visitors to the state. Similar controversies are continuing in 2016 over so called "religious freedom" laws in North Carolina and Mississippi that critics regard as allowing discrimination against LGBT people. Are these an expression of a partisan political position, or are critics of the statute applying a principle that does seem central to athletic competition: that no one should be excluded on the basis of certain characteristics, such as race, gender, and sexual orientation, that are not freely chosen?

The line between sports organizations taking strong partisan political stands on one hand and standing up for values closely related to those central to competitive sport on the other is indeed blurred, but perhaps still worth examining closely. I have argued elsewhere that educational institutions, such as colleges and universities, normally ought not to endorse partisan values since such institutions need to serve as referees for partisan discourse among their faculty and student body. Who would have confidence in a referee already committed to the side of one's opponent? Equally important, partisanship might discourage the formation of an intellectually diverse student body and faculty. Would pro-choice faculty or students, for example, find a university that was explicitly anti-abortion attractive?[1]

Be that as it may, the same logic does not apply with full strength to professional sports teams. Such professional teams are businesses, and in the view of some, the only obligation of a business is to make a profit. On this view, it is not the job of a for-profit business, including professional teams, to promote discourse in a fair framework for debate. Nevertheless, businesses, including sports teams, may well have moral obligations; for example, to promote the safety of their workers and of consumers. In my view, if they were permitted to do so, sports teams would go much too far in becoming active political agents for a great many highly controversial causes. Sports teams in particular have moral reasons, however, for embracing certain values, such as nondiscrimination on the basis of race, gender, sexual orientation, and religion. These values are not only an extension of moral principles embedded in fair sporting competition, but they may also be required to protect their players, employees, and fans from discrimination.

Of course, individual athletes retain the same rights to speak out on major issues as other citizens. Although many athletes have chosen to stay out of politics, some sports stars such as Mohammed Ali have been highly visible spokespersons on controversial issues, as we will see later in our discussion.

Accordingly, the claim that sports and moral controversy can and should be kept in entirely separate realms seems extremely difficult to defend in uncompromising form, although it is much more defensible when applied to highly partisan issues and debates. The Olympics, from its origins in ancient Greece to today, were meant to express and encourage values such as friendship among athletes from around the world (or from the different city states in ancient Greece) and promote virtues such as respect for excellence and for opponents. This itself is a political stance, although it may not be partisan but rather a defense of core values central to the practice of sport at its best.

**You claim equality and openness to all are core values of sport, or at least of sport at its best, but hasn't sport also been an instrument for perpetrating unjust inequalities?**

It certainly is true that sport sometimes has been a medium for implementing or supporting unjust discrimination. Racial segregation was a practice in Major League Baseball until 1947 when Jackie Robinson courageously broke the color line. The Professional Golfers Association had a Caucasians-only clause in its bylaws until as late as 1961 and black golf players, like black baseball players before them, generally played on their own circuit. As a result, we will never know how superb golfers such as Teddy Rhodes and extremely talented base-ball players such as LeRoy "Satchel" Paige and "Cool Papa" Bell would have fared, had they been able to compete in their primes against the top white players of their day.

Outside the United States, major soccer matches have been tainted by racist and more recently anti-Semitic chants by spectators, and even some racist taunts by players. Thus, as widely reported, spectators at a Dutch soccer game yelled out such slurs as "Jews burn the best" and "Hamas, Hamas, Jews to the gas."[2] While playing in Poland, a Nigerian player was pelted with bananas by unruly fans. Similarly, in a 2014 match between Barcelona and Villareal in Spain, a banana landed in front of Brazilian player Dani Alves, who picked it up, took a bite, and reportedly remarked that he was grateful for the extra potassium. Many other top players took Alves's side, eating bananas and posting pictures of themselves under the slogan, "We are all monkeys."

In addition to race, there also are issues of gender equity in sport. Prior to the passage of Title IX in the United States, although there were professional leagues for women in tennis and golf, women and girls were virtually excluded from participation in most high school and intercollegiate sports.

The claim that sports can be as meaningful to women as men probably needs no defense today, but an anecdote from the early twentieth century may illustrate the point. My Aunt Sally lived well into her 90s, but as she finally lost memory after memory to dementia, one that remained was of playing girls basketball on the Lower East Side of Manhattan during her years in high school. At that time, girls were considered too delicate to play the full-court game they play today, so one group played only on offense and another stayed on the other side of the court and played only defense. But on several occasions before she died, even though she couldn't remember many details of her life such as where she worked, she would tell me, "I wish I had had a chance to play offense."

Despite the formal and informal exclusion of women from most competitive sports in the United States through much of the twentieth century, outstanding female athletes made their mark. These included Althea Gibson in tennis, Wilma Rudolph in track and field, and Babe Zaharias in golf, a player who was so skilled she sometimes competed against men on the PGA Tour as well as on the LPGA, the women's circuit. However, the overall picture was that sports was a male-dominated practice, with exceptions in some sports regarded as "feminine," such as tennis, swimming, and golf.

Racial segregation in sports and gender-based exclusion from sports pose a problem not only to the philosophy of mutualism we discussed earlier but also to the very ideal of striving for excellence. Even when we consider these practices within the context of the ideal practices of the sports themselves, they are objectionable in that they eliminate worthy opponents from the field. It should go without saying that discrimination based on race and gender—and this also goes for religion, sexual orientation, social class, and other characteristics—is unjust for fundamental moral reasons, perhaps most important for demeaning other human beings who are persons in their own right and so should be treated with respect. The ethics that, as we have discussed, are intrinsic to sport reinforce this argument against discrimination of all stripes; people should be evaluated by their contributions to an endeavor rather than by characteristics irrelevant to their very nature as persons—as human beings equally and inherently deserving of respect and concern.

In any case, let's pursue this theme of equality in sport further, starting with issues raised by the major piece of legislation affecting gender equity in the United States, Title IX and its consequences.

### What is Title IX and what moral issues arise with its implementation?

Title IX is a section of the Educational Amendments, legislation passed by Congress in 1972. It states that "no person shall, on the basis of sex, be excluded from participation in, be denied the benefits of, be treated differently from another person or otherwise be discriminated against in any interscholastic, intercollegiate, club or intramural program offered by a recipient" of government financial support. After its passage, there were controversies over such issues as whether the legislation applied to only to a specific program within an educational institution that directly received support from the government, such as the Biology Department, or to the whole institution, and whether individuals could sue for redress or only the relevant government agencies could pursue investigations into charges of discrimination.

Despite lack of clarity about these issues, the impact of Title IX was swift and significant. For example, in the academic year 1970–1971, only 300,000 girls participated in interscholastic sports compared to nearly 4 million boys. But by 1978–1979, over 2 million girls were participating in high school sports, a number that has increased even more since. In 2013–2014, over 3,267,000 girls participated in high school sports, the 26th straight year participation of females increased, and a record 4.5 million boys participated as well.

Moreover, many of the ambiguities in the law were clarified over time. The Supreme Court, in *Grove City v. Bell* (1984), ruled that Title IX applied only to those programs within educational institutions that directly received federal funds. However, the Civil Rights Restoration Act passed by Congress a few years later clarified the original legislation, mandating that Title IX applied to the entire institution, making clear that Title IX applied to athletic programs that normally do not receive government aid.

In 1990, the Office of Civil Rights of the US Department of Justice issued important guidelines for determining whether an institution actually complied with Title IX. Perhaps the most important aspect of the guidelines became known as the three-part test. According to this test, an institution is in compliance if it meets any of the three criteria paraphrased as follows:

1. The proportion of athletes of each gender is virtually the same as the proportion of each gender in the student body as a whole.
2. There is a history of expansion of opportunities for the underrepresented gender; that is, adding sports teams for the gender that had lesser opportunities for participation in the past.
3. The interests and abilities of the underrepresented gender are "fully and effectively accommodated" by the existing program.

It is important to remember that an institution need only satisfy any one of the three prongs to be in compliance, a point sometimes forgotten by critics of Title IX.

In 1992, a unanimous Supreme Court ruled that individuals who successfully filed suit under Title IX were entitled to punitive damages, adding teeth to the existing legislation.

Title IX raises a number of ethical issues. We will consider two of the principal objections raised by critics. First, the critics argue that the proportionality requirement amounts to a quota that favors women. A consequence of this, they argue, is that the easiest way to meet the quota is not to add opportunities for women but to eliminate them for men. Second, some theorists argue that the widely implemented "separate but equal" model of women's sports, allowed and perhaps encouraged by Title IX, dooms women's sports to inferior status. Separate but equal, in the critic's view, is no more acceptable when applied to gender than it was when it was applied to race in the United States before the civil rights movement. Let us consider each of these criticisms in turn.

### Does the proportionality requirement of Title IX establish a quota for women sports?

The proportionality prong of the three-part test does establish a numerical standard. For example, if in University X, 60% of the students are male and 40% female, just about 40% of the athletes also should be female. There is room for small variation from year to year, but the proportions must be almost the same as in the student body as a whole.

Is this a quota? The meaning of "quota" is itself unclear, but note that an institution need not satisfy the proportionality requirement to comply with Title IX. It can satisfy one of the other two prongs instead. So if a quota is a numerical target that must be met, proportionality is not a quota.

Some have argued that proportionality uses the wrong numerical standard. In a case in which the proportionality prong was challenged, Brown University argued that women ought to be represented in a university's athletic program, not in proportion to the overall proportion of females in the general student body, but in comparison to those interested in participating in athletics.[3] In effect, the argument postulated that women might be less interested in participating in athletics than men, and so expecting the proportion of women athletes to mirror the proportion of women in the student body was not only unrealistic but also unfair.

Proponents of the claim that women are less interested than men in participating in competitive athletics might point out that in one recent survey conducted by the National Federation of High Schools Association in the academic year 2006–2007, while the number of female participants in high school sports broke the 3 million mark for the first time, over 4 million males participated as well. If fewer females than males are participating in high school sports, doesn't that demonstrate less interest in participation by females?

The court in the Brown University case rejected the claim that women are less interested in participation than men as a basis for overriding the proportionality requirement. I suggest that we should view this claim about a disproportional interest in sports between men and women with suspicion as well. We have to keep in mind that women were discouraged from participation in many forms of athletics for a long period of time in the United States, and as a result girls may still not receive the same encouragement as boys do to participate in athletics. Because young women still, decades after the passage of Title IX, form their preferences with regard to sports in the wake of longstanding discrimination that has resulted in an ongoing if subtle and even unintended discouragement, these preferences cannot be considered fixed and should not be taken at face value. With any luck, in time, as society—parents, the media, schools—fosters conditions that encourage more young women to pursue sports, more and more will feel empowered to participate in them.

This is not idle—or idealistic—speculation; females' interest in participating in athletics has increased since the passage of Title IX. Moreover, even if it turns out that women do have somewhat less interest in participating in sports, it is much too early, as the court indicated, to take present preferences, which themselves may be the result of past exclusion, at face value.

Moreover, there is a dynamic interplay of cause and effect between promotion of opportunities for women in sport and participation in women's sports. That relationship between promotion and participation is likely to help to bring more gender balance to sports. For example, as an increasing number of sports fans follow women's intercollegiate softball, due undoubtedly to increases in the skill of the players and significantly enhanced television coverage of the Division I NCAA Championship, we are likely to see an uptick in participation at less elite levels in which the game is played. To take another example, women who have not played at the varsity level in secondary levels may be drawn to certain sports that were not offered or not as attractive to them at the secondary level once they are in college. Thus, once in college, women may be attracted to sports such as rowing and cross country, where at least at many smaller institutions that compete at less athletically elite levels of intercollegiate sport, rosters are not limited and there is room for less experienced athletes to join a team and compete.

All this suggests that if sufficient opportunities are offered, women will take advantage of them. Thus, the criticisms considered so far do not undermine the requirement of proportionality. As the court in the Brown case reasoned, it is just too soon after the passage of Title IX and the growth of opportunities for women to simply assume that any differences between the genders in participation in sport are fixed or to be taken as evidence that women are less interested in playing than men.

### Doesn't proportionality lead to the elimination of men's sports, often without increasing opportunities for women? Is that fair?

It is true that since the implementation of Title IX, there have been significant cuts in intercollegiate teams for men. Universities have all too frequently eliminated lower profile men's sports, such as gymnastics, swimming, track and field, and more than 150 wrestling programs, allegedly in an attempt to satisfy the proportionality requirement. Moreover, such cuts do not necessarily result in the addition of opportunities for women. Some schools may have deigned it more worthwhile to reduce the number of male athletes in a given sport—or cut the sport in question altogether—than raise the number of spots for women to even out with those for men. For example, if our hypothetical University X has a ratio of 50% males and 50% females in the student body but has 500 male athletes and only 400 females, it can satisfy proportionality by cutting 100 slots for men, which also would be much less costly than adding 100 slots for women.

However, proportionality may not necessarily be to blame for such cuts. Instead, unwillingness to ask for reasonable cuts in men's high-profile and sometimes revenue-producing programs, which perhaps already receive too many of overall funds allocated to athletics at a given institution, may be more to blame. For example, if big-time football programs cut one game per season, or restricted long-distance travel to away games, or reduced the size of their rosters or their enormous recruiting budgets, the savings could be used to help pay for additional women's teams without requiring elimination of any men's programs.

Even more important, institutions can comply with Title IX without satisfying the proportionality test. As we have seen, they can demonstrate a history of expanding the women's program or, more likely, show that they "fully and effectively" accommodate the interests of their student body, thus satisfying either of the other two criteria—only one of which, remember, they need to meet in order to comply

It does seem true, however, that the proportionality requirement can create an incentive for cutting men's teams without adding teams for women. Such a strategy seems to contradict the spirit of Title IX, however, which surely was intended to increase athletic opportunities for females.

Perhaps existing legislation should be amended to place a burden of proof on institutions that cut men's teams, and which do not otherwise comply with Title IX, to make a reasonable case that other options for promoting women's athletics such as transferring funds from high-visibility men's sports are not feasible.

Nancy Hogshead-Makar, a former Olympic Gold Medalist swimmer, and attorney for the Women's Sport Foundation, argues that cutting men's teams may not be unjust just as it is hardly unjust when, by necessity, parents pay less attention to their first child once the next child is born.[4] However, as I've argued elsewhere, the analogy does not always apply to the cutting of men's sports teams. The new baby is actually getting attention that previously went to the only child, but resources saved from cutting men's teams do not always go to add opportunities for women.

In any case, although the proportionality requirement does raise some troubling issues, it sets an important benchmark that institutions should try to meet. The objections to it can be mitigated, I suggest, if it is made significantly more difficult to comply simply by eliminating opportunities for men without adding any for women.

*High schools and colleges generally have separate teams for men and women in most intercollegiate sports. Does this philosophy of separate but equal doom women's sports to permanent inferiority? Are major sports such as soccer, basketball, football, and hockey male biased because they favor strength, height, and body mass?*

Although the separation of men's and women's sports has become the default method of achieving equality, critics argue that as in the case of racial segregation, separate is inherently unequal. According to these critics, male sports will be regarded as superior because at similar levels of competition, males perform at a superior level. Some of these critics regard popular major sports as male biased because they favor strength and power. Because women generally are smaller and less strong than men at the same level of play, the best athletes in these popular sports almost always will be male.

Let's consider these points in turn, beginning with the analogy between racial segregation and the provision of separate sports teams for each gender. There is an important difference between the two practices that puts them on a radically different ethical footing. That is, racial segregation was imposed by a powerful group on a relatively powerless one against their will, was designed to limit the opportunities of the victims, and expressed prejudice, contempt, and hatred for them. In contrast, the provision of separate sports programs for men and women is designed to increase opportunities for women, is not imposed on them against their will, and does not express prejudice, hatred, and contempt for women. Rather, so the argument goes, the split between men's and women's sports recognizes physiological differences between men and women and provides opportunities for women to compete that would be absent if they had to struggle for places on a team roster by competing against bigger and stronger males.[5] (This point would not apply to sports where men lacked a physiological advantage, such as riflery and some equestrian events. Perhaps such sports should not provide separate competitions for men and women.)

Is this reply decisive? Two sorts of responses might be made to it. One might say that, in the interest of equality, we ought to develop or more effectively promote sports in which males are not physiologically advantaged.[6] These might include gymnastics, figure skating, equestrian events, or the creation of new sports that emphasize traits such as agility, grace, and flexibility rather than strength and power. Although this suggestion has merit, some caveats need to be kept in mind. First, such sports may prove to not be as popular as currently very popular sports like soccer, lacrosse, and basketball with young women who are prospective athletes. Although exposing young people to a variety of sports is a good idea, it doesn't follow that already popular sports will become less so as a result.

Second, and more important, I suggest we question the assumption that women's sports are inferior to men's sports simply because the men's team normally would beat the women's team at the same level of competition.

Women's sports often have a different style and require different strategies that make them equally interesting to knowledgeable spectators. Women's basketball, for example, may emphasize setting screens for teammates and passing to the open shooter, whereas men's basketball may emphasize athleticism to different extents but each can be equally interesting. I myself would just as soon watch the outstanding University of Connecticut women's basketball team because of the beauty of their style of play as watch many professional games in the NBA. Similarly golf fans probably can learn as much by studying the swings of top female players on the LPGA Tour as they can by watching the somewhat more powerful but sometimes less efficient swings of stronger male players. It is arguably not a matter of the male or the female sports being superior but of learning to appreciate the best qualities of each.

Moreover, mutualism, as we discussed in Chapter 1, emphasizes the role of challenge in sport and the interest in seeing who best responds to it. Thus, a highly competitive high school girl's playoff game in front of screaming local fans can be just as competitive and as interesting as a late-season professional game between weak teams, whose fans are unenthusiastic, and in which neither has a shot at winning a championship.

Critics might respond that women normally are not the best in their sport. The top women athletes, even though they are far superior to almost all male athletes, are not as good as the very top males in their sport. The epitome of basketball excellence is found in the NBA championship, soccer excellence in the men's World Cup, or on a top Olympic men's team, or in the men's Final Four of the NCAA Division I playoffs. Or so the argument goes.

If that argument is sound, the only true way for women to earn equality is to compete with men and get better through testing themselves against the best. Thus, I believe that golf star Michelle Wie was right to test herself when she still was a teenager by trying to play on the men's tour. Even if her efforts were by some standards not successful (and subjected her to considerable criticism), they pushed the limits for women and perhaps enabled her to grow into the sort of player who later would go on to win the Women's U.S. Open in 2014.

There is a strong case, I suggest, that men's sports should be open to women who qualify and who want to compete, although we also need to take into account that if many top women gravitate to men's sports, the overall level of competition for women's sports would drop as a result. Moreover, men and women can compete equally in sports where there is no significant gender bias.

However, I suggest that the best egalitarian strategy in this area is to better educate fans, and perhaps some athletes themselves, to better appreciate the nuances of the women's game. In fact, the achievements of women athletes may already be appreciated equally to those of men by fans in some sports. Tennis fans, for example, seem to admire the more extensive volleying in the women's game at least as much as the more powerful serves in the men's game. Female stars, such as the Williams sisters, play for prize money similar to those on the men's tour.

On this view, women's sports are subtly different from their male counterparts, but the difference does not imply inferiority. The *pluralist* strategy of promoting separate sports programs for men and women not only creates much greater opportunities for women athletes than would be the case if we assimilated the two and women had to compete directly with men, it also creates the opportunity to appreciate nuanced difference in the ways in which athletes pursue a mutual quest for excellence.

The pluralist approach does not deny that sports biased toward female body characteristics ought to be supported and more such sports developed. It does deny that just because men at comparable levels of competition are bigger and more powerful than women that men's sports therefore are better: both men and women are engaged in the attempt to meet the challenges of their sport. Shouldn't we aim to appreciate the subtle differences in their approaches to sports and to appreciate them equally?

### Have sports been progressive with respect to promoting racial equality and respect?

Although a question this general does not admit of any broad yes or no answer, it is valuable nevertheless because it allows us to disentangle a number of lines of inquiry that are worth exploring. For one thing, there have been many major events in sports that have helped advance the cause of equality for African Americans. The outstanding performance of the African American athlete Jesse Owens at the 1936 Olympics held in Berlin, where he won four gold medals, provided an obvious rebuttal to the vicious racist theories advanced by Hitler and the Nazis and their myth of "Aryan" superiority. Jackie Robinson's breaking the color line in Major League Baseball in 1947 was transformative in many ways in advancing the cause of civil rights in America. The success of so many black athletes today contributes to the view that sports provide a level field. Prominent social scientist James Q. Wilson, as we already noted, cites sports teams as one of the few institutions in America where significant ties of trust and cooperation emerge regularly across racial boundaries.[7]

However, there is another side of the picture.[8] When John Carlos and Tommie Smith, two African American athletes, gave the Black Power salute during their medal ceremony to call attention to racial injustice and segregation in the United States and South Africa, they were widely criticized for bringing politics into sport and for their apparent endorsement of what was regarded as a radical group. Black golfers such as Charles Sifford were the victims of racially based harassment, taunts, and even threats when they first broke the color line on the Professional Golf Association Tour, but they did pave the way for the success of one the greatest golfers of all time, Tiger Woods.

Today, the lack of black coaches and administrators in some professional sports leagues, including the NFL, remains a point of significant concern. Racist chants and taunts at soccer games in many countries continue to be, as we have seen, a major problem. In 2014, Donald Sterling, then the owner of the professional basketball team the Los Angeles Clippers, was banned from the NBA for life by Commissioner Adam Silver for making racist comments that were caught on tape. Sterling's remarks were especially surprising and disturbing because the NBA players are disproportionately athletes of color.

We have also explored in Chapter 5 the claim that scholarship athletes in elite Division I intercollegiate programs, a disproportionate number of whom are black, are exploited, or at least treated unfairly, when they do not share in the financial rewards such athletic programs sometimes produce. However, I suggested we should not fully endorse this claim by arguing that its force depends upon whether these athletes are given or are denied a genuine chance to acquire a solid college education.

Some writers have argued that the success of African American athletes actually has actually harmed the black community by exalting success on the playing field over success in the classroom. In addition, some have argued that portraying African Americans as successful through athletics has effectively reaffirmed stereotypes that hold that black people are primarily physical rather than intellectual beings.[9]

When we emphasize athletic success and fail to integrate academics and athletics, as I have argued that we must do, we can end up neglecting the education of our athletes. This can be especially true for poorly funded schools, whose students sometimes lack adequate parental guidance and are especially vulnerable to peer pressure. In such circumstances, young people may rightly or wrongly view athletics as one of the very few routes to future success. On the other hand, if schools make a robust attempt to harmonize athletics and academics, participation in sports can be an extremely useful tool promoting success in the classroom as well as on the field, as we saw earlier.

Moreover, we ought to question the supposed dualism between physicality and intellectuality—between expression through the body and through the mind. In particular, although sports are games of physical skill, that does not imply they are *only* games of physical skill. As we have seen in our earlier discussion, success in sports requires the use of complex strategies, including making intelligent decisions, and the exercise of such virtues as dedication, coolness under pressure, and the willingness to learn from criticism and improve as a result. Thus, the distinction between physicality and intellectuality may be too sharply drawn to reflect what actually goes on in competitive athletics. The claim that black athletes excel because their race tends to have more physical skills than intellectual ones is nonsense for this reason, among others.

Finally, black athletes such as Olympic star Wilma Rudolph, boxer Muhammed Ali, Major League Baseball players Jackie Robinson and recently Ernie Banks, and Tim Duncan of the NBA, to name just a very few individuals out of the many that might have been selected, have been role models in a way that transcends athletics and exemplify moral virtues from which we all can benefit.

This sketch suggests that although there have been important progressive steps toward racial equality taken through sports, racial animosity and prejudice have not been absent from the world of sports. But even though the history of modern sport may present a mixed picture of racial progress, and the significance of sport for racial equality is debatable, the ethics of athletic competition points toward inclusion and equality, not exclusion or racial discrimination.

Athletes engaged in a quest for excellence should want to play against worthy opponents and with highly skilled teammates, so as to generate the best challenges for all involved in a contest. Excluding some athletes because of athletically irrelevant qualities such as race violates this principle.

This point indicates that the ethics of sport are not isolated or in a different moral universe from more general ethical principles. Mutualism, for example, rests on broader moral principles, such as respect for persons as fellow competitors and overall fairness in competition. Perhaps our discussion shows just how such values can apply in competitive sports.

### Should team nicknames, such as Washington Redskins, Cleveland Indians, and Notre Dame Fighting Irish, be changed to avoid the use of racist slurs in sports?

This issue has become quite controversial, with the use of "Redskins" being at the center of the controversy. Many regard the term as a racial slur, tracing its use back to wars with the Indians, the practice of scalping, and the demonization of them for a long period of American history. Some scholars, on the other hand, find a more benign origin to the use of the term, citing that is was used by Indians themselves as well as by whites.[10]

In any case, one side, including many Indian groups, sees the nickname as a slur directed against them, while perhaps the majority of Washington fans defend it as a way of honoring Indians as well as on grounds of the traditions associated with the team. Owner Dan Snyder has vowed never to change it.

Whatever the origins of the term "Redskins," it not only is regarded as a slur by many Indians who face significant discrimination in some areas of the country and who bear the burden of a fraught past of oppression and horrendous violence, which this terms conjures up.[11] Indeed, dictionaries refer to the term as offensive. I would ask how readers of this book would feel if a way of referring to a group to which they belonged and which they regarded as insulting was used as a nickname for a sports team. In addition, many of the symbols used by team mascots such as feathers and drums were used in Native American religious ceremonies. Again, would each of us want our own religious symbols or icons used for cheering at sports events?

In any case, I suggest the use of derogatory terms such as "Redskins" is particularly questionable from the moral point of view. I don't deny that sometimes a nickname, like Notre Dame University's nickname of the "Fighting Irish," can be transformed from a slur (its original use may have been to express prejudice against the Irish by implying they were drunken brawlers) to what is now arguably a source of pride. But that surely is not the case with "Redskins."

Other nicknames like the Cleveland Indians and Kansas City Chiefs also single out Native Americans but arguably do not have the derogatory associations called up by the use of "Redskins." Nevertheless, this kind of cultural appropriation raises moral issues separate from those that surround the use of a slur or derogatory term. Although political correctness can lead us astray at times, I nevertheless suggest that we ought to question the ethics of powerful majorities offending minorities by using slogans, nicknames, and chants that are not only offensive to the groups they may stereotype (say by portraying Indians as especially warlike, for example, through the use of "the Tomahawk Chop" as a cheer) but which also may encourage discrimination against group members as well.[12]

We have seen that one of the key values underlying an ethical approach to competitive sports is respect for persons as worthy opponents and fellow competitors but also as people like ourselves who have a justifiable claim to be treated fairly and respectfully. We need to ask ourselves if dominant majorities comply with such norms by treating those in more vulnerable positions in ways they regard as not only disrespectful but which also may demonstrate prejudice by relying on offensive stereotypes of others.

### Has elite sport been turned into a commodity, and has this harmed the integrity of the game?

Elite sports, especially at the professional level, entertain millions of fans and have become big business as a result. Professional franchises sometimes are valued in the hundreds of millions of dollars or even more, and salaries of players and coaches have skyrocketed into the millions. Even at the intercollegiate level, the NCAA Division I men's basketball tournament is one of the prime sporting events of the year in the United States with enormous numbers of fans not only watching but also participating in contests to pick the winners, ranging from office pools to online competition. College football bowl games are big business for the institutions involved and for the communities in which they are held, and NFL games, especially the Super Bowl, are major events on the American sporting schedule. In the United Kingdom, the Premier League, the major league of soccer there, is a major enterprise where players are paid huge sums, receive large fees to endorse various products, and teams bring in revenue not only from ticket sales but from sales of merchandise and the media. The Premier League is the most-watched football (soccer) league in the world, and it is said to be broadcast to over 600 million homes and a potential TV audience of 4 billion people.[13] In effect, big-time sports have become a commodity to be marketed and to be pursued for profit. Is this development a good or bad thing for sports?

The Harvard philosopher Michael Sandel has written eloquently about the dangers of extending the marketplace too far, of what we can call "commodification."[14] He argues that when certain goods are given a monetary value and sold on the market to the highest bidder, their social significance or meaning changes, often for the worse and to the detriment of our communal life.

Let's first consider an example outside of sports. In the United States today, seriously ill people in need of a kidney in order to survive must hope that a compatible donor is willing to voluntarily donate a kidney. Although healthy individuals have two kidneys and can live an active and healthy life with only one, the supply of kidneys available for transplant is far less than the number of patients who need a kidney transplant to survive.

One proposal to remedy this shortage is to establish a system through which potential donors can sell their kidneys to willing buyers on the open market. The argument in defense of this proposal primarily is utilitarian; namely, both parties will benefit from the transaction. The buyer would rather pay the price and have the kidney than not do so, and the seller would rather have the money than the normally redundant kidney.

Although such a proposal is attractive, and may be justified, all things considered, it faces serious objections as well. One is based on fairness and distributive justice. The wealthy would be able to outbid others for the desperately needed kidneys, whereas those with the most incentive to sell would be the poor. According to critics, the poor would constitute a class of organ donors, in effect an organ farm, for the wealthy. There may be ways to modify the proposal to sell kidneys on the market to avoid this criticism, perhaps by providing government subsidies or charitable donations that would enable the less affluent to purchase kidneys. However, let us turn to a different kind of criticism that reflects concern about how the market corrupts the social significance of ethically meaningful actions.

At present, the act of donating a kidney is one which requires compassion for the plight of another, which requires courage, and which binds us together as members of a common community in which mutual assistance is a recognized social norm. A market in kidneys, one may argue, would transform this, turning kidney donation into the pursuit of personal gain. Indeed, in a world where the selling of life-saving organs on the market was the social norm, donors might be looked at as dupes or "marks" who allow themselves to be taken advantage of by others, rather than as compassionate members of a caring community. In such a world where profit reigns beyond its proper bounds, the ethical significance of kidney donations would be corrupted beyond recognition.

Readers may be wondering how this applies to sports. When big time-sports become a business regulated by market norms rather than internal ones, such as a quest for excellence, its internal values are at risk of being undermined or lost. Let's consider some examples.

Basketball at its best is a game of constant movement in which the physical conditioning of the players is crucial to success. However, the addition of "TV time-outs," frequent breaks in the action of televised games to allow for advertisements on the media, not only breaks the momentum of the contest but devalues the efforts of well-conditioned players who do not need such breaks, thus changing the very strategy of the contest.

Sandel himself cites the example of changing the names of major sports stadiums from ones that specify a city or a team or honor an individual to ones that showcase (and advertise) corporate involvement in sport. In addition, ticket prices often are raised for postseason championships. This practice not only prices many loyal fans out of the market but also may lead to different and less enthusiastic or knowledgeable fans attending the big event, changing the crowd dynamic and the atmosphere at the game.

Elite, highly visible college sports also are affected as institutions forsake traditional rivalries to join super conferences or leagues in which the teams compete against each other to determine the championship of the group. Super conferences, made up of the most elite competitors with national followings can generate more money from television and secure more visibility for their teams than available to leagues composed of a mixture of teams at different levels of skill and attractiveness to large audiences. However, the formation of these super conferences, sometimes national in scope, leaves less space on the schedule for traditional rivalries or competition with local institutions that are of special interest to both players and fans in the area in which they might take place.

The danger, of course, is that as sports are regarded more and more as a business or as entertainment, central values crucial to good sports may be lost or eroded. Games can be "dumbed down" to be made more understandable to fans and generate more entertainment value. Perhaps an example is the addition of the designated hitter in Major League Baseball, a player who only bats and never plays the field on defense. This designated hitter often replaces pitchers, who are not normally effective batters, in an attempt to generate more offense and please fans who may want to see high-scoring games. This rule allows for more scoring and more home runs, but it makes the game less nuanced by taking away strategic choices, such as whether to remove the pitcher from the game by allowing a pinch hitter, a one-time substitute batter, to enter the game. At worst, sports might become more and more like professional wrestling, where the contest might be replaced by an entertaining script written in advance of actual play. I myself recently attended a professional basketball game and was dismayed by how much the spectacle of loud announcers, blaring music played during the action of the game, giant screens showing advertising or the fans themselves as much as play, eclipsed the actual action on the court. More important, television and the Internet have made sports almost omnipresent in our lives. If fans want to see a major sports contest, they normally can find a way to see or follow live action on some form of media. Fantasy sports, often a form of gambling, has become a multi-million-dollar industry, allowing fans to become even more involved in sports by selecting plays for their fantasy teams and winning or losing according to how their teams perform. Critics argue that even apart from greater opportunities the media have supplied for gambling, they also have eclipsed the idea of sports as a mutual quest for excellence, with the pursuit of profit.

**What are the benefits of commercialization of sports, particularly the high visibility of elite sports on mass media?**

Markets have many virtues. Not only are they efficient in many circumstances, but they also respect the choices of individuals by allowing individuals to allocate their resources or income as they themselves see fit. However, it is not so much the market itself to which critics of the commercialization of sports object. Rather, as we have seen, it is its extension to goods that should be exempt from market valuation.

Critics of the commercialization certainly have a point when they warn of the dangers of turning sport into pure entertainment where the major or sole aim of sports franchises is to make a profit. However, the commercialization of sport also has been beneficial in a variety of ways. For one thing, the media have made prominent sporting events available to a mass audience in ways that were unknown as late as the 1950s and 1960s. For example, when I was growing up, if one did not live near the home of a Major League Baseball team, one had to travel hundreds of miles to see a game or try to pick up radio broadcasts of contests as best one could. Now, games in virtually all major sports are available on television, and fantasy sports leagues have become a major business.

In addition, games are not only widely available on television, but some of the changes of the rules in major sports not only make the game more entertaining but also a better game as well. That is, making the game sell better sometimes makes it a better game as well. The introduction of the shot clock in basketball, which limits the time the team on offense can hold the ball without shooting, not only leads to a faster paced game by preventing stalling but also requires teams to test all their skills rather than just holding the ball once they get a lead. Similarly, although the designated hitter rule in Major League Baseball has been criticized for making the game less nuanced, it can be defended as eliminating the normally uninteresting spectacle of a weak hitting pitcher being overmatched by a skilled pitcher.

Moreover, as a number of observers have noted, sports can be viewed as a moral laboratory, or at least a public venue in which moral issues emerge for our consideration. Media coverage of high-visibility sports, in other words, puts moral issues right into the public eye. The framework of sport allows for debate on contentious issues in a less polemical way than is the case with hot-button issues in the political realm.

For example, the Deflategate scandal in the NFL has helped to clarify the distinction between cheating and gamesmanship. The former, as we have already seen, implies arbitrary violation of a public system of norms to obtain a competitive advantage, whereas the latter normally involves an attempt to test the mental toughness or focus of the opponent by acts that do not violate rules or principles applying to the sport. Regardless of whether the illegal deflation of the footballs used by the Patriots in a playoff game was intentional, and regardless of the degree to which star quarterback Tom Brady was involved, if he was involved at all, interest in the case brought issues of integrity and sportsmanship into the public eye.

*How can we preserve the upside of commodifying sports
while minimizing the dangers of corruption raised by the critics?*

Although it will be difficult for sports, on the whole, to reap
the benefits of becoming more and more market driven and
massively promoted through a wide range of media while also
preserving the ethics that make sports so valuable, we might
be able to find a way forward that maintains such a balance.
This will depend on sports authorities, such as the commis-
sioners of professional leagues, the NCAA, the IOC, and the
governing bodies of such sports as golf, to name just a few.
They have a special function of preserving the integrity of the
sports they regulate.

Competitors in elite sport ranging from individuals to
teams have an incentive to pursue victory and the financial
and personal rewards that go with it by any means they are
permitted to put to use. Just as Hobbes thought we needed
a sovereign to control the war of all against all in the state of
nature, sports authorities need to control the struggle for competitive success to ensure that the challenge of the sport is preserved. That is why, in golf, the United States Golf Association
and the Royal and Ancient, the two organizations that set the
global standards for the game, regulate equipment by rigorously testing the effect of technological innovations on play.
Similarly, in other sports, equipment that significantly reduces
the challenge of the sport, such as the full-body swim polyurethane and neoprene suits that gave swimmers such a boost in
2008 through 2009, was banned by the appropriate governing
bodies as of 2010.

Sports authorities then have a fiduciary role in protecting
the integrity of their sport. That is one major reason why the
charges of extensive corruption brought in 2015 against top
officials of FIFA by the US Department of Justice and Swiss
authorities are so disturbing. If these allegations are true, the
officials charged were more concerned with lining their own
pockets than protecting "the beautiful game" and helping it
flourish.

In any case, the governing bodies of major sports have an ethical responsibility to preserve their sport from excessive commercialization that dilutes the very game they also are trying to market to a mass audience. For example, the commissioner of the NBA might consider some reduction in the number of games played in the regular season in an effort to reduce overuse injuries to the players. Similarly, although hard fouls that risk injury to opponents may be entertaining to some in the audience at NBA games, perhaps further changes in the rules in order to provide the players with more opportunity to exhibit their artistry and their athleticism would be both good business and good for the game as well. The commercialization of sports, then, has benefits as well as costs.

Although sports often are entertaining for participants and spectators alike, they should not be reduced to mere entertainment. Rather, it is because they have integrity and an inner core of values of their own that they have the capacity to fascinate in the first place.

### Should athletes be role models?

The commercialization of sport has enhanced its value as entertainment. The availability of major sports on various media makes many top athletes household names. Although admiration for top athletes is hardly a new phenomenon, and was present in ancient Greece as recounted in Homer's *Iliad*, the media have brought top performers in competitive sport into our homes and in such contests as the Olympic Games and the World Cup to a worldwide audience. Although top athletes in ancient Greece, such as Achilles, were regarded as exemplars of important virtues, do today's top athletes have duties or moral obligations that are magnified by their fame and fortune? Are elite athletes of today merely entertainers, should they also accept special moral responsibilities arising from their status, and if so what does athletic performance have to do with ethical responsibility?

Former NBA star and now broadcaster Charles Barkley famously asserted, "I am not a role model ... Just because I can dunk a basketball doesn't mean I should raise your kids." As we have seen, however, sports are inherently value laden, even though they need not intersect with partisan values. So, then, what are the implications for the social obligations of athletes themselves?

Jokingly, but also to make a point, Barkley conflates two separate issues. Just because one is a role model does not imply one also has responsibilities for raising other people's children. In particular, one might be a role model in different respects. Thus, a scientist might be a good role model for how to conduct inquiry, if he or she weighs evidence fairly and judiciously and does not leap to conclusions, but may not be a role model in other areas, such as how be a good parent. Moreover, the judicious scientist might be a good role model for students but perhaps not for those who have to make immediate decisions based on minimal evidence in emergencies. So being a role model involves three variables: the individuals who are models, the group for whom they are models, and the respect or characteristic that they model. The scientist in the aforementioned example models fairness and judiciousness in evaluating evidence for students or others who engage in sustained research and critical inquiry. Similarly, teachers in the classroom can model for their students how to debate controversial topics in a civil but forceful way, without demonizing opponents.

When we ask whether athletes are or should be role models, we need to specify the group they should be models for and the respect in which they should be emulated. To keep our discussion within bounds, let's focus on whether athletes should be models for children and younger athletes in how they conduct themselves in competition. This does not involve them functioning as all-around exemplars on how children should lead their lives, as Barkley suggests, but focuses only on their conduct as competitors.

Clearly, athletes can be bad role models if they conduct themselves poorly during play; for example, by fighting, openly criticizing and embarrassing teammates, and defying reasonable requests by coaches. Perhaps more important, they can undercut values central to athletics by cheating, by deliberately trying to injure opponents, and by engaging in particularly egregious acts of gamesmanship.

Rightly or wrongly, children and adolescents do look up to their favorite star athletes and try to emulate them. Part of what is so sad about Tom Brady's possible involvement in the Deflategate scandal is that, if true, it will let down the many young athletes who admire him; it would endorse the idea that it is all right to make yourself an arbitrary exception to the rules that apply to others or, in other words, to cheat. (Of course, Brady's supporters may with some plausibility regard him as innocent—and may be correct in their view.)

Accordingly, if we accept the idea that athletics is best conducted as something like a mutual quest for excellence, or at least not like a cutthroat Hobbesian war of all against all, athletes do have a special obligation to uphold the core values of their practice. Just as professors have a special duty to present evidence on controversial issues in their field fairly, even if they eventually take a stand on matters themselves, so athletes need to uphold values of fairness and respect for excellence and for the opponent.

It may be relatively uncontroversial to say athletes should be at least minimal role models on the field, protecting and applying basic norms of sportsmanship. It is much more questionable whether they have any special obligation to be role models off the field, which probably is what Charles Barkley was referring to when he claimed he was not a role model. Clearly, it is wrong for athletes to be abusive, commit crimes, or commit acts of violence against others. But do they have a duty to go above and beyond basic moral norms—in other words, do they need to be exceptional?

Clearly, any response to this question will be highly debatable. But perhaps an analogy may help focus our thinking and advance the discussion. Let's return to our judicious scientist who fairly evaluates and presents all sides of a scientifically debatable issue before coming to his own conclusions. Suppose, however, this scientist who is renowned and even has been rewarded for presenting debates on contentious issues with respect for all sides, acts the opposite way as a parent, spouse, or friend. That is, he thinks the worst of others on the flimsiest of evidence, is suspicious of family members on minimal grounds, and mercilessly heckles the officials at his children's basketball games, even though in fact he has very little understanding of the rules or strategies of basketball. He not only seems to be hypocritical but undercuts the very values of judiciousness and fairness that he supports professionally. Surely, he is guilty not only of a kind of moral schizophrenia but, more important, he is guilty of publically disrespecting values he himself regards as important and has every reason to support.

Athletes who abuse others, commit crimes, and otherwise behave badly are arguably in the same boat. As athletes, they should recognize the humanity of opponents and treat them as persons, and they should support compliance with the rules and principles that apply to their sport. Indeed, they themselves often have personally profited from exhibiting internal virtues of sport on the field, including exerting the effort to improve, remaining cool under pressure, and keeping their temper when reacting to provocation that would hurt their team, perhaps by resulting in their ejection from the contest.

If they are admired for exhibiting such traits on the field, doesn't that imply a special responsibility to exhibit them off the field as well?

Perhaps something like the following principle deserves consideration: namely, if one exhibits certain virtues in one context and personally gains as a result, one has a special obligation, all things being equal, to exhibit and support such virtues in other contexts as well.

How might this principle be supported? One suggestion is that if others, especially young people, emulate you partly as a result of your virtuous behavior on the field, and sometimes become better people themselves as a result, it is wrong to reject or undercut the very same values in different contexts when your behavior could undo the good it has done in inspiring those who look up to you. As in the case of the hypocritical scientist, such conflicting behavior calls your own commitment to those values into question. Young athletes might conclude from your off-the-field behavior that honorable acts on the field are just a façade and the real you, the one they should emulate, is not the individual who acts virtuously on the field but the one who acts badly off it. In other words, with special honor comes special responsibility.

Athletes who exemplify one set of values on the field and another set off it not only call their own personal commitment to those values into question but can undermine adherence to them by others as well. Perhaps, for example, the children of the scientist in our previous example come to believe that his judiciousness in the academy is only a façade adopted for personal advancement whereas the real value they should emulate is "my team, right or wrong."

Of course, this discussion is at best only a preliminary approach to a complex issue. It surely faces many objections. For example, if the argument applies both to the professor and the athlete, how does it establish that athletes as a group have a *special* obligation to be role models that does not also fall on others? Aren't commitment and dedication valued in virtually all forms of work, for example? A preliminary reply might be that athletes, although not unique in these respects, are in a special position, because of their visibility in the public eye and because their play illustrates or expresses core values of sport to such a large audience. In particular, elite athletes in major sports have profited by exposure through the media, by commercialization including the sale of sports apparel marketed under their name. But if they should be expected to show allegiance to such internal values of sport as respect for the opponent, concern with excellence, and dedication to improvement, arguably it would be objectionable for them to undercut adherence to such values by disrespecting others off the field and calling into question the very values they may exemplify during play.

Our discussion does not suggest that athletes are or should be regarded as substitute role models for parents, teachers, neighbors, and coaches. At most, it suggests that athletes often are regarded as and should act as role models, not that they are the most important role models for children or young people to have. A wise and loving parent, a dedicated cancer researcher, or an inspiring teacher may be and very well should be the key role models in the lives of young people. It does not follow, however, that athletes lack any moral responsibility at all in this area, or that their status as sports stars carries no moral responsibility at all with it.

*But are the core values of sport always morally sound? Isn't this assumption itself unwarranted, given all that in fact is wrong with sports, as much of your own discussion throughout this book indicates?*

These are great questions and fair ones. Perhaps the view of sports that emerges from our discussion is much too rosy and as a result is morally distorted. Let's do justice to it and examine it more fully in the concluding chapter.

# 7

# CONCLUDING COMMENT

## THE TWO SIDES OF THE FORCE, OR ARE SPORTS SO GREAT AFTER ALL?

*Are the core values of sport always morally good ones?*

The mutualist presents sports as ethically defensible and even as promoting human flourishing. Some wonder: doesn't this perspective ignore less attractive core values of sport that are not ethically defensible? These questions can be taken in two ways. First, they might be asking whether sports *as actually practiced* comply with ethical guidelines about how sport *should be* conducted, including those suggested by mutualism. It seems obvious that competitive sports often fail major ethical tests, as I hope our discussion has brought out. The pursuit of winning as the supreme goal of competition, the transformation of elite, high-visibility intercollegiate sport into a business, racism exhibited by spectators at major soccer contests, and issues of gender discrimination are just some of the problems that have and continue to plague contemporary sports at various levels of competition.

However, our discussion has sought to set out standards, which are claimed to be central to the ethical practice of sports. These standards, if complied with, constitute the elements of not only an ethically defensible conception of sports but a morally valuable one as well. Mutualism is one conception of how sports may be conducted ethically; perhaps critical discussion of the sort we have engaged in will lead to the defense or development of other perhaps even more morally favorable approaches. But is even this too rosy a view of sports? Is it easy to separate less morally attractive features of sport from the practice itself? Or, given standard features of human motivation, is it virtually impossible to do so? As one writer, John Russell, has noted, sports, rather than constituting only a mutual quest for excellence, also are a form of "ritualized physical conflict."[1] Russell argues further that motives such as dislike of the opponent and desire to be dominant often can contribute more to good performance than simply the duty to challenge one's opponent so that each competitor can perform at their best. He cites the remark of Leo Durocher, the manager of the New York Giants baseball team in the 1950s: "Nice guys finish last." For every good sport who wants opponents to play their best to create a challenge, there are others who just want to "kick butt" and win.

Russell even suggests that the kind of cooperation between opponents emphasized by mutualists, where competitors try their best to challenge their opponents to also do their best in a mutual quest for excellence, is morally suspect or at least not an exemplar of virtue as mutualists might claim. Such cooperation may be more like a temporary alliance for personal gain rather than a genuine moral bond between opponents.

This critique of mutualism suggests that there is an inherent conflict between the pursuit of excellence, on one hand, and moral values such as equity and sportsmanship, on the other. Russell himself expresses some ambiguity about how the conflict should be resolved, confessing that he might well trade off a bit of ethics for a much bigger dose of excellence. But is such a trade-off really necessary?

Let's begin our examination of this critique by considering cooperation between opponents who in effect agree to try their best to create a meaningful test of their abilities and promote the pursuit of excellence. Perhaps the agreement between athletes to cooperate in this way, even if they arrive at it voluntarily, is nevertheless only an alliance of convenience entered into only for personal (or team) advantage. Even if so, however, each athlete nevertheless is respecting the other's choice and each exercises personal autonomy in choosing. Thus, each is acting and being treated as a moral agent, an autonomous self, which is itself of moral significance.

Even more important, even if such agreements start out as mere alliances of convenience, athletes can and often do internalize the norms of the mutual pursuit of excellence. In other words, the agreements can develop moral status as the competitors themselves accept the ethics of fair competition.[2] Just as some students initially might not cheat on exams out of fear of getting caught but later do not cheat because they have internalized academic standards of excellence and intellectual honesty, so athletes as they develop may internalize core values of good sports. Thus, whereas some elements of cooperation among competitors in sport may arise only from agreements based on self-interest, that need not be the case as the competitors mature and come to endorse the ethics of good sports.

However, we cannot deny the claim that rivalry is central to the notion of athletic competition. Rivalries can often generate dislike and even hatred for opponents. Mutualists might suggest, however, that rivalries can be kept within moral boundaries if sports are taught in ways that reflect important principles, such as respect for opponents and recognition of excellence, even when exhibited by an opponent. An athlete can really want to win against a major rival without necessarily disliking or hating the opponents. Indeed, one may want to beat someone badly just because one respects the game. Indeed, one might want them to play their very best so one's victory over them becomes especially significant. Moreover, mutualism does not imply that athletes must always like, let alone be friends with, opponents. So long as they treat their opponents fairly and with respect, friendship, while it might be desirable, is not required.

Dislike and hatred for an opponent can be effective motivators, and perhaps too often are at work in sports. Nevertheless, they do not seem necessary to good competition and may even be less effective than the desire to be the best in the competition, even against competitors one actually likes. Hatred in particular seems alien to the mutualist ideal of sport; remember that what mutualism most requires is treating an opponent fairly and with respect as a fellow human being.

Just as the force in the movie *Star Wars* has two sides, one promoting good and the other evil, there may be values such as rivalry that when taken to extremes may undermine what I have suggested is an ethical approach to athletic competition. Rivalry kept within proper bounds, however, need not lead to hatred of the opponent; instead, it can lead to the intense desire to meet to challenge of playing an especially worthy fellow competitor. (Indeed, the Rules of Golf specifically refer to opponents as "*fellow* competitors.") If adherence to a defensible ethic of sports becomes widespread, perhaps the "dark side" of sports can be kept in much greater check than it is today.

### What do you regard as the main themes that emerge from the discussion of sports in this book?

We covered too much ground to summarize in any brief review, but I regard the following three themes (a somewhat arbitrary number) as especially important.

First is the rejection of the Hobbesian model of competition in sports as resembling a war of all against all, and its replacement by a revised understanding of athletic competition. My favored model is mutualism, the mutual quest for excellence through challenge, but other approaches that also recognize the personhood of all competitors and the virtues of meeting interesting challenges may emerge from further discussion.

Second is the idea that participation in sports, as well as watching and studying them, can have educational value. Despite some of the distortions in elite, highly visible intercollegiate athletics, a case can be made that Plato was on the right track in regarding athletics as having significant educational value.

Third, there is a core of values central to athletic competition when it is carried out ethically that coheres with broader ethical perspectives. This might be called an inner morality of sports.[3] The values in this core include respect for others as persons equal to ourselves and the importance of a fair framework to ensure that competition takes place on a level playing field. We have not fully implemented these ideals either in sport or in the broader society, but principles embedded in the best understanding of what athletic competition entails might provide support for such values not only in sport but also for implementing them in society as well.

Finally, because I am not very good at sticking to only three points, let me conclude with a personal wish or hope. I hope that the discussion of issues in this book has been fair to different positions, including those not my own. Above all, I hope that the book illustrates how rational and civil inquiry can help us make progress even on difficult issues. Even if there is no guarantee of certainty in ethics, critical inquiry can not only advance our understanding but also provide us with justifications for our conclusions. It also allows us to consider and examine ideas that might prove to be even better.

The more our conclusions survive critical scrutiny, the stronger our grounds for holding them. The more criticism brings out their weaknesses, the stronger the case for replacing them with better ones. Ethics does not give us certainty, but ethical argument can help us arrive at conclusions that can withstand the test of criticism, or if not, stimulate new arguments that promote moral progress and moral growth. Indeed, inquiry itself presupposes many of the values we have found in sports at their best, including an openness to the contributions of others, a degree of impartiality toward our own views, and intellectual honesty in assessing reasons, our own as well as those of others. Above all, I hope this book has contributed to appreciation of critical inquiry, and that by participating in it, we all have learned not only something about good sports but also of the value of critical discourse itself.

# NOTES

**Prologue**

1. Arnold Rampersad's *Jackie Robinson: A Biography* (1998) is a fascinating biography of Robinson's life. Roger Kahn's *Rickey and Robinson* (2014) explores the relationship between Robinson and Dodger executive Branch Rickey, who recruited him to break the color line and counseled him on what he had to do to succeed.

**Chapter 1**

1. The influential but obscure twentieth-century philosopher Ludwig Wittgenstein raised the possibility that there are no common characteristics that all games share in his *Philosophical Investigations* (1951).
2. The quotation is from the late Bernard Suits, whose book *The Grasshopper: Life, Games, and Utopia* (2005) is an analytically acute but often humorous attempt to show not only that there are features common to all games that define them but also that utopia itself may consist of a life of game playing. The account of games presented here is indebted to Suits's analysis, although I myself would not claim that all games share common characteristics.
3. This point was made by Suits in *The Grasshopper*.
4. John Russell (2014).
5. This distinction was developed in an influential article by Scott Kretchmar (1975).
6. For a fuller discussion of this point, see Ronald Dworkin, *Justice for Hedgehogs* (2011).
7. Peter French discusses amateurism and its role in England in preserving class distinctions (French, 2004).
8. For a spirited defense of the view that coaches have a moral duty to attempt to correct bad calls in their favor, see Russell (2013).

9. Tom Verducci's article, "Totally Juiced," *Sports Illustrated*, 96, June 3, 2002, 34–48, is an excellent source on these points as is the Mitchell Report by Senator George Mitchell to Major League Baseball (2003).

10. For fuller discussion, see Dworkin (1977) and Russell (1999).

11. Russell (1999).

**Chapter 2**

1. For example, see Keating (1964).

2. See Tannsjo (1968).

3. See Simon, Torres, and Hager (2015), especially Chapters 2 and 3.

4. Such a view is defended by John Russell (2014).

5. I am indebted here to the discussion of this point by Kretchmar and Elcombe (2007).

6. These points have been developed by Nicholas Dixon (1999), and I am indebted to his discussion.

7. For a fuller and especially insightful discussion of this issue to which I am indebted, see Torres and Hager (2013).

8. Such a view is argued for by John Russell (2013a).

9. Gert (1998).

10. This example is from Russell (2013a).

11. A summary of events involved in this scandal, and indications of its deep complexity, can be found at http://www.nytimes.com/interactive/2015/05/27/sports/soccer/sepp-blatter-fifa-timeline.html?_r=0#/#time376_11008.

12. See Leaman (2007).

13. But is this point complicated by the possibility, suggested by a pre-publication reviewer, that a hockey coach might claim that his most valuable player is an enforcer (i.e., one who is good at intimidating the opposition through hard physical contact)?

14. For an acute extended discussion of gamesmanship to which I am indebted, see Howe (2004).

15. For a version of such a view, see Summers (2007).

16. This point is made by Summers (2007).

17. Quoted by Holmes, Baxter, and Peltz (2011).

18. Dixon (2010).

19. This may also be the case in Major League Baseball. Moreover, any administration of a rule prohibiting retaliation for hit batters in baseball may be too cumbersome or bureaucratic to work effectively. For an argument to this effect, see Browne (2015).

20. I am indebted on this point to Mark Hamilton's acute discussion of make-up calls (2011).

21. Hamilton (2011) makes a similar point.
22. This was pointed out by James Keating (1964) in his own discussion of sportsmanship.
23. Keating (1964).
24. See Feezell (1986) for a view defending a position similar to the position sketched in this paragraph.
25. Such a view has been suggested by several scholarly articles, including Butcher and Schneider (1998) and defended in Simon, Torres, and Hager (2015).

## Chapter 3

1. For a summary of findings, see http://kidshealth.org/parent/nutrition_center/staying_fit/exercise.html. For a more academic paper, see Giannini et al. (2007). For a discussion of the effect of participation on girls, see Parker-Pope (2010).
2. I have argued this previously. See Simon, Torres, and Hager (2015).
3. Lasch (1977).
4. Helpful information can be found at the Sports Concussion Institute Web site at http://www.concussiontreatment.com/concussionfacts.html.
5. For a thoughtful defense of such a view on which I draw, see Russell (2005).
6. I owe this point to Leslie Francis.
7. See Simpson (2004).
8. Date from www.stanfordchildren.org.
9. See Lackman (2015).
10. A moving account of Ali's present state and a tribute to his social significance can be found in Tim Layden's article in *Sports Illustrated*, "Ali: The Legacy" (2015).
11. www.healthresearchfunding.org.
12. Kristol (1971).
13. See Gert (1998) for an account of how we should understand an evil, such as death or loss of freedom. For Gert, an evil, roughly, is a harm no rational person would want to suffer, or want those he or she cares about to suffer, without an overriding reason.
14. See Hampton (1996).
15. Nicholas Dixon (2001) has argued for such a reform.

## Chapter 4

1. This case is discussed by Alun Hardman (2014).
2. I owe this point to Leslie Francis.

3. I first made this suggestion in 1984 (Simon 1984), and it is developed in Simon, Torres, and Hager (2015).
4. For an acute but highly analytic discussion of coercion, see Wertheimer (2014).
5. For an acute discussion of the view that PEDs make some sports too easy, see Gardner (1998).
6. See Simon (1984) for the development of this argument as presented at the conference.
7. See Holm (2010) for an insightful discussion of this point, to which I mostly follow.
8. A similar argument, on which I draw, has been made by Lavin (1987).
9. Sigmund Loland (2001) had argued forcefully for this point. It might be replied that surpassing the best previous performance and setting a new record by however small an amount is a major achievement. But should setting such a record be the primary goal of competition?
10. For discussion, see Dixon (2007).
11. Simon, Torres, and Hager (2015)
12. Such a view has been defended by Claudio Tamburrini (2007).
13. See Loland (2001) for a fuller defense of this point.
14. A possible exception is the kind of liberalism based on the work of Mill that advocates the development of autonomy and critical thinking as virtues the state should promote in its citizens. Arguably these values enhance the capacity to decide for oneself and are too thin to be described as "imposing a way of life on citizens."
15. Sandel (2013).
16. Sandel (2007).
17. This point is suggested by Morgan (2008).

**Chapter 5**
1. For discussion of the parallel between athletics and critical inquiry in ancient Greece, see Reid (2012).
2. A member of the Philosophy Department who worked closely with the women's basketball team also was alleged to have acted improperly.
3. Data on the financial status of intercollegiate athletic programs is available under the heading of "Research" at NCAA.org.
4. Knight Commission (2010).
5. Knight Commission (2010).

6. See French (2004) for such an argument.

7. For a summary of Smith's contributions off the court, see, for example, the tribute to him by Richard Goldstein in *The New York Times* (Feb. 8, 2015), "Dean Smith, Champion of College Basketball and of Racial Equality, Dies at 83."

8. Hawkins (2013).

9. Source: http://sports.usatoday.com/ncaa/salaries/. Of course, coaches not employed by athletically elite major powers or in lower visibility sports make far less and in Division III of the NCAA generally are paid on the same scale as other faculty.

10. See, for example, "Exploitation," *Stanford Encylopedia of Philosophy*, stanford.edu/entries/exploitation/ 2012 for fuller discussion.

11. For an acute discussion of the complexities of understanding exploitation, including a discussion of how mutually advantageous exploitation might apply to college athletics, see Wertheimer (2014).

12. Alan Page quoted in Berkow (1983).

13. See Shulman and Bowen (2001) for comparisons of how athletes at educationally elite institutions fare after graduation when compared to students at large. Graduation rates can be found at ncaa.org.

14. Of course, many would argue that that is just what elite Division I men's football and basketball (and to some extent high-level women's basketball) already are.

15. Ogilvie and Tutko (1971) is an early but influential article expressing doubt about the kind of character sports build.

16. See Simon (1994).

17. French (2004) argues for such a view, especially with respect to football.

18. Some critics claim that a line of empirical studies show that athletes, rather than developing morally because of their participation in sport, actually regress morally and score lower than nonathletes when asked to respond to moral dilemmas described by the investigators. See, for example, Ogilivie and Tutko (1971) and the later work of Bredemeier and Shields cited later.

19. Bredemeier and Shields (2001).

20. Bredemeier and Shields (2001).

21. Drew Hyland (1984) has developed the case for such a view.

22. Wilson (2007).

23. See Shulman and Bowen (2001) for data and an overall critique of the effect of athletics even at highly selective institutions across divisions of the NCAA.

24. See Parker-Pope (2010).
25. See the report from *USA Today* already cited in note 9.
26. See Torres and Hager (2013) for a fuller discussion of this point.
27. This example was proposed and discussed by Fry (2000).
28. Reid (2013).
29. Fry (2000).
30. This example also is discussed in Simon (2013). The dilemma, as far as I know, was originally posed by Fry (2000).
31. See, for example, "Anti-Semitism in the Stands," *The New York Times*, April 18, 2015, available at NewYorkTimes.com/2015/04/19/opinion/sunday/anti-semitism-in-the-soccer/stands.html).
32. This may be an example of the soft paternalism we discussed earlier.
33. See, for example, Kretchmar (2013).
34. Kretchmar (2013).
35. This was pointed out in one of my classes by a student, Jackson Kushner. I myself have argued for a similar point in Simon (1978–1979).
36. Kretchmar acknowledges the importance of hard work in his paper (2013) on this topic.
37. For example, see Simon (2008).

**Chapter 6**
1. See Simon (1994) for a fuller discussion of university neutrality.
2. From a *New York Times* editorial, April 18, 2015.
3. *Amy Cohen et al. v. Brown University*, U. S. Court of Appeals, 1st Circuit, 1983.
4. Hogshead-Makar (2013).
5. This point was also argued in Simon, Torres, and Hager (2015).
6. For an early but still influential discussion of these and other related issues, see English (1978).
7. Wilson (2007).
8. I am indebted here to discussions with my colleague Todd Franklin.
9. For such an argument, see Hoberman (1997).
10. See http://www.slate.com/blogs/lexicon_valley/2013/12/18/redskins_the_debate_over_the_washington_football_team_s_name_incorrectly.html for a discussion of the origin of the term.
11. See www.racismagainstIndians.org for some examples.
12. Thus, according to one Web site, parents had to remove children from school for being called the names of the school mascots (see racismagainstindians.org).

13. Statistics are from an article in *The London Times*, "History and Time Are Key to Power of Football Says Premier League Chief," available at http://www.thetimes.co.uk/tto/public/ceo-summit/article3804923.ece.
14. Sandel (2013).

**Chapter 7**
1. Russell (2014).
2. Such a view is developed in Butcher and Schneider (1998).
3. The inner morality of sports is a central theme of Simon, Torres, and Hager (2015).

# RECOMMENDED READINGS AND REFERENCES

The following books are recommended for further reading. The texts pursue some of the issues raised in this book in more depth, engage with scholarly literature more fully, or approach issues considered here from different angles. The anthologies contain many of the articles cited in the notes at the end of each chapter and are designed to provide an overview of the field of philosophy of sport.

## Texts

French, Peter. 2004. *Ethics and College Sports: Ethics, Sports, and the University*. Lanham, MD: Rowman and Littlefield.

Reid, Heather. 2012. *Introduction to the Philosophy of Sport*. Lanham, MD: Rowman and Littlefield.

Simon, Robert L., Cesar Torres, and Peter Hager. 2015. *Fair Play: The Ethics of Sport*. 4th ed. Boulder, CO: Westview Press.

Suits, Bernard. 2005. *The Grasshopper: Life, Games and Utopia*. Buffalo, NY: Broadview Press. (Originally published in 1978 by the University of Toronto Press.)

## Anthologies and Reference Works

Holowchak, M. Andrew, ed. 2002. *Philosophy of Sport: Critical Readings, Critical Issues*. Upper Saddle River, NJ: Prentice-Hall.

McNamee, Mike, and William J. Morgan. 2015. *Routledge Handbook of the Philosophy of Sport*. New York: Routledge.

Morgan, William J. ed. 2007. *Ethics in Sport*. Champaign, IL: Human Kinetics.

Torres, Cesar, ed. 2014. *The Bloomsbury Companion to the Philosophy of Sport*. London: Bloomsbury.

### References

Berkow, Ira. 1983. "College Factories and Their Output." *New York Times,* January 18: D25.

Bredemeier, Brenda and Shields. 2001. "Moral Growth Among Athletes and Non-Athletes: A Comparative Analysis." *Journal of Genetic Psychology* 147:7–18.

Browne, Alister. 2015. "One for One: A Defense of Pitcher Retaliation in Baseball." *Journal of the Philosophy of Sport* 42:379–392.

Butcher, Robert, and Angela Schneider. 1998. "Fair Play as Respect for the Game." *Journal of the Philosophy of Sport* 25:1–22.

Dixon, Nicholas. 1999. "On Winning and Athletic Superiority." *Journal of the Philosophy of Sport* 26:10–26.

Dixon, Nicholas. 2001. "Boxing, Paternalism, and Legal Moralism." *Journal of the Philosophy of Sport* 27:323–345.

Dixon, Nicholas. 2010. "A Critique of Retaliation in Sports." *Journal of the Philosophy of Sport* 37:1–10.

Dworkin, Ronald. 1977. *Taking Rights Seriously.* Cambridge, MA: Harvard University Press. See especially Chapter 4, "Hard Cases" (pp. 81–130).

Dworkin, Ronald. 2011. *Justice for Hedgehogs.* Cambridge, MA: Harvard University Press.

English, Jane. 1978. "Sex Equality in Sports." *Philosophy and Public Affairs* 7:269–277.

Feezell, Randolph. 1986. "Sportsmanship." *Journal of the Philosophy of Sport* 13:1–13.

French, Peter. 2004. *Ethics and College Sports: Ethics, Sports, and the University.* Lanham, MD: Rowman and Littlefield.

Fry, Jeffrey. 2000. "Coaching a Kingdom of Ends." *Journal of the Philosophy of Sport* 27:51–62.

Gardner, Roger. 1989. "On Performance Enhancing Substances and the Unfair Advantage Argument." *Journal of the Philosophy of Sport* 1:59–73.

Gert, Bernard. 1998. *Morality: Its Nature and Justification.* New York: Oxford University Press.

Giannini, Cosimo, Tommaso de Giorgis, Angelika Mohn, and Francesco Chiarelli. 2007. "Role of Physical Exercise in Children and Adolescents with Diabetes Mellitus." *Journal of Endocrinology and Metabolism* 20:173–184.

Goldstein, Richard. 2015. "Dean Smith, Champion of College Basketball and of Racial Equality, Dies at 83." *New York Times,* February 9: A1.

Hampton, Jean. 1996. *Political Philosophy.* Boulder, CO: Westview Press.

Hamilton, Mark. 2011. "The Moral Ambiguity of the Makeup Call." *Journal of the Philosophy of Sport* 38:212–228.

Hardmun, Alun. 2014. "Sport and Technological Development." In *The Bloomsbury Companion to the Philosophy of Sport*, edited by Cesar Torres, 279–294. London: Bloomsbury.

Hawkins, Billy. 2013. *The New Plantation: Black Athletes, College Sports, and Predominantly White NCAA Institutions*. New York: Palgrave Macmillan.

Hoberman, John. 1997. *Darwin's Athletes: How Sport Has Damaged Black America and Preserved the Myth of Race*. New York: Houghton Mifflin.

Hogshead-Makar, Nancy. 2013. "The Ethics of Title IX and Gender Equity for Coaches: Selected Topics." In *The Ethics of Coaching Sports: Moral, Social, and Legal Issues*, edited by Robert L. Simon, 193–214. Boulder, CO: Westview Press.

Holm, Soren. 2010. "Doping Under Medical Control: Conceptually Possible but Impossible in the World of Professional Sports?" In *The Ethics of Sports: A Reader*, edited by Mike McNamee, 186–193. London: Taylor and Francis.

Holmes, Baxter, and Jim Peltz. 2011. "The Code Made Me Do It." *Los Angeles Times*, August 5, A4.

Howe, Leslie. 2004. "Gamesmanship." *Journal of the Philosophy of Sport* 31:221–225.

Hwang, Jung Hyun, and Scott Kretchmar. 2010. "Aristotle's Golden Mean: Its Implications for the Doping Debate." *Journal of the Philosophy of Sport* 37:102–121.

Hyland, Drew. 1984. *The Question of Play*. Lanham, MD: University Press of America, a division of Rowman and Littlefield.

Kahn, Roger. 2014. *Rickey and Robinson: The True, Untold Story of the Integration of Baseball*. New York: Rodale.

Keating, James W. 1964. "Sportsmanship as a Moral Category." *Ethics: An International Journal of Social Political and Legal Philosophy* 75:25–35.

Knight Commission on Intercollegiate Athletics. 2010. *Restoring the Balance: Dollars, Values and the Future of College Sports*. Available at knightcommission.org/restoringthebalance

Kretchmar, Scott. 1975. "From Test to Contest: An Analysis of Two Kinds of Counterpoint in Sport." *Journal of the Philosophy of Sport* 2:23–30.

Kretchmar, Scott, and Tim Elcombe. 2007. "In Defense of Competition and Winning." In *Ethics in Sport*, edited by William J. Morgan, 165–180. Champaign, IL: Human Kinetics.

Kretchmar, Scott. 2013. "Bench Players: Do Coaches Have a Moral
    Obligation to Play Benchwarmers?" *The Ethics of Coaching
    Sports: Moral, Social, and Legal Issues*, edited by Robert L. Simon,
    123–138. Boulder, CO: Westview Press.

Kristol, Irving. 1971. "Pornography, Obscenity, and the Case for
    Censorship." *New York Times Magazine*. March 28.

Lackman, Jon. 2014. "Is It Wrong to Let Children Do Extreme Sports?"
    *New York Times Magazine*. Available at http://www.nytimes.com/
    2015/05/17/magazine/is-it-wrong-to-let-children-do-extreme-
    sports.html?_r=0

Lasch, Christopher. 1977. "The Corruption of Sports." *New York Review
    of Books*, April 28: 24–30. Available at http://www.nybooks.com/
    articles/archives/1977/apr/28/the-corruption-of-sports/

Lavin, Michael. 1987. "Sports and Drugs: Are the Current Bans
    Justified?" *Journal of the Philosophy of Sport* 14:34–43.

Layden, Tim. 2015. "Ali: The Legacy." *Sports Illustrated*, 123: 60–67.

Leaman, Oliver. 2007. "Cheating and Fair Play in Sport." In *Ethics
    in Sport*, edited by William J. Morgan, 201–207. Champaign,
    IL: Human Kinetics.

Originally published in 1981 in *Sport and the Humanities: A Collection
    of Original Essays*, edited by William J. Morgan. University of
    Tennessee: Bureau of Educational Research and Service.

Loland, Sigmund. 2001. "Record Sports: An Ecological Critique."
    *Journal of the Philosophy of Sport* 28:127–139.

Morgan, William J. 2008. Review of Michael Sandel's "The Case Against
    Perfection." *Journal of Intercollegiate Sport* 1:284–288.

Morgan, William J. 2008a. "Markets and Intercollegiate Sports: An
    Unholy Alliance." *Journal of Intercollegiate Sport* 1:59–65.

Morgan, William J. 2012. "Broad Internalism, Deep Conventions, Moral
    Entrepreneurs." *Journal of the Philosophy of Sport* 39:65–100.

Morgan, William J. 2013. "Interpretivism, Conventionalism, and the
    Ethical Coach." In *The Ethics of Coaching Sports: Moral, Social,
    and Legal Issues*, edited by Robert L. Simon, 61–77. Boulder,
    CO: Westview Press.

Ogilvie, Bruce C., and Thomas A. Tutko. 1971. "Sport: If You Want
    to Build Character, Try Something Else." *Psychology Today*,
    October, 61–63.

Parker-Pope, Tara. 2010. "As Girls Become Women, Sports Pay
    Dividends? *New York Times*, February 15. Available at http://well.

blogs.nytimes.com/2010/02/15/as-girls-become-women-sports-pay-dividends/?_r=0

Potter, Stephen. 1947. *The Theory and Practice of Gamesmanship: The Art of Winning Games without Actually Cheating*. London: Rupert Hart-Davis Publishers.

Rampersad, Arnold. 1998. *Jackie Robinson: A Biography*. New York: Random House.

Rawls, John. 1971. *A Theory of Justice*. Cambridge, MA: Harvard University Press.

Reid, Heather. 2012. *Introduction to the Philosophy of Sport*. Lanham, MD: Rowman and Littlefield.

Russell, J. S. 1999. "Are Rules All an Umpire Has to Work With?" *Journal of the Philosophy of Sport* 26:27–49.

Russell, J. S. 2005. "The Value of Dangerous Sports." *Journal of the Philosophy of Sport* 32:1–19.

Russell, J. S. 2013. "Coaching and Undeserved Competitive Success." In *The Ethics of Coaching Sports: Moral, Social, and Legal Issues*, edited by Robert L. Simon, 103–120. Boulder, CO: Westview Press.

Russell, J. S. 2013a. "Is There a Normatively Distinctive Concept of Cheating in Sport (or anywhere else)?" *Journal of the Philosophy of Sport* 41:1–21.

Russell, J. S. 2014. "Competitive Sport, Moral Development, and Peace." In *The Bloomsbury Companion to the Philosophy of Sport*, edited by Cesar Torres, 228–244. London: Bloomsbury.

Sandel, Michael. 2007. *The Case Against Perfection: Ethics in the Age of Genetic Engineering*. Cambridge, MA: Harvard University Press.

Sandel, Michael. 2013. *What Money Can't Buy: The Moral Limits of Markets*. New York: Farrar, Straus and Giroux.

Shulman, James L., and William G. Bowen. 2001. *The Game of Life: College Sports and Educational Values*. Princeton, NJ: Princeton University Press.

Simon, Robert L. 1978–1979. "An Indirect Defense of the Merit Principle." *The Philosophical Forum* X: 224–241.

Simon, Robert L. 1984. "Good Competition and Drug-Enhanced Performance." *Journal of the Philosophy of Sport* 11:6–13.

Simon, Robert L. 1994. *Neutrality and the Academic Ethic*. Lanham, MD: Rowman and Littlefield.

Simon, Robert L. 2013. "The Ethical Coach: An Interpretive Account of the Ethics of Coaching." In *The Ethics of Coaching Sports: Moral,*

*Social, and Legal Issues*, edited by Robert L. Simon, 41–60. Boulder, CO: Westview Press.

Simon, Robert L., Cesar Torres, and Peter Hager. 2015. *Fair Play: The Ethics of Sport*. 4th ed. Boulder, CO: Westview Press.

Simpson, Joe. 2014. *Touching the Void*. New York: Harper Collins.

Suits, Bernard. 2005. *The Grasshopper: Life, Games and Utopia*. Buffalo, NY: Broadview Press. (Originally published in 1978 by the University of Toronto Press.)

Summers, Chuck. 2007. "Ouch . . . You Just Dropped the Ashes." *Journal of the Philosophy of Sport* 34:68–76.

Tamburrini, Claudio. 2007. "After Doping, What? The Morality of the Genetic Engineering of Athletes." In *Ethics and Sports*, edited by William J. Morgan, 285–297. Champaign, IL: Human Kinetics Publishers.

Tannsjo, T. 1968. "Is Our Admiration for Sports Heroes Fascistoid?" *Journal of the Philosophy of Sport* 25:23–34.

Torres, Cesar, and Peter Hager. 2013. "Competition, Ethics, and Coaching Youth." In *The Ethics of Coaching Sports: Moral, Social, and Legal Issues*, edited by Robert L. Simon, 167–184. Boulder: CO: Westview Press.

Vonnegut, Kurt. 1968. "Harrison Bergeron." In Vonnegut's *Welcome to the Monkey House*. New York, Random House. (This story was first published in *The Magazine of Fantasy and Science Fiction* in 1961.)

Wertheimer, Alan. 2014. *Coercion*. Princeton: Princeton University Press.

Wilson, James Q. 2007. "Bowling with Others." *Commentary* 124:28–32.

Wittgenstein, Ludwig. 1953. *Philosophical Investigations*. G. E. M. Anscombe and R. Rhees, eds. Oxford: Blackwell.

# INDEX

Abrahams, Harold, 17
Ali, Mohammad, 83, 183, 198
Aristotle
 the Golden Mean, 14, 39, 62–64,
  113, 121
Armstrong, Lance, 91, 94, 104–105
athletes
 as role models, 87–88, 168, 198,
  208–213
attention deficit hyperactivity
 disorder (ADHD)
 and Ritalin, 93

Barkley, Charles, 209
Bell, James "Cool Papa," 184
Bentham, Jeremy, 18
Black Lives Matter, 181
Blatter, Sepp, 44. *See also* FIFA
boxing
 and dangerous sports, xviii, 68,
  70, 77, 82–89
 and *Million Dollar Baby*, 82
 and prohibition, 82–89
Brady, Tom, xi–xii, 47, 206–210.
 *See also* Deflategate
brain, injury to, 75. *See also* CTE
Brand, Myles, 139
Bredemeier, Brenda, 154
broad internalism, ix, 26–27, 114, 116
Brundage, Avery, 180

Canesco, Jose
 and, *Juiced: Wild Times, Rampant
  'Roids, Smash Hits and How
  Baseball Got Big,* 104
Carlos, John, 9, 196
*Chariots of Fire,* 17
cheating, 11, 40
 as deception, 41
 as legitimate in sport, 45–47
 and systems of rules, 41–44
 vacuity of cheating, 40–41
Cheetah Blades
 and Oscar Pistorius, 90, 115
Christopher, Matt, 38
chronic traumatic
 encephalopathy (CTE), 75.
 *See also* concussions
coaches
 as educators, 147, 151–155, 158,
  161–164, 176, 178
 ethical issues in coaching,
  161–164, 170–173
 ethical responsibilities of,
  161–173
 and youth sports, 161–164,
  167–173
coercion
 nature of, 84, 101–102
 and performance enhancing
  drugs, 100–102

college sports. *See* intercollegiate
    sports
commercialization of sport
    (commodification), 201–208
communitarianism, 131, 155
    civic communitarianism, 88
    and genetic enhancement,
        124–130
    and violence in sport, 85–86
competition
    critiques of, 28–32
    mutualism and
        competition, 33–35
*Concussion*, 75
concussions, 14, 73–75, 99.
    *See also* chronic traumatic
        encephalopathy
constitutive rules, 3–6, 12–13, 22,
    34, 41–46, 65–69, 150
cost-benefit analysis
    complications of, 74–77
critical inquiry, xiv, 15–17,
    149–150, 156, 199,
    218–219
    and impartiality, 110–111
    and justification, 18, 218–219

dangerous sports, 68, 70, 77–82
    and boxing, 82–84
    for children, 80–82
*Dark Angel,* 127–128
Davis, Mo'ne, 37
Deflategate, xi–xii, 47, 206–210.
    *See also* Brady, Tom
Di Canio, Paulo, 23
disability in sport
    Oscar Pistorius and cheetah
        blades, 90, 115
    *PGA Tour v. Casey Martin,*
        115–116
discrimination, 182, 184–186, 214.
    *See also* racism; Title IX
Dixon, Nicholas, 55–56
Dworkin, Ronald, 23–25

exercise
    difference from sport, 4–7, 69
    and public health, 69–70
exploitation, 141–143
    and "the new plantation," 141

fairness, 2, 18, 20–23
    and distribution of playing
        time, 170–173
    and performance enhancing
        drugs, 102–103
    and unfair advantage, 97,
        102–103, 111
fantasy sports
    and gambling, 205
FIFA, 23, 44, 92, 181. *See also*
    Blatter, Sepp
    and corruption, 44, 94, 207
Flood, Curt,169. *See also*
    reserve clause
    and the reserve clause
football, 4, 51, 66, 87, 98, 133,
    137–138, 151–152, 191
    and brain injury, 14, 75
    dangers of, 14, 70–75
    (*see also* chronic traumatic
        encephalopathy)
Fraleigh, Warren, xv
*Friday Night Lights, 168*

Galarraga, Armando, 57
games, xiii, xvi, 4–7, 12–13, 21
gamesmanship, 1, 22, 47–48, 210
gay marriage, 182
genetic enhancement
    and designer children, 117,
        120–121
    ethics of, 117–130
    and inequality, 121–123
    somatic v. germ-line, 117, 119
    therapy v. enhancement, 117–119
    and transhumanism, 119
Gerrard, Paul, 22
Gert, Bernard, 41, 223n

Gibson, Althea, 185
Golden Mean. *See* Aristotle
*Grove City v. Bell*, 187

Hamilton College, xvi–xvii, 74,
    152, 158
harm principle. *See* Mill, J. S.;
    paternalism
Hawkins, Billy
    and "the new plantation," 141
health
    and sports, 68–72
Henry, Thierry, 1–2, 57
Hobbes, Thomas, 30–32
    and human nature, 32
    and the state of nature, 34, 56,
        114, 210, 207, 210, 217
Hogshead-Makar, Nancy, 192
Holzman, Red, 10
Homer
    and *The Iliad*, 132, 208
human nature, 28, 32–34, 118
*Hunger Games*, 31

ideals
    of the good life, 97
    of sport, 106–108, 123–124
intercollegiate sports
    and academics, 150–153, 156–160
    and character, 146–161
    coaches as educators, 158,
        161–170
    as entertainment, 140–141
    as "the new plantation," 141
    O'Bannon lawsuit, 145–146
    professionalization, 141–145
    reforming Division I, 173–178
    as revenue producing, 137–138
    scandals and academic fraud,
        135–136
interest in sports
    alleged gender differences,
        188–190
    explanations of, 6–7

International Association for
    the Philosophy of Sport
    (IAPS), xiv
International Olympic Committee
    (IOC), 180, 206–207

justice, xiii–xiv, 18, 20, 141, 155,
    180, 201. *See also* fairness
    corrective justice, 51–58

Kant, Immanuel, 19, 42, 53,
    155, 164
kidneys, free market in, 202–203
Knight Commission, 136–138
Kristol, Irving, 85

Ladies Professional Golf
    Association (LPGA), 185, 194
Lasch, Christopher, 73
liberalism, 124, 131
    liberal eugenics, 130
    and performance enhancing
        drugs, 97–98
libertarianism, 97–100, 124,
    129, 131
    libertarianism of sport,
        120–121, 124
Loland, Sigmund, 112
Long, Lutz
    and 1936 Berlin Olympics,
        60–63
luck, influence of, in sport, 33
    and the genetic lottery, 103, 122
    and significance of winning,
        35–37, 51

Mack, Reddy, 25–26
Martin, Casey, 115–116
Mazeroski, Bill, 36
Mill, J. S., 18
    the harm principle, 77–79, 83,
        85–86, 95–97, 99–100
    and paternalism, 77–78, 95–97
*Million Dollar Baby*, 82

*Mitchell Report*, 104–105
moral education. *See* virtue

National Basketball Association
    (NBA), 145, 176
National Collegiate Athletic
    Association (NCAA), 134,
    136–139, 144–145, 182
    Division I, xvi, 134, 136,
        138–139, 141, 149, 159–160,
        173–174
    Division III, xvi, 74, 134, 138,
        151, 159, 179
    and exploitation of athletes,
        141–142
    graduation rates of NCAA
        athletes, 139
    suggestions for reform,
        174–179
National Football League (NFL),
    35, 74–75, 85, 97, 170, 201
National Hockey League
    (NHL) 5–6
neutrality, critical institutional
    and moral education,
    148–149
New England Small College
    Athletic Conference
    (NESCAC), 159–160
New Orleans Saints
    and bounties, 14, 85, 170
new plantation, the, 141. *See also*
    Hawkins, Billy
nicknames
    team nicknames and racism,
    199–201

O'Bannon Ed
    O'Bannon lawsuit, 145–146
officials, 2, 13, 21, 50, 210
    and make-up calls, 52, 56–60
Olympic Games, 90, 132, 183
    1936 Berlin Olympics, 60,
        63–64, 196

massacre of Israelis at 1972
    Munich Olympics, 180
one and done in college
    basketball, 136, 175–176
open future, the right to, 120–121
Owens, Jesse
    and 1936 Berlin Olympics, 60,
        63–64, 196

Paige, LeRoy "Satchel," 184
parents, 72
    and dangerous sports, 80–82
    and genetic enhancement,
        120–121
    and youth sports, 70–71,
        80–82, 161
paternalism
    and boxing, 83–84
    for children, 70–71
    J. S. Mill's critique of,
        77–78, 95–97
    and performance enhancing
        drugs, 95–97
Paterno, Joe
    and Sandusky scandal,
        136–137
performance enhancing drugs
    definitions of, 91–94
    evaluation of, 94–112
    and paternalism, 95–97
    and rational choice, 103–104
    and unfair advantage, 102–104
    See also *Mitchell Report*
performance enhancing
    equipment, xii, 105–109, 113
    Polara golf ball, 90, 106
    swimsuits, polyurethane, 90,
        106, 113–114
*PGA Tour v. Casey Martin*, 114–116
Plato, 3, 145
    and education, 132–133, 145,
        162–163, 179, 218
    and *Euthyphro*, 133
    and the *Republic*, 13

pluralism in women's sports
    criticism of separate but equal,
        184, 192–196
Potter, Stephen, 47
Premier League, 23, 201
Professional Golfers
    Association (PGA), 114–116,
        163, 184

racism, xiv
    Caucasian clause of PGA
        Tour, 184
    influence of sport on racism,
        146, 158–159, 198
    and "the new plantation," 141
    segregation in sports,
        xii–xiii, 9, 184
    in soccer, 184, 214
    team nicknames, 199–201
rational choice
    and performance enhancing
        drugs, 103–104
Rawls, John, 155
reason, role of in ethics. *See* critical
    inquiry
Reed, Willis, 10
Reid, Heather, 132, 163
relativism, 15–18
reserve clause, 169. *See also*
    Flood, Curt
retaliation in sports, 52–56
    and vigilantism, 55–56
Rhodes, Teddy, 184
rivalry
    as counterexample to
        mutualism, 215–217
Robinson, Jackie, viv, 9, 184,
        196, 198
Rudolph, Wilma, 185, 198
rules
    constitutive, 3–5, 12, 34, 41, 46,
        66, 123, 150
    rules v. principles, 24–26
Russell, John, 25, 42, 44, 215

Sandel, Michael, 125–126,
        202–203
Scalia, Anthony, 116
Shields, David, 154
Sifford, Charles, 197
Silver, Adam, 197
Simpson, Joe, 79
Smith, Dean, 138–140
Smith, Tommie, 9, 196
Smith, Will, 75
Soccer War (Hundred Hours
        War), 181
social function theory
    as explanation of interest in
        sport, 9–11
sports
    and challenge, 4–5, 8, 11–14, 16,
        21–22, 35–37, 76
    and competition, 28–35
    dangerous sports, 26–27
    definition of sport, 3–6
    explanations of interest in, 6–7
    as moral laboratory, 206
    sports vs. games, 2–6
sportsmanship
    definition of, 60–62
    as required or
        encouraged, 62–65
*Star Wars*, 217
Stevenson, Betsy, 161
Suits, Bernard, 221n2
Swank, Hilary, 82

Tamburrini, Claudio, 122
tanking
    ethics of, 65–66
Title IX, xviii, 144, 184–188
    effects of, 186–187
    history of, 186–188
    as promoting separate but
        unequal, 192–196
    and proportionality, 188–192
    three part test, 187
*Touching the Void*, 79

transhumanism. *See* genetic
    enhancement
trash talking, 48–51

utilitarianism, 18–19, 155, 202

values
    civic communitarianism, 88
    civic, intellectual and partisan
        values, 156–158
Virdon, Bill, 36
virtue, xii, 8, 13, 19, 82, 122,
        183, 198
    coaching and character, 19,
        147–153, 158, 163–166
    empirical research on sports
        and character, 153–156
    and moral education, 133, 156–158
    and role models, 211–212

Weiss, Paul, xv
Wie, Michelle, 195
winning
    importance of, 35–40
    in youth sports
Woods, Tiger, 157, 197
World Cup, 112, 194, 208
    2009 playoff, 1–2, 57
    and corruption in FIFA, 44,
        94, 207

youth sports
    and coaching, 14, 18,
        21–22, 159–164,
        170–172, 181
    and emphasizing winning, 14,
        37–40, 159–164, 168

Zaharias, Babe, 185